W9-COU-058

Betty Gottland
(TD)

2:00 – Thurs.

Papers on Acting

Edited by

BRANDER MATTHEWS

With a Preface by Henry W. Wells
*Curator of the Brander Matthews Dramatic Museum
of Columbia University*

A DRAMABOOK

 HILL AND WANG · NEW YORK

PN2061
M26

Copyright 1958 by Hill and Wang, Inc.
Library of Congress Catalog Card Number: 58-6066

ALL RIGHTS RESERVED

This volume is published by special arrangement with the
Brander Matthews Dramatic Museum of Columbia University.

Manufactured in the United States of America
by The Colonial Press Inc.

CONTENTS

176190

PREFACE

Between 1914 and 1926 a series of twenty-one small books were published by The Brander Matthews Dramatic Museum, at Columbia University, under the general direction of the distinguished founder of the Museum, whose name it bears. By the first decade of the present century Brander Matthews had established himself as a prominent figure in drama and the stage. Born in New Orleans, in 1852, he shortly became a resident of New York City, his home until his death in 1929. He commenced teaching at Columbia College in 1891. In 1900 he was assigned to the first chair of drama established in any university. This distinction has been kept in mind by the subsequent designation of his academic position as the Brander Matthews Chair of Dramatic Literature, occupied in turn by G. C. D. Odell, Joseph Wood Krutch, and Eric Bentley.

At approximately the time of his fortunate shift from the teaching of English literature in general to the history and theory of the stage, a visit to the small theatre museum in the Paris Opera House suggested to him the establishment of an institution of similar purpose in New York. The nucleus was his own large collection of books, pamphlets, programs, pictures, stage models, puppets, and memorabilia of the theatre. After an informal existence, during which the collection was divided between his home and the University, the Museum was officially organized in 1911 and housed on the Columbia campus. It was the first of its kind in this country. Important materials were acquired from Europe and the Orient, often as gifts from Brander Matthews' wide circle of acquaintance. With the help of an endowment, the general work of the Museum continues to the present.

Although the editorial labor for several further publications by the Museum was largely completed before Brander Matthews' death in 1929, the series of volumes, like so many other projects associated with the theatre and the arts, terminated with the beginning of the economic depression. The collection is best understood as a record of one of America's most stimulating minds in theatrical research. Among Matthews' many eminent friends were several of the authors of the papers themselves. He was a playwright, critic, scholar, reviewer, and author of some twoscore books, a man of surprisingly wide interests and activities, an enthusiastic advocate of language reform, one of the founders of The Authors Club, The Players Club, and similar institutions, a prolific contributor to newspapers and periodicals, and widely known for his "Sunday Evening Salon." At his death he left to Columbia University a wide correspondence received from his friends in this country and abroad. Indeed, he was almost as familiar a figure in London and Paris as in New York. Among his chief books are *The Development of Drama, Studies of the Stage, Molière, Shakespeare as a Playwright, Principles of Playwriting,* and *Essays on English.*

Brander Matthews was essentially a collector—of books, works of art, friends, anecdotes, ideas. Possessed of an extraordinarily acquisitive and eclectic mind, he neglected nothing, forgot nothing. His roving wit, though often dry, was even more ingratiating than caustic. None of his multitudinous labors remains today more typical or valuable than this compilation of papers comprising the two companion volumes* that now bring to the public the fruit of a career at its height nearly half a century ago. It was for several years the pleasure of the present writer to be Brander Matthews' assistant in his University classes and a youthful participant in the activities of his literary circle; it is an equal pleasure to introduce to a new group of readers essays whose selection confirms the good judgment of one of America's most searching scholars of the stage.

HENRY W. WELLS

Curator of the Brander Matthews
Dramatic Museum

---

* The first volume, *Papers on Playmaking,* was published in August 1957.

Papers on Acting

Art and the Actor

by

CONSTANT COQUELIN

Translated by Abby Langdon Alger

With an Introduction by Henry James

Introduction

It was nearly seventeen years ago and the first time that the writer of these remarks had taken his seat in that temple of the drama in which he was destined afterwards to spend so many delightful evenings, feel the solicitation of so many interesting questions and welcome so many fine impressions, these last crowned by the conviction that the Théâtre Français was such a school of taste as was not elsewhere to be found in the world. The spectator of whom I speak felt the education of his theatric sense fairly begin on the evening M. Coquelin was revealed to him in *Lions et Renards*—and revealed in spite of a part of rather limited opportunity. Many parts since have continued the revelation, these more important, more marked for success (Émile Augier's comedy to which I allude was, not undeservedly, a failure); but I have retained in its vividness my image of the hour, and of all that this actor in especial contributed, because it was the first step of an initiation. It opened a door through which I was in future to pass as often as possible into a world of delightful, fruitful art. M. Coquelin has quitted the Comédie, his long connection with that august institution has come to an end, and he is to present himself in America not as a representative of the richest theatrical tradition in the world, but as an independent and enterprising genius who has felt the need of the margin and elbow-room, the lighter, fresher air of a stage of his own. He will find this stage in the United States as long as he looks for it, and an old admirer may hope that he will look for it often and make it the scene of new experiments and new triumphs. His visit is in fact itself a new experiment, the result of which can scarce fail of interest for those who watch with attention the evolution of taste in our great and lively land. If it should be largely and strikingly successful that sacred cause will quite of necessity, I think, have scored heavily.

It is nevertheless to be noted that foreign performers, lyric and dramatic, descending upon our shores by the thousand, have encountered a various, by no means always an assured,

2

fortune. Many have failed, and of those who have succeeded it is safe to say that they have done so for reasons lying pretty well on the surface. They have addressed us in tongues that were alien and to most of us incomprehensible, but there was usually something in them that operated as a bribe to favour. The peculiarity of M. Coquelin's position and the cause of the curiosity with which we shall have regarded the public's attitude toward him are in the fact that he offers no bribe whatever, none of the lures of youth or beauty or sex or of an insinuating aspect, and none of those that reside in a familiar domestic repertory. The question is simply of appreciating or not appreciating his admirable talent and his not less admirable method. Great singers speak, or rather sing, for themselves; music hath charms, and the savage breast is soothed even when the "words" require a handy translation. Distinguished foreign actresses have the resource of a womanhood which a chivalrous people is much more willing than not to take for lovely. Madame Sarah Bernhardt was helped to relieve the burden of the French tongue to the promiscuous public by being able to add to her extraordinary cleverness her singular beauty, and then to add ever so many wonderful dresses and draperies to that. M. Coquelin will have had to please with nothing like the same assistance; he is not beautiful, he is not pictorial, and his clothes scarcely matter. The great Salvini has successfully beguiled us in Italian, but has had the advantage of the bravest address to the eye of which a man can be well capable, and of representing with his romantic type characters that have on our stage a consecration, a presumption, in their favour. M. Coquelin's type is not romantic, and whatever in him is most immediately visible would seem to have been formed for the broadest comedy. By a miracle of talent and industry he has forced his physical means to serve him also, and with equal felicity, in comedy that is not broad, but surpassingly delicate, and even in the finest pathetic and tragic effects. To enjoy the refinement of his acting, however, the ear must be as open as the eye, must even be beforehand with it; and if that of the American spectator in general learns, or even shows an aptitude for learning, the lesson conveyed in his finest creations, the lesson that acting is an art, and that the application of an art is style, and that style is expression and that expression is the salt of life, the gain will have been something more than the sensation of the moment—it will be a new wisdom.

In M. Augier's comedy which I have mentioned and which was speedily withdrawn, there was frequent reference to the "robe of innocence" of the young Vicomte Adhémar, an interesting pupil of the Jesuits, or at least of the clerical party, who, remarkable for his infant piety and the care taken to fence him in from the corruptions of the town, goes sadly astray on coming up to Paris and inflicts grievous rents and stains on that precious garment. I well remember the tone of humbugging juvenile contrition in which Coquelin, representing the misguided youth, confessed that it was no longer in a state to be worn. He had a little curly flaxen wig, parted in the middle, a round and rosy face and a costume resembling the supposed uniform in New York to-day, of that illusive animal the dude; yet he was not a figure of farce, but a social product, so lightly touched in as he was definitely specified. I thought his companions as delightful as himself, and my friendliness extended even to the horrible stalls in which at that time one was condemned to sit, and to the thick hot atmosphere of the house. I suspect the atmosphere has never been cleared since then—that the place has never had a thorough airing; but certain mitigations have been wrought, new chairs and wider passages supplied, with frescoes on the ceilings and fresh upholstery in box and balcony. It is still however of the dingy and stuffy old theatre I think, haunted as it then more sensibly was by the ghosts of the great players of the past, the mighty presences of Talma and Mars and Rachel. It has seemed to me ever since that the "improvements" have frightened these sacred shades away; the ancient lack of ease was a part of the tradition—a word which represents the very soul of the Comédie and which, under the great dim roof that has echoed to so many matchless sounds, one pronounces with bated breath. The tradition was at that time in the keeping of MM. Régnier, Bressant, Delaunay and Got, of Mesdames Plessy, Nathalie and Favart, to say nothing of the subject of this sketch, the latest comer in the great generation of which these were some of the principal figures. Much has been changed with the lapse of the years, and M. Coquelin, though still in the happy prime, was the other day almost a senior. Régnier, Bressant, Delaunay had disappeared, and from the boards of the Français the most robust depository of the tradition in the younger line—for to this title our visitor has certainly a right—has also vanished. Gone is the brilliant, artificial, incomparable Plessy; gone is that rich and wise *comédienne*, the admirable, elderly, discreet, the amusing and touching Nathalie; gone is poor Madame Favart, whose utterance I remember I couldn't understand the first time I saw her (she was still playing quite young persons and represented, in a very tight dress, the aristocratic heroine of

Lions et Renards), but whom I afterwards grew to admire as an actress of high courage and a great tragic range.

It took a certain time for a new spectator to discriminate and compare, to see things, or rather to see persons, in the right proportion and perspective. I remember that the first evenings I spent in the Rue de Richelieu I thought everyone equally good, I was dazzled by the general finish, by the harmony unbroken, a regulated tone and observed propriety which at that time affected me as an almost celestial order. Everyone *was* good—I don't say it of everyone to-day; even if afterwards the new spectator perceived differences. He was to discover indeed that, such is the grossness intermixed with the noblest human institutions, there could be sometimes a failure of taste behind that stately *rampe*. And now he has heard common voices, has had the shock of the imperfect illusion there, has seen the dead letter of the famous tradition uninformed by a free spirit. He has seen gentlemen put down their hats with great accuracy on the first chair on the right of the door as they come in, but, even when the further convincing grace might be much required of them, achieve very little more than that. He has seen actresses for whom all the arts of the toilet, all the facility of the French-woman and all the interest they had in producing the right impression could not conduce to the representation of a lady. These little roughnesses, however, inherent, as I say, in every mundane enterprise, were not frequent enough for the general glamour to suffer from them. I nevertheless rejoice to-day in a certain confidence of having even at the very first dimly discerned the essence of the matter, the purest portions of the actor's art, to abide in young Coquelin—he was then young—with unsurpassable intensity. It concerns his history that he was born at Boulogne-sur-Mer in 1841, and was christened Benoît-Constant; that his vocation defined itself at the earliest age, and that he became a pupil of the Conservatory in 1859. From this nursery of histrionic hopes he entered the Théâtre Français, where he at once drew attention to his presence. At the age of twenty-three he was a *sociétaire* of the great house. His features, his cast of countenance, the remarkable play and penetration of his voice, which combines the highest metallic ring with every conceivable human note, marked him out for parts of extreme comic freedom as well as for the finer shades of what is called character. Much before I had seen him I was to retain the impression of the liveliest, received from a friend's account of him in Théodore de Banville's touching little poetic piece *Gringoire,* where, in the part of a medieval Bohemian of letters condemned to hanging by Louis XI and reprieved when the halter is already round his neck—I have not seen the piece for a long time and rather forget the argument—he showed a mastery of that mixture of the appeal to the pity of things with the appeal to their absurdity which always so succeeds with the French. *Gringoire* is an excellent example of that range, and has taken its place in M. Coquelin's regular repertory, where he has matched it, in comparatively recent times, with M. Coppée's *Luthier de Crémone;* a like sensitive and slightly morbid personage this last, represented by the actor with wondrous discretion, delicacy and fancy, and dear to the French public from the fact that he may be introduced to families and young ladies. The pathetic, the "interesting" —including, where need be, the romantic and even the heroic, these and the extravagantly droll mark the opposite terms of our performer's large gamut. He turns from end to end of this scale, he ranges between his extremes, with incomparable freedom and ease. Into the *emploi* of the impudent extravagant serving-men of the old comedies, the Mascarilles, the Scapins, the Frontins, the Crispins, he stepped from the first with the assurance of a conqueror; from hand to foot, in face, in manner, in accent, in genius, he was cut out for them, and it is with his most shining successes under that star that his name has become synonymous for the public at large. If his portrait is painted for the foyer of the Comédie—which was doubtless long since the case—it should perhaps be in particular as the Mascarille of Molière's *Étourdi.*

This must have been, I think, the second part in which I gaped at him, when Delaunay, with but little less nature and art and effect of his own delightful kind, was the incorrigibly scatter-brained hero. I see Mascarille, I hear him, the incarnation of humorous effrontery and agility, launch again his prodigious voice over the footlights, fairly trumpet his "points" to the dome and give an unparalleled impression of life and joy. I have acclaimed him in the character many times since then, and found it, save for his astonishing image of the false marquis in the *Précieuses Ridicules,* the most exuberant in his repertory. Of this fantastic exuberance, the special chartered license of the whole family, he is a master whom one watches very much as one watches some supreme dancer or trickster on the vertiginous tense wire, feeling him as certain to pile danger high as not to risk his neck by excess. This safe playing with the danger of excess—which is a defiance of the loss of balance under exhilaration—connects itself with the actor's command of the effects that lie entirely in self-possession, effects of low tone, indications of inward things. The representative of Don Annibal in the *Aventurière,* of Don César de Bazan in *Ruy Blas,* under both of which names this master is superb, is also the representative of various prose-talking and concentrated gentlemen of to-day (the Duc de Septmonts in the *Étrangère* of the younger Dumas, the argumentative, didactic Thouvenin in the same author's *Denise*) caught in various tight places, or suspicious of them, as gentlemen must be in a play, but with no accessories *à la* Goya to help them out. The interpreter of the tragic passion which is the subject of *Jean Dacier,* a piece I have not seen for many years, lurks in the stupendously droll and dreadful evocation of M. Loyal, the canting little pettifogger or *clerc d'huissier,* who appears in a single brief scene of the last act of *Tartuffe* and into whom M. Coquelin, taking up the part for the first time in the autumn of 1885, injected an individuality of grotesqueness and baseness which gave him, all in the space of five minutes, one of his greatest triumphs.

The art of composition is in the various cases I have mentioned the same, but the subjects to which it is applied have nothing in common. I have heard members of the public say with complacency: "Coquelin has great talent, he does ever so many different things, but somehow he is always the same Coquelin." He is indeed always the same Coquelin, which truth to himself crowns our comfort, considering the damage that in so gallant a genius any breach of his identity might have wrought. It is exactly by being fixed so firm at his center that he is able to reach out, reach ever so far, to the perfect Jean Dacier one night and to the perfect Don Annibal another. If it be meant by the remark that he makes Don Annibal resemble Jean Dacier, or gives the two personages something in common that they could not really have possessed, no criticism could well be less just. What it really points to, I suppose, is the infallibility and punctuality of the great artist's method, the fact of its *always* reporting his observation and his experience, just as the postman always delivers the letters he starts out on his round with. The letters are various, but the postman remains the postman. It is, however, above all by his voice that M. Coquelin is (in the degree denounced, I suppose) exposed and betrayed, that voice which no art of composing a particular character or adopting a particular tone can well render a less astounding organ at one moment than at another. Don César is Coquelin and M. Thouvenin is Coquelin, because on the lips alike of Don César and of M. Thouvenin sit a range and a use of tone, a directed application of it, which are peculiar to the artist who commands them and are surely the most wondrous in their kind that the stage has ever known. It may be said that his voice does fairly give him away, that he cannot escape from it, and that whatever he does with it he still pays the penalty of reminding us that only he can command such service.

This idiosyncrasy it is in short that, by so intimately connecting him with his characters, connects them inevitably with each other and shuts them up together as prisoners of war, so to speak, are shut up in their ring fence. Its life and force are such that we seem at times to hear it run away with him, take a "day off" and engage in antics and exercises on its own account. The only reproach it would occur to me to make to a *diseur* so endowed is that he may perhaps at moments show as the victim rather more than as the master of his gift, may occasionally lose the idea while he listens to the form. That beguilement is doubtless not to be grudged, however, as a reward to so much toilsome forging and polishing of the vocal arm; the result gives us something unsurpassably addressed to the stage, where the prime necessity of the least thing done, as well as of the greatest, is that it shall "tell" for every creature in the house. When this master speaks the sound is not sweet and caressing, though it adapts itself beautifully, as I have hinted, to the most human effects; it has no analogy with the famous romantic murmur of Delaunay, a thing of ineffable quavers and enchanting cadences, dying falls and semitones calculated to a hair's breadth. It is not primarily the voice of a lover, or rather— for I hold that any actor, given the indulgence of the public to this particular easy appeal, may be a lover with any voice —it is not primarily, like that of M. Delaunay, the voice of love. There was no urgent reason why it should be, for the passion of love is not what M. Coquelin was cut out to represent or has usually been concerned with.

He has usually had to represent the passion of impudence, and it is, I think, not too much to say that in this portrayal he has won his greatest victories. His inimitable force of accent enables him to place supremely before us the social quality which, beyond question, leads straightest to social success. The valets of Molière and Regnard are nothing if not impudent; impudent are Don César and Don Annibal; impudent, as I remember him, M. Adolphe de Beaubourg in *Paul Forestier;* impudent the Duc de Septmonts; impudent even—or at least decidedly impertinent—the copious moralist M. Thouvenin. I select thus but a handful of instances from

our actor's immense repertory; there are doubtless others at
least as much to the point in parts in which I have not seen
him. He is believed moreover—and nothing could be more
natural—to have aspirations of the liveliest character in
respect to Tartuffe, and it may be predicted that on the day
he embraces that fine opportunity he will give a supreme sign
of his power to depict the unblushing. It need hardly be
remarked that the Mephistopheles which he is at the moment
I write rumored to have his eye on in an arrangement of
Goethe's drama will abound in the same sense. If M.
Coquelin's art of tone meanwhile is not the art of sweetness
it is in an extraordinary degree that of firmness and distinctness, that of penetration, of the power to "carry" sound and
sense. I hear it as I write ascend again like a rocket to the
great hushed dome of the old theatre, under which, vibrating
and lashing the air, it seems to have sprung from some
mechanism of still greater science even than the human
throat. In the great cumulative tirades of the old comedy,
which grow and grow as they proceed, but the difficulties of
which are pure sport for our artist's virtuosity, it flings down
the words and the verses as a gamester precipitated by a run
of luck flings *louis d'or* upon the table. I am not sure that the
most perfect piece of acting I have seen him achieve, in the
sense of the exhibition of things intensely felt and reacted
upon, is not a prose character, but to appreciate to the full
his mastery of form, his authority, as they say, we must
listen to and enjoy his delivery of verse; since it represents
all the breadth of the difference, of the abyss, one may
indeed say, between the French dramatic manner and any
claim to a manner open to ourselves in the same connection,
that verse has remained among M. Coquelin's countrymen,
till within recent years, the supposedly most congruous
language of comedy—a distinction from any familiarity with
which our theatre was long ago to fall away, save in so far
as parts of the Shaksperean comedy saved it. That armor-
plated assurance, that perfection of confidence which is but
the product of the most determined study, shines forth in
the example before us, at any rate, in proportion as the
problem is complicated. The problem does not indeed as a
general thing become so in the old rhymed parts psychologi-
cally speaking; but in these parts the question of elocution,
of delivery, of *diction,* or even simply the question of breath,
bristles both with opportunities and with dangers. It is true
as a rule that wherever M. Coquelin has a very long and
composite speech to utter, be it in verse or prose, there one
gets the cream of his talent, or at least of his virtuosity.

There one perhaps even sees why it is sometimes critically declared of him that he is not an actor in anything like the same sense in which he is a *diseur;* the criticism with which the genius of his country so restlessly invites the artist ever to reckon dealing thus in a discrimination not familiar from any act of frequency among ourselves.

Our distinctions in that order are between smaller things, things too, I think, in every way less apprehended; so that we never have for instance such a matter to consider as the wondrous length of some of the speeches in French plays, and of the detailed responsibility laid thereby on exponents. The longest continuous aggregation of lines that has had to face French footlights, not excepting the famous soliloquy of Figaro in the second comedy of Beaumarchais, and that of Charles the Fifth in *Hernani,* is, I should suppose, the discourse placed in the mouth of our above-mentioned M. Thouvenin in the last act of *Denise.* It occupies nearly four close pages in the octavo edition of the play—oh those delightful octavo editions, with their projection into literature of the dignity of the theatre, unless indeed one says their projection upon the theatre of the dignity of literature!—and if it is not in strictness a soliloquy, being the product of an age posterior to that innocence and enjoying an audience on the stage as well as in the house, it is a delivered address, an uttered homily, a series of insistent remarks on many things. English or American spectators would have sunk into settled gloom by the time the long rhythm of the thing had declared itself, and even at the Théâtre Français the presumption was against the actor's ability to take safely into port a vessel drawing such a prodigious depth of water. M. Coquelin gave the affair life, light, colour, natural movement and that variety any absence of which would have wrecked it—gave it in short an interest that made it a triumph. We held our breath not altogether perhaps to hear what Thouvenin would say—it didn't quite come to that, but certainly to hear how Coquelin would bring Thouvenin through. Such a success as this case represents the actor's art at its highest and serenest, because built up straight from the humanity and all the moral facts that underlie it.

"Saying" things is on our own stage quite out of fashion—if for no other reason than that we must first have them to say. To *do* them, with a great reinforcement of chairs and tables and articles of clothing, of traps and panoramas and other massive carpentry, is the most that ever occurs to our Anglo-Saxon star of either sex. The ear of the public, that field of the auditive intelligence which is two-thirds of the comedian's battle-field, has simply ceased to respond for want of use; for where in very fact is the unfortunate comedian to learn to speak? Is it the unfortunate public, sitting all on this side in deepest darkness, that is to teach him? From what sources shall the light of usage, of taste, of tact, the breath of harmony and the tone of civilization, the perception in a word of anything approaching to a standard, have descended upon the society itself out of which the actor springs? Gone at any rate are the days—if they ever really were with us—when any situation not grossly obvious, any interest *latent* in anything and thereby involving for its issue our finer attention and our nobler curiosity, could look for help from the play of tone, *the* great vehicle of communication. What this comes to is that histrionic lips have ceased— so far as they ever began!—to be able to tell a story worth telling or to gratify a taste worth gratifying. The brilliant stage-carpenter, that master of supreme illusion the scene-painter, that mistress of inordinate variety, or of the only variety we may look to, the dressmaker, have taken over the whole question.

One September night ten years ago, a frequent haunter of Paris, though returning to it but after a considerable absence, was drawn to the Comédie by M. Lomon's *Jean Dacier,* four acts in verse and of a highly tragic cast. When this spectator came out he was too excited to go home, to go to bed, to do anything but live the piece over and walk off his agitation. He made several times the circuit of the Place de la Concorde, he patrolled the streets till night was far gone and his emotion had somewhat subsided. It had been produced by Coquelin's representation of the hero of the piece, and no tribute to the actor's power could have been more hearty and unrestricted. Many years have passed since then; the play, for reasons social and political, I think, rather than artistic, has not been repeated, and the visitor of whom I relate this harmless anecdote has consequently had no chance of renewing his impression of it. He has often wondered whether his recollection is to be trusted, whether some shade of a mistake, of extraneous fortuitous felicity doesn't hang about it. That evening abides with him none the less as well-nigh the most memorable ever spent by him in a theatre. Was there something in his inward condition that happened exceptionally to help the case, or was the whole thing really as fine, and was Coquelin's acting in particular as splendid, as his subsequent ecstatic perambulation would have proved? Why on the one hand should Coquelin's acting not have been splendid, and why on the other, if it was as splendid as I have ever since

ventured to suppose, has it not been more celebrated, more
commemorated, more of a household word? I fail to have
noted any general awareness of this eminent triumph, and in
fact to remember anywhere catching so much as a reference
to it. Inexcusably, I admit, I have retained no memory of
the action on its fate of the overwhelming attention of M.
Sarcey, who must have had at such a crisis in our artist's
career innumerable remarks to make. Why, at any rate, social
and political reasons to the contrary notwithstanding, has the
play never again been brought forward, allowing its effect to
have been even but half as great as I thus fondly suppose it?
Whatever the answer to this question my own impression
must warrant me—Jean Dacier is a part which, now that he
is his own master and may claim his property where he finds
it, M. Coquelin will consult the interests of his highest
reputation by taking up again at an early day.

As the beauty of this creation comes back to me I am
almost ashamed to have described his strong point just now
as the representation of impudence. There is not a touch of
that excess in the portrait of the young republican captain
who has sprung from the ranks and who finds himself, by
one of the strange complications of circumstances that occur
in great revolutions, married before he can turn round to the
daughter of his former seigneur, the lord of the manor, now
ruined and proscribed, under whom he grew up in his Breton
village. The young man, naturally, of old, before being swept
into the ranks, has adored in secret, and in secret only, the
daughter of the noble house, divided as he is from her by the
impassable gulf which in the novel and the drama, still more
than in real life, separates the countess and the serf. The
young woman has been reprieved from the scaffold on condition of her marrying a republican soldier—cases are on
record in which this clemency was extended to royalist
victims—and the husband whom chance reserves for her is
a person who was in the days of her grandeur and his own
obscurity as dust beneath her feet. I speak of chance, but as
I recover the situation it was not purely fortuitous, inasmuch
as Jean has already recognised the object of his passion—he
naturally escapes recognition himself—as she passes the windows of the guard-house at Nantes in the horrible cart of the
condemned. A "republican marriage," with the drum-head for
the registrar's table, has just been celebrated before the
spectator's eyes and those of the appalled young man; a
stout Breton damsel (not in this case a royalist martyr) has
cheerfully allowed herself to be conjoined by a rite not even
civil, and of scarce more military grace than if performed

by a court-martial, with one of her country's defenders. This strikes the note of Jean's being able to save his former mistress—the idea flashing upon him as he sees her—if she will accept a release at such a price. But how can she herself know whether or not she accepts it?—she is too dazed, too bewildered and overwhelmed. The revulsion is too great and the situation too shocking to leave her for the moment her reason; and an extraordinarily striking passage, as well as one of the most consummately performed things I remember to have seen, was the entrance of Madame Favart as the heroine at this stage of the piece. She has at a moment's notice been pulled down from the tumbril, and with her hands just untied, her hair disordered, her senses confounded, and the bloody vision of the guillotine still in her eyes, she is precipitated into the roomful of soldiers with the announcement of the inconceivable terms of her pardon in her ears. The night I saw the play the manner in which Madame Favart, in this part, rendered in face and step all the amazement of the situation, drew forth a long burst of applause even while she still remained dumb.

The ceremony is concluded before this party to it regains her senses, and it is not till afterwards that she discovers the identity of her accomplice. I recall as a scene to which the actress's talent gave almost as much effect as Coquelin's own the third act of *Jean Dacier,* the episode of the poor room that sees the young republican captain introduce her as his bride—where the waiting *éclaircissement* takes place of course between the couple so portentously brought together. As I thus refer to it a certain analogy with the celebrated cottage-scene in *The Lady of Lyons* occurs to me; but I was not struck with this in watching the play. The step the young man has taken has, it appears, been only to save the life of his unwitting mistress; this service rendered, he wishes but to efface himself, worship her though he does, without insisting on the rights of a husband. The situation is of course foredoomed to still richer romance and still sharper tragedy; by the time Marie, whose noble surname I forget, apprehends in her companion the moral beauty of this effort of sacrifice, by the time a new passion on her side begins to supplant her first impression of his plan to take a base advantage of her, by this time it is inevitably too late and we are close up against the catastrophe. I forget how the climax occurs; I roughly recover it as determined by Jean's taking or appearing to take part in a secret movement for putting the life of the girl's father, his old feudal superior, so to speak, in safety as against his own colleagues, the republican chiefs. The attempt, the virtual treachery to *them*, comes to light after it has succeeded, and the young man's life, either by his own hand or by military justice, is the terrible forfeit. What I am most distinct about is that while the curtain falls the once proud Marie, who has fathomed the depths of his heroism, flings herself upon his inanimate form. All this is of the finest high pitch—the interest of M. Lomon's play, you see, must have been intense; and my theory would be that M. Coquelin's rendering of his part was a marvel. Not formed by nature for depicting romantic love, he triumphed over every obstacle superficially presented to his zeal, and gave signal support to the interesting truth that if a player have in him the active imagination of his opportunity, which is the root of the matter, with a superiority in two or three of the arts of suggestion, his mere outward facts needn't at all interfere with the consistency of the figure he desires to impose.

Without the root of the matter, as in every other art, nothing else, however it may disconnectedly pretend, has any contributive virtue—whereas that inward force may occasionally cause the physical desert itself to flower, or to seem to for the hour, which comes to the same thing. The impression of the ear, it can scarce be too often repeated, may always at the worst charm away the objections raised by the eye; though I have never known the impression of the eye to charm away a protest strongly made by the ear. In proof of the former of which propositions, one may ask, who does not recall from experience some case of the happy process so exhibited? The immediate alarm, after the rise of the curtain or on the entrance of the apparently ill-starred figure, has been dispelled, genius taking its time to intervene; the omens have been boldly reinterpreted and the claim to interest and convince us made good. Vivid for me to this day my disconcertment, long years ago, by the prime aspect of that sincerest of artists and most attaching of heroines Aimée Desclée, who "came on" in *Froufrou,* the part she was to launch on its prodigious career, only to surround herself at once with the cloud of doubts that she was within the next ten minutes so triumphantly to sweep away that no one of them lifted its head again during the whole of the piece. I cherish that memory for its supremely exquisite support of the truth most precious in all this connection, the truth that expression and persuasion so depend on the actor's intelligence, on its being of the finest possible order for the particular application, and so take effect in proportion as it *is* of such an order, that other measurements and tests cease in comparison to be urgent. I see some of these indeed claiming on behalf of the pantomimist, the *mime* pure and simple; but even then what are his motions, what is his play of face, but so many tones and syllables, so many signified mute words, all making sentences and with the sole difference of their being addressed to the mental instead of the physical ear? Language is not the less in question for its but *appearing* to be uttered; when the art is consummate we fail to distinguish between appearance and sound. All of which brings me round again without inconsequence to my point, on behalf of Coquelin's Jean Dacier, that youth, passion, patriotism, tenderness, renunciation, everything gallant and touching and that causes the sense to thrill and melt, are embodied for me, without attenuation by the years, in the little republican officer with the meagre material presence, the weather-worn uniform, the *retroussé* nose and that far-ringing, nerve-stirring voice which in certain of the patriotic couplets of the first act played through the place like a clarion. I note moreover that the part is tragic without a moment's look-in, as the phrase goes, of that apology for truth when truth becomes difficult which is known in the theatre as the "relief" of an altered pitch. The strings of the lyre are individual, and when the tune and the harmony are all in the graver ones I hate to find the others irrelevantly twanged.

It comes over me further, to revert, that if that admirable old Alsatian country schoolmaster in the *Ami Fritz,* of whom our intending visitor makes so inimitable a figure, is not tragic, neither is he in any degree impudent. I recall this character as a finished image of quaint old-world geniality and morality, of patriarchal and peaceful *bonhommie.* Wondrously elaborated, yet never exaggerated, it reproduces the individual in his minutest particularities, and yet keeps him closely related to the medium, the sheltered social scene, in which he moves—keeps him perfect in tone, perfect above all in taste. The taste in which MM. Erckmann-Chatrian's schoolmaster is embalmed I judge it would be impossible to M. Coquelin under any betrayal of opportunity whatever to depart from. It bears him company as a classic temperance—not less in the grotesque unctuousness of M. Loyal abovementioned than in the extravagance of the grimacing, chanting, capering footman of the *Précieuses.* Which comes back, as I have already hinted, to his letting go of the treasure of style as little in his lowest comedy as in his highest. His presentment of the Duc de Septmonts in the *Étrangère,* to which I have already alluded, is an instance of his highest and of the conditions in which he draws upon the treasure

most considerately and quietly. I have left myself no space
to devote to this consummate creation, which I had in mind
in speaking just now of his Jean Dacier as surpassed for
"importance" but by one other case in his repertory. (I can
only answer of course for those I have seen, and there are
several I have unluckily missed. Among these are three or
four characters of the last few years, such as the chief in the
Député de Bombignac, and the chief in Octave Feuillet's
Chamillac, figures, I believe, with nothing whatever in common save an intimate actability, of which he appears to have
taken with equal ease an extraordinary advantage. Such light
studies of the infinitely modern as the former of the things
just named, and as the hero of *Un Parisien,* happily within
my ken, are a new extension of his range, and help to represent in him that liveliest of the self-respecting actor's ideals,
and the greatest honour of the craft, I think, the placing at
the two ends of his scale the most different images conceivable.) It is not on our artist's lighter efforts, however, that I
should waste words—his marvellous virtuosity just *finds* ease
in material out of which his weaker brethren have to extract
it by the sweat of their brow; and it is more to the purpose
that if Jean Dacier is his highest flight in the line of rhymed
parts the Duc de Septmonts is his finest stroke in the field of
a closer realism. Fine indeed the aesthetic sense and the
applied means that can invite, that can insidiously encourage,
a conception so to mature and materialise, and that can yet
so keep it in the tone of life as we commonly know life, keep
it above all "in the picture" in which it is concerned and in
relation to the other forms of truth that surround it, forms
it may not barbarously sacrifice. M. Coquelin's progress
through this long and elaborate part, all of fine shades and
pointed particulars, all resting on the keenest observation as
well as appealing to it, resembles the method of the "psycho-
logical" novelist who (when he is in as complete possession
of his form as M. Coquelin of *his*) builds up a character, in
his supposedly uncanny process, by touch added to touch,
line to line, illustration to illustration, and with a vision of
his personage breathing steadily before him. It wouldn't take
much more than my remembrance of the Duc de Septmonts
at the Français to make me pronounce his exponent really the
Balzac of actors. The fact that his farewell to the great
theatre (taken in conjunction with some other recent com-
motions, some other rifts within the lute, now indeed a goodly
number) will have upon the classic scene itself belongs to a
range of considerations which, though seductive, are not
open to us here. But it is impossible not to follow with

interest, in fact with a lively suspense, the future of the distinguished seceder; his endowment, his capacity, his fortune up to this time, with the remaining possibilities of such an ambition, have so the weight of assurance, the exploring, conquering air. He is an image of success as well as of resolution, and with so much of the booty of his general quest appropriated, we look to see where the rest of it may be stored. If he draws it forth, as well he may, in forms as yet unsuspected and undiscovered, his career must still have a scope, and our attention a thrill, at least proportionate to what the past has done for us. The defect of his activity, if I may "drag in" again that note—no very assured one at the best—is a certain technical hardness, an almost inhuman perfection of surface; but the compensation of this on the other hand is that it suggests durability and resistance, resistance I mean to the great corrupting contact with the public. May that virtue in him not break down under such a test as our American conditions have it in their dread power to apply!

HENRY JAMES

1886-1915

Art and the Actor

For some time past, much attention has been devoted to the members of our profession; the actor and the theatre have been discussed again and again; an attempt has been made to prove that we are a race of beings set apart from the rest of the world, whether viewed from a social or an artistic point; some have even gone so far as to call us mere parrots. I shall now try to prove that the actor is an artist, and has the same title to a place in the state as any other citizen.

In the first place, what is *art,* and what do we understand by it, if not the interpretation of nature and of truth, more or less tinged by a peculiar light, which does not alter the proportions, but yet marks the salient features, heightens their colors, displays their fidelity to nature, so that our minds are more deeply and forcibly affected by them?

Is it not the actor's duty to cast this light?

The poet has for his material, words; the sculptor, marble or bronze; the painter, colors and canvas; the musician, sounds; but the actor is his own material. To exhibit a thought, an image, a human portrait, he works upon himself. He is his own piano, he strikes his own strings, he molds himself like wet clay, he paints himself!

But you may say this is not work for an artist, because the idea that he embodies is not his own, and the characteristic feature of art is creation. Creation, indeed! Common-sense answers this objection at once, since the very word *creation* is the one which we use to express the first performance of a part; and the term is strictly correct. If you do not believe me, believe Victor Hugo, who says of Mlle. George, in *Marie Tudor,* "In the poet's own creation, she creates something which surprises and enchants the author himself."

I also find in the Memoirs of Marmontel:

[Mlle. Clairon] was yet more sublime in the character of Electra. This part, which Voltaire himself required to be declaimed like one long lamentation, acquired a beauty hitherto unknown even to him; for when he saw her play it in his theatre at Ferney, he exclaimed, "This is not my work, but hers; she has created her part!"

Here we have the opinion of both Marmontel and Voltaire. Is not the poet's surprise significant? If he felt it, how much more must others experience it! Nor have they failed to do so; in proof, read their prefaces, postscripts, and dedications.

Victor Hugo also wrote, on the day after the first performances of *The Burgraves,* this opinion of Geffroy:

> M. Geffroy, who, as painter and actor, is twice an artist, and a great artist, gave to the personality of Otbert the predestinating physiognomy which such poets as Shakespeare know how to conceive, and such actors as Geffroy to embody.

A curious extract from the elder Dumas, in regard to *Henri III,* follows:

> Michelot has been reproached by many for his conception of the part. I am the one to be blamed. I, in some measure, forced M. Michelot to play the part in accordance with documents which critics consider incorrect. Since then, he has taken another view of the part—that which he first chose—and has been much applauded: the case has been tried. . . . I was wrong.

Speaking of Firmin:

> He finds in his part, not only delicate distinctions unperceived by the author, but those expressions of the soul which seize and shake the soul.

The dedication of *Angèle* is:

> To the actors who played *Angèle:* My friends, we have had a family triumph; let us accept and share it.

I also find in Halévy's memoirs:

> In 1835 Nourrit played the part of the Jew Eleazar. In the account given me by M. Scribe of the plot of *La Juive,* and of the way in which he intended to treat the subject, the part of Leopold, the Christian, lover of the Jewess Rachel, was meant for Nourrit; the father was to fall to the share of Levasseur, and the cardinal to Dabadie. But when I examined the score, I was struck by the new

meaning which a tenor voice would impart to the music, Nourrit's voice to the part of the father. This also gave me the voice and talent of Levasseur, as the Cardinal, who is a father also.

M. Scribe agreed with me, and with one accord we gave the poem to Nourrit to read, leaving him free to choose his own part. A few days later, he said, "My choice is made; I feel the instincts of a father." Nourrit, in thus falling into our plan, was moved by a sincere love of his art. The tenor usually clings to his prerogatives as a *lover;* he dreads lest he should lose the fascination of youth forever, should he make himself up as an old man—fears to leave with his audience, especially the feminine portion of it, a lasting memory of an ugly mask, and the premature marks of that fatal age which the actor's art is so skillful in concealing: but Nourrit was young enough, and felt himself strong enough to confront this danger, and he generously sacrificed himself for the common interest. He also gave us excellent advice. There was a *finale* in the fourth act, for which he begged us to substitute an aria. I wrote the appropriate music, and Nourrit asked M. Scribe's permission to write the words himself. He desired to choose the most sonorous syllables, as well as those most favorable to his voice. M. Scribe, generous because he was rich, readily consented to the singer's request, and Nourrit shortly after brought us the words of the air, 'Rachel, quand du seigneur la grâce tutelaire.'

You see that Nourrit also was both commentator and creator.

And of Frédérick Lemaître, Lamartine wrote in his preface to *Toussaint l'Overture* "that a great actor had veiled the imperfections of the work beneath the splendors of his genius."

I do not deny that these dedications may contain a spice of exaggeration, caused by the friendly feeling resulting from long labors in common, and by a certain benevolent impulse arising from a joyful success—we are most amiable when we are happiest; but I feel sure that the portion of truth is large enough to make them an important testimony from those best calculated to give it.

Yes, the actor creates, even when interpreting the dreams of a genius like Racine, Corneille, or Hugo; even, stranger yet, when the character is one conceived and executed by one of those rare masters who were themselves actors, like Shakespeare and Molière.

This is because there is always a considerable distance between the type dreamed of and the type actually living and breathing; because it is not enough to create a soul—a body must be provided for it as well; and not only must this body be its complete and living expression, but it must have its peculiar manner of coming and going, of laughing, crying, walking, breathing, talking, and moving; and all these modes of being, doing, and suffering must fit together—form a real individuality, such a person as we meet every day, recognize, love, and greet affectionately, and this habit which the character needs is furnished by the actor, and the actor alone.

This outer shell which the actor provides for a character, even for one of Shakespeare's conception, ends by becoming so thoroughly its own that there are certain bits of stage action, certain make-ups, invented by Garrick or by Kean, which are now appropriated by every Hamlet and Othello; there are certain traditions at the Théâtre Français, unmentioned by Molière, without which Molière is never played, and which the spectator, becoming a reader, mentally supplies as he sits by his fireside, as one supplies omissions in an incomplete copy.

Further yet, there are certain masterpieces—somewhat antiquated, it is true—which are greatly admired when read, but which all agree in pronouncing impossible of representation—let us be bold; which all would call stupid if performed, and which would be so if intrusted to ordinary actors. But let a man of talent come forward; let him take possession of the work buried beneath the dust of indifference—or respect, which sometimes produces the same results as indifference; let this man step in, lavish his powers and his genius upon it, and behold, the mummy bursts its cerements, is once more fresh and blooming, and the mob rushes to gaze and goes wild with enthusiasm, and the forgotten masterpiece draws crowded houses! In this case, art is not content with creating, it brings the dead to life!

Let us add that there are but few masterpieces so perfect that the actor cannot find something to add to them, if so willed. Much more frequent are the parts wherein an author of second, third, or any rank leaves his interpreter everything or almost everything to do. What remains to us of all the classicist dramas of the Empire or the Restoration—*Leonidas, Marius, Charles VI,* etc.? Nothing but the memory of Talma. Only try to read them through. You come to the passages where you know that Talma was sublime, and you puzzle your brains with the question, "But how the mischief did he do it?" The answer is simple: he turned creator. You read the scene—you find naught save the words of Arnault or Pichat, and it is meaningless; he put the spirit of Talma into it—it was vivid, it was great, it was sublime! And you tell me that this is not art? Pray tell me what it is, then.

I hold that acting is an art; analogous to that of the portrait painter, for instance. The type which the actor must reproduce (and this is a difficulty unknown to the painter) is not always set before him; he must begin, as we may say, by conjuring it out of empty air like the magician. The author, if he have talent and genius, holds up a perfect image before the mirror of his mind; in other cases—most frequently, as I said before—the actor has but a sketch, a rough model to work from; yet again, he is forced to borrow from the common fund—that is, human nature—and to paint in imagination, by dint of observation and reflection, the figure to be realized later on.

Very great actors sometimes have the splendid good luck to create out of whole cloth, almost in spite of their authors; to invent types which will live side by side with the offspring of Molière's brain. Every one must know that I refer especially to Frédérick Lemaître and his immortal creation, Robert Macaire.

I will let Frédérick speak for himself, quoting his account of the first performance of the *Auberge des Adrets:*

The story of this gloomy melodrama, transformed into a burlesque, after being written in all due earnest, has been so falsified that it may not prove uninteresting to give the true origin of this odd fancy, which proved to be but the prologue to a comedy destined ten years later to wound to the quick the susceptibility of more than one office-holding Robert Macaire, or order-wearing Bertrand.

When the reading, which took place at the theatre, ended, I went away deeply discouraged at the thought that this part of Macaire was to be my first creation.

How could I make the public accept this mysterious and melancholy plot, which was wrought out in a style in no wise academic? Without appearing ridiculous, how could I portray a character so grossly cynical? a highway assassin, frightful as the ogre of any fairy tale, and carrying his impudence to the extent of curling his whiskers with a dagger, while eating a bit of Gruyère cheese!

I really did not know which way to turn; when one evening, as I sat poring over the pages of my manuscript, I began to see how excessively farcical all the situations and speeches of Robert Macaire and Bertrand might appear, if taken jocosely and acted accordingly.

I at once shared with Firmin—a clever fellow, who, like me, felt ill at ease with a serious Bertrand—the wild, crazy idea which had crossed my brain. He thought it superb! But we had to beware of suggesting this change of base to the authors, who were convinced that they had produced another *Cid*.

Firmin and I firmly resolved to execute our plan, let it cost what it might; we arranged all our stage effects together, without breathing a word of our secret to any one; and on the night of the first performance we made an entrance at which we had not even hinted at the rehearsals.

When the audience saw the two bandits take their positions near the footlights, in the attitude so often copied since, muffled in costumes which have become traditional—Bertrand in his huge gray coat, with its inordinately long pockets, both hands crossed over the handle of his umbrella, erect, motionless, face to face with Macaire, who measured him with a swaggering stare, his crownless hat on one side of his head, his green coat flung back, his red trousers covered with patches and darns, his black bandage over one eye, his lace cravat and dancing shoes—the effect was overwhelming.

Nothing escaped the eager shrewdness of a public excited to the utmost by so new and unforeseen a spectacle. The kicks lavished upon Bertrand, Macaire's squeaky snuff-box —every allusion was seized with the more hilarity, from the fact that the rest of the piece was played by the other actors with all the gravity and earnestness which their parts required.

Audinot and Sénépart, our managers, attained a success which they were far from expecting; for they frankly confessed, some time after, that they had had but little confidence in the piece.

The authors, Benjamin Antier and St. Amand, who were later to become my collaborators in *Robert Macaire*, resigned themselves to their fate like sensible men, and were easily consoled for their failure to melt their audience to tears as they had dreamed, without shedding any on their own account when they saw the nightly receipts mount up to a figure hitherto unknown in the annals of the theatre.

But their third accomplice, a certain Dr. Polyanthe—a dramatic author through the force of circumstances, who, if he had not most fortunately stopped short, might have managed to murder as many melodramas as he did patients

—vowed eternal vengeance against me. He went about everywhere, declaring that I had slaughtered his play! He, at least, had paternal instincts.

And again, how much help did Frédérick Lemaître have from the authors of *Paillasse* or of *The Old Corporal* (in which he played the part of a deaf-mute), or of countless other parts? We must remember that the same man who invented Robert Macaire was also the marvelous interpreter of Ruy Blas; we can then comprehend the full force of the expression used by Victor Hugo in giving an account of the evening of November 9, 1838, on which he says Frédérick made the part, not a performance, but a *transfiguration*. This is the right word; this is the supreme effort of the actor's art.

And may we not apply this fitting title, transfiguration, to Régnier, when he played in *La Joie fait peur, Gabrielle,* the *Adventurière,* or *Romulus;* to Samson, as the peer of France in the *Camaraderie,* the Marquis de La Sieglière, Bertrand de Rantzau, or Sganarelle (in *Don Juan*); to Delaunay, when he plays Fortunio, Perdican, or the enchanting Horace of *The School for Wives;* to Got, whether he be Duke Job, Giboyer, or his incredible priest in *Il faut jurer de rien;* to Dumaine, in *Patrie!;* to St. Germain, in *Baby?*

The memories which I have evoked recall another of the arguments often used against us. The actor does not create, it is said, because he leaves nothing of himself behind after death. This is indeed the great misfortune of our art. Talma deplored it on his dying bed. And yet it is not an absolute truth, since Frédérick, as we have just seen, left behind him a type which is still vigorous and strong. But even were it rigorously true, why should we hesitate to exercise an art because the creations of that art are perishable? Is the actor the only sufferer from a similar cause? What is left to us of Apelles, and all the great painters of antiquity? A memory, as of the actor Callipides, the contemporary of Phidias. How long do the creations of art usually endure? Alas! that is a question of more or less. How many sublime works of poets, painters, and sculptors have vanished forever! Creation is one thing; durability another. Marble is more lasting than canvas, verses more enduring than marble, but time devours them all. Suppose that, as the result of a natural and fatal law, at the moment that Michelangelo died, by the same stroke of an invisible hammer, death had reduced to powder all his works, from the Moses to the Last Judgment: because the work and the workman perished at the same instant, should you say, "Michelangelo was no artist; he did not create"?

The actor is in a similar predicament. His statues perish with him. Nothing remains of them, as of those of Praxiteles, but memories—sometimes too flattering, but more often not sufficiently so. I repeat it, this is the misfortune of our art: it cheats us of that supreme consolation of unappreciated genius, the appeal to posterity. However, misfortune though it be, it is no degradation. We are to be pitied for it, that is all. Love us the more for it, dear charitable public, since you are at once our present and our future, and our immortality dies with the echo of your applause!

I have used the word *memories*. It is through this, in fact, that we survive, as well as by the occasional shock which some one of us, more powerful than the rest—a sort of artistic leader—imparts to a whole era. A great actor calls forth plays. Witness Burbage in the time of Shakespeare; witness Frédérick or Bocage. Others may create a school, revolutionize the traditional costume, delivery, and the general rendition of the masterpieces of the age, and thus apparently renovate and renew them.

"The actor is an artist, then? And now tell us his aim."

Well—we might say, in a very general way, that it is the same as that of all women: to please.

Only, with an actor ambitious for himself and his art, it is to please by satisfying the nobler or more delicate instincts of the public; by charming with a display of the beautiful; by transporting with the spectacle of grandeur; by rousing healthy laughter or reflection through the representation of the truth.

If we come to the question whether actors are really useful—that is, whether the pleasure which they provide, and which I have just defined, is profitable to mankind—this is plainly a question of the utility of the theatre itself; and I would refer my reader to what has been written on the subject by masters interested therein, like Corneille, Molière, Shakespeare, and, in antiquity, Aristotle, in his chapter on this question.

To me, I must own that it seems puerile to question the utility of an institution which responds to so manifest a want on the part of humanity.

In the age of stone, rough or polished, this want generated savage pantomimes, mock challenges, and combats. After the deluge—let the reader observe that I pass directly on to this point—we find it once more among religious orders, inspiring those mystery plays which were veritable dramas, such as *The Death and Resurrection of Adonis*. Every primitive race has had similar performances. Wherever society exists, there we find the theatre; and it is always at the moment that the nation leaves barbarism triumphantly behind that the theatre assumes its complete and final form, and wings its flight proudly upward. It is pre-eminently a peaceful and supercivilized art; and it is among races especially amiable and social, like the Greeks and the French, that it attains its highest degree of splendor, and from among whom it sends its most brilliant rays to gild the ancient or modern world.

What does the theatre actually do? It sets man face to face with himself. It paints his destinies for his own inspection. For, the theatre being a thing of many sides, its utility is of diverse kinds, and extends from mere amusement and simple physical relaxation to the highest lessons of morality. A pleasant comedy by Labiche, which makes us as cheery as its author for the time being, is profitable in quite another way than *Cinna* or the *Horaces*. And as I have mentioned the works of Corneille, let me say that it seems to me difficult to deny that they contain as much that may be usefully applied as the finest treatise on duty, and that these plays must ever be a national reserve of patriotism and dignity in moments of trouble or of danger. But, finally, if the utility of the theatre is not always so great—if it does not correct our vices, as it claims to do, by showing us our common weaknesses and infirmities, by making us laugh or cry over them— it at least teaches us to bear with one another, to forgive one another; in a word, it makes us more sociable, it makes us more human.

The theatrical world is divided into two opposing camps in regard to the question whether the actor should partake of the passions of his part—weep himself in order to draw tears—or whether he should remain master of himself throughout the most impassioned and violent action on the part of the character which he represents; in a word, remain unmoved himself, the more surely to move others, which forms the famous paradox of Diderot.

Well, I hold this paradox to be literal truth; and I am convinced that one can only be a great actor on condition of complete self-mastery and ability to express feelings which are not experienced, which may never be experienced, which from the very nature of things never can be experienced.

And this is the reason that our trade is an art, and this is the cause of our ability to create!

The same faculty which permits the dramatic poet to bring forth from his brain a Tartuffe, or a Macbeth armed and equipped, although he, the poet, be a thoroughly upright and honest man, permits the actor to assimilate this character, to dissect and analyze it at will, without ceasing to be for an instant distinctly himself, as separate a thing as the painter and his canvas.

The actor is within his creation, that is all. It is from within that he moves the springs which make his character express the whole gamut of human consciousness; and all these springs, which are his nerves, he must hold in his hand, and play upon as best he can. I do not say that this can be done without difficulty and fatigue; it may be carried to utter exhaustion; that is a mere matter of temperament. But each must regulate his own expenditure of force.

The actor makes up his personage. He borrows from his author, he borrows from stage tradition, he borrows from nature, he draws on his own stock of knowledge of men and things, on his own experience and imagination; in short, he sets himself a task. His task once set, he has his part; he sees it, grasps it—it does not belong to him, but he inhabits its body, is fairly it!

This is why the true actor is always ready for action. He can take up his part, no matter when, and instantly excite the desired effect. He commands us to laugh, to weep, to shiver with fear. He needs not to wait until he experiences these emotions himself, or for grace from above to enlighten him.

Talma was playing Hamlet one night. While waiting for his cue he was talking in the wings with a friend; the callboy, seeing him smiling and apparently thinking of anything but his lines, came up: "M. Talma, your entrance comes directly!" "All right, all right, I am waiting for my cue." His scene, the scene with the Ghost, began off the stage, the spectators hearing Talma before they saw him. He went on with his conversation very gayly; the cue came, he pressed his friend's hand, and—a smile still on his lips, that kindly hand in his—he exclaimed:

> Angels and ministers of grace, defend us!

and his terrified friend started back, and a shudder ran through the audience.

Did this prevent him from being natural? By no means. But the artist's brain must remain free, and all emotions, even his own, must expire on the threshold of his thought. These are two very different regions. Is the actor the only person in whom these phenomena occur? Allow me to quote a fact, although it may seem foreign to my subject.

A friend of M. Victor Massé assured me very recently of the truth of a story which I had frequently heard: it was at the bedside of his mother, whom he adored, of his mother suffering from the disease destined to be fatal, all hope of recovery being lost—it was then and there that the master, inspired, despite the most poignant grief, composed—what music do you think? The lively, gay, and tripping airs of the *Noces de Jeanette!*

And examples abound of this mutual independence of head and heart in the artist. One more shall suffice me. Talma is again my hero. It is said that when he learned of the death of his father, he uttered a piercing cry; so piercing, so heart-felt that the artist always on the alert in the man instantly took note of it and decided to make use of it upon the stage, later on. This characteristic trait shows us the artist looking down upon his own emotions and studying them, as it were from a superior plane, yielding to them that he might store them up for future use and reference. And just as their sorrows often serve great poets as the inspiration of their best verses, so ours may serve us in the creation of great parts.

We find the same trait in this man when on his deathbed: regretting not life but art, which was the interest and the honor of his life, he studied with an artist's eye his poor, emaciated body, and said to a friend, plucking at his withered neck, "That would have been fine in Tiberius!" The fact of the matter is that, had he been able, he would have dragged his perishing frame to the theatre to incarnate the tyrant. There he would have used just that amount of sickness and suffering required by his part, and would have commanded the remainder to cease to exist. In the same way—to go back —in repeating his cry of orphaned woe upon the boards, he would have ruled his own emotion: what do I say? he would have experienced none! In both cases he would have been the actor, and nothing but the actor, master and monarch of all of humanity within him; a sufficiently great actor to imitate, without the aid of disease, the sharpened features and withered neck of Tiberius, as well as to discover for himself, by the sole light of his genius, without the loss of a father, the cry which nature wrested perforce from his lips.

Therefore the actor needs not to be actually moved. It is as unnecessary as it is for a pianist to be in the depths of despair to play the Funeral March of Chopin or of Bee-thoven aright. He knows it; he opens his instrument, and your soul is harrowed. I would lay a heavy wager, on the contrary, that if he should give way to any personal emotion, he would play but ill; and by analogy, that an actor who regarded his own emotions otherwise than as material to be utilized, or who made the passions of his part absolutely his own, would be likely to fare badly; emotion sobs and stammers, alters and breaks the voice. He would cease to make himself audible. The natural effect of passion is to destroy all self-government; we lose our heads, and how can we be expected to do well rather than ill, when we cease to know what we are doing?

A certain degree of excitement may not be injurious, but I should never place great value on the wit or the affection of a man who only displayed those qualities after partaking of champagne or of truffles.

I do not intend to deny the existence of what are called strokes of genius, but I think that genius is displayed far better by an entire and enduring mastery of self than by intermittent flashes—sublime, if you will, but incoherent and incomprehensible; a trump only turned up by mere chance. And then, nothing is more likely to produce inspiration than good hard preparatory work, the fertilizing of the brain by meditation, and constant rehearsing of the character.

The opinion which I maintain has been upheld by all truly great actors: Talma, Rachel, Samson, Régnier, and Mme. Dorval. The opposite opinion is a prejudice of the crowd. It is in virtue of this prejudice that this same crowd which will not suffer—with great show of reason, indeed—that the actor should reveal so much as a glimpse of his own feelings, his household cares, through his assumed character, and which permits, nay, commands us to play side-splitting farces when we feel more like crying our eyes out—it is in virtue, I say, of this simple prejudice that this same crowd waits at the theatre door for the villain of the piece, to greet him with a warm reception. When M. Provost played the character of Sir Hudson Lowe, at the Porte Saint-Martin, he was obliged to have a strong bodyguard to escort him from the theatre every night.

This brings us to the hotly contested question of stage convention, as opposed to realism—to naturalism, as it is now called.

To my mind, nothing is great, nothing is beautiful, which is unnatural; but here again I feel obliged to repeat, acting is an art, and consequently nature can be reproduced by it only with that species of luster and relief without which there can be no art.

I may say further, that nature pure and simple would produce but a slight effect upon the stage.

And this is very easily understood. Multiply your scenic devices, produce marvelous effects, ruin yourself in absurdly accurate details, in costumes fitted to drive a Benedictine or a collector mad with delight, and you cannot make the scene upon which the stage action occurs a real one.

You are at the theatre, and not in the street or at home. If you suppose the scene to occur in the street, or in a private house, the effect is somewhat similar to that produced by setting a life-sized figure up on a high column; it no longer appears life-size.

You have a special and peculiar medium; you must use it in an appropriate manner.

Let us take an example—the voice. Should I speak on the stage as I do in a parlor, in the same friendly tone with which I inquire for your health, I should not be understood, or even heard. Your room, which I can cross in a few strides, is quite a different thing from the vast space where from fifteen to eighteen hundred people are hanging on my words, each having an equal right to hear me. To produce an effect equal in value to that produced within the four walls of your room if I were talking alone with you I must raise my voice, accent my words more strongly; and to be clearly understood, I must introduce tones and expressions which in private I should not require to use, because in private you would be thoroughly conversant with my character.

This is a necessary convention. It entails similar concessions in regard to gesture; and these, taken as a whole, are the result of optical laws. Given this background, the stage— isolated, elevated, brightly lighted—and that collection of conventional properties, the footlights, wings, scenery, the actors themselves—for an actor is himself a convention—we must absolutely modify the conditions of real life to suit this background, if we would produce the illusion of real life upon the spectators.

I can scarcely enter into the details of these important conventions; their study would be too special, too technical; but I must note one essential point, and this is that, as a lifelike effect is to be produced on these fifteen or eighteen hundred people assembled together, whom we call the public, we must take into account their intellectual status and their degree of culture. The Parisian public is not to be deceived by the same illusions that would suit an audience of savages. A crowd of children is content with the very rude apparatus required by a Punch and Judy show, nor was much more skill required to amuse an audience in the time of Shakespeare; we are far more difficult to please nowadays. In a word, the law of enhancement, of setting things in relief, is eternal, because it is an artistic law; but stage effects change with the progress of time and civilization.

The ruder manners of our ancestors possibly made fierce rollings of the eyes and of the *r*'s a theatrical necessity. The gentler manners of the present day render this kind of exaggeration superfluous. The pitch has been lowered.

I am not in favor of the singsong style, and I detest bombast. But if, for example, a general intellectual disturbance should occur tomorrow, as it did in 1830; if the nation, being overwrought, became passionate, violent, and unreasonable— I think it probable that a similar revolution would follow in the theatrical world, and we should be obliged to raise the pitch to keep ourselves in tune.

In treating this question thus passingly, I assume, as is evident, the peculiar point of view of the actor. If I were to examine the matter more closely, I should refer to the very beautiful preface which the younger Dumas has just added to his play of the *Étrangère*. I have the satisfaction of holding the same opinion as that master, son of another master mind, from whom he has inherited so much; I mean in a theatrical way. M. Alexandre Dumas, it seems to me, gives us an admirable definition of our art and a clear explanation of the reasons which render an absolute fidelity to truth and nature impossible upon the stage.

To sum up my assertions: We must not destroy all truth in the theatre by too frequent use of conventions; but neither must we destroy the theatrical illusion by too great fidelity to fact. And by theatrical illusion I mean the pleasure in search of which people go to the theatre—that theatrical pleasure, partly composed indeed of the illusion that they are seeing a reality, but mingled with a feeling of personal safety and a sincere conviction that they are assisting only at an illusion.

This sense of security must never be destroyed. If by dint of realism or artifice you succeed in making your spectator forget absolutely that he is witnessing a mere spectacle, he ceases to be amused; he becomes an actor instead of a spectator, and what is worse, a well-gulled actor, for he is the only sincere one.

Theatrical joys are analogous to the pleasure of the wise Lucretius, who loved to watch a storm at sea from the shore. If this philosopher had been forced to embark, his pleasure would have speedily vanished.

Therefore, try to produce an apparent truth; but let it be true only in seeming. There is a whole class of sentiments and sensations which it is never well to excite at the theatre, for the irrefutable reason that they would prevent people from frequenting it. What are they? That is for you, actors or authors as the case may be, to discover; for it is generally a matter of delicate shades and distinctions. But I will name an example of an opposite kind: Paulin-Ménier, in *The Lyons Mail*.

Here we have a creation worthy of a master hand. With what supreme art this knavish figure was drawn! The gestures! the facial expression! and the inimitably vulgar accent! Do you remember?

Wasn't that nature itself? It was real, but it was not repulsive; it was alarming, but not frightful. This was art, and excellent art, too. There was the stroke of genius, the little touch which makes a picture by Teniers or Jan Steen a masterpiece. The spectator, amused or terrified, was never disgusted; he never felt impelled to rise and leave the hall. Mark that, I beg; we must never make our audience feel anxious to leave. What I say may be commonplace; but I, for my part, fail to see how a theatre can be maintained without an audience.

But, cry the purists, is that the only object of the theatre —amusement? Then make it an exhibition of women!

I do not say so. Not that I am opposed to exhibiting women, if art is to find a profit in it; that is to say if, by exhibiting them, we excite a purely theatrical pleasure in the spectator's breast, and not a pleasure of a lower, I might say more shameful, kind. But I do not forget the maxim, *Castigat ridendo mores;* only I would not omit one jot or tittle of it.

Yes, the theatre corrects our morals, but by ridicule and laughter. Suppress that tiny gerund *ridendo*, and you suppress the theatre; you change it to a penitentiary. Now a stage box, even a closed box, is not a confessional: if the theatre were such, are you very sure that we should find eighteen hundred people ready to go there every night? Rigid moralists assure us that men, and women too, sometimes seek the pleasures of the playhouse at church; but I never heard them say that men, or women either, ever sought for ecclesiastic instruction at the playhouse.

And let it be thoroughly understood that I use the word *ridendo* in its broadest sense. It means not only laughter, but, in a more general sense, pleasure—that which I call theatrical pleasure: a kind of gratification, I repeat, compounded of truth and deception, blended in unequal proportions, according to the nature of the play; a pleasure, in fine, which is but one variety, a very special and lively variety, of that delight always produced by art of whatever kind.

I have tried to establish the fact that the actor pursues an art; that this art has its difficulties, its utility, and its grandeur. Let me close by an attempt to establish the actor's proper position in modern society.

Among the Greeks, the true forefathers of the stage, the actor was held in very great esteem. We recall Callipides, who commanded the fleets of Athens, without therefore being obliged to renounce the buskin and the lyre.

This was partly because theatrical representations then partook of a religious and patriotic character. They were the results of Bacchic worship, and the priest of the god always presided over them.

At those splendid competitions where Æschylus and Sophocles vied with each other, all Greece eagerly hastened to gather and applaud in the vast ampitheatre, and it was like the national anniversaries of the present day; at least, like those held in France on the first of May and the thirtieth of June.

The Chorus in these ancient tragedies was composed to a certain degree of the people themselves; and through the mouth of their leader, in the parabases of Aristophanes, they deliberated upon affairs of state, in language worthy of Athens —that Athens which was formerly what our Paris now is, the admiration of philosophers and the distraction of all men.

In the Middle Ages the drama still retained somewhat of these characteristics, without the same poetic worth.

In the church, too, the drama was born with mystery plays and miracle plays; and our Brotherhood the Passion is the direct ancestor of the Théâtre Français.

In the immense length of the dramatic performances, which sometimes lasted for weeks at a time, in the public stages erected in the market place, in the vast crowds of people which thronged thither, we discover a rude resemblance to the dramatic festivals of Athens; as we also find the coarse witticisms of Aristophanes, with cruder, I was about to say more realistic tints, in the loose language of these old compositions, licentious in form and often audacious in thought as they are.

In those days church and theatre fraternized. How does it happen, then, that the church, so maternally inclined toward mystery plays and miracle plays, has picked so bitter a quarrel with us since?

I greatly fear that the quarrel dates back only to the time of the old farce; to the days of that dear Jack Pudding with whom I must have been hail-fellow-well-met in some previous state of existence.

Yes, I fear me that the quarrel began then with the daring dramatic satires of that excellent but unfortunate fellow who, as we all know, ventured to put upon the stage our Mother Church herself in the guise of a foolish parent, and his Holiness the Pope under the transparent title of the Obstinate Man.

The trouble began then; but it was not until later on, in Molière's time, that all reconciliation became impossible, and in the antipathy lavished upon us it is not difficult to distinguish a rankling resentment against *Tartuffe*. We share in the proscription of Molière. Nor would I complain of that.

There, methinks, in the rancor aroused by that immortal work, lurks the explanation of the long road traversed from the days of the actor Genest, whom the church canonized, to the actor Molière, whom she refused to bury in consecrated ground.

Still we must acknowledge that Mother Church has become somewhat appeased since then. She sometimes allows us to enter her precincts; she consents to bury us—perhaps with pleasure. But there still exist traces of the excommunication pronounced against us in days of yore; that stigma of inferiority which has so long weighed down the actor still remains an article of faith to many people, even among the most enlightened classes. In a word, the prejudice exists, it prevails, softened only and subdued by the progress of civilization in France since the Revolution.

And in fact, it is natural enough that a form of thought so vivid and of such wide circulation as that employed by the theatre should be regarded with anxiety and suspicion by all those old constitutional bodies, easily alarmed by an increasing degree of intellectual life and animation. Even now, nearly one hundred years after its first performance, I doubt if the magistracy would leave a representation of *The Marriage of Figaro* in any very indulgent mood.

But how happens it that this prejudice has still such weight with even a liberal public? for many receive us in their homes—nay, invite us thither—who are yet vaguely disturbed and distressed by any suggestion of perfect equality. We are petted, we are admired—I speak of actresses now; but if we pass certain limits, if we let fall the slightest claim to certain rights, lo and behold! the prejudice rears its snaky head and darts forth as fierce and forked a tongue as in the good old times.

I have no desire to refer to the rights which the public considers that it holds over us. I shall not inveigh against the hiss, which is assuredly the most odious of all noises, but which is a means of showing its displeasure to which the audience certainly has a right—a right placed under the sacrosaintly guard of one of Boileau's verses.

Nor against the throwing of onions and eggs, that waste of good victuals being now of rare occurrence, even in rural districts.

Nor against the apologies which an audience, sometimes more despotic than the laws of Christian charity or even simple justice would allow, occasionally exacts from some ill-fated actor, or, what is still worse, from some nervous, suffering actress who may perhaps have lost her lines or her patience.

Nor against cabals. And here I pause; but what does all this prove, if not the species of subjection under which the public, often unwittingly, still desires to hold the actor, the more or less favored slave of its good pleasure? a subjection more apparent in the provinces, where the old customs are kept up, prejudices included; where, furthermore, the actors, being but birds of passage, can scarcely have those regular relations with the public which a little talent on the one hand and good will on the other so readily transform into friendly intercourse.

And finally, let us suppose Molière to be born again among us. Undoubtedly, in consideration of the masterpieces which he would give you, you would forgive him for appearing on the stage. Assuredly the president of the Republic, no prouder in this particular than Louis XIV, would be charmed to add a leaf to his dinner table for him, were it merely as an elector, and would hand him a chicken's wing with the same engaging gesture as the sun of royalty did formerly; but would there not be many among the most fervent admirers of his genius, among those who most warmly applauded the actor and author in the character of Alceste, who would deem it a great mistake ever to allow the man with the green ribbons to become the man with the red ribbon?

It may be said that in our days Molière would never play in comedy. How can we tell? Who can say, and why might not the same fate which made him a comic actor before it made him an author play him the same romantic trick today? For we know the strength of his passion for our art, and his noble reply to Boileau, who urged him from respect for his own play, *The Misanthrope,* to throw off the sack of Scapin and abandon the stage: "What are you thinking of? I am honored by remaining." Honored! think of that! Molière honored! This phrase is worth pondering. Men like Molière are not to be numbered by legions!

It is a strange thing—painful, indeed, to my vanity as a Frenchman, a vanity which does not exceed decent bounds with me, although an actor's vanity is usually represented as overweening—it is a painful thing, I say, to know that this prejudice, strong as it is in France, is already abolished in other countries.

There is no trace of it in England, where—not to mention Shakespeare, because comparisons are odious—Garrick's name is graven in Westminster Abbey side by side with those of the most illustrious men. It does not exist in Germany, nor in Italy, nor in Russia, nor in Belgium, where actors receive the honorable distinctions denied them in France; nor in Sweden, where Mme. Ristori experienced as royal honors as if she had been a Rosa Bonheur; nor even in Austria, where I know a certain old actor in retirement who occasionally returns to tread the boards with his wonted fire despite his eighty years, and who has received a patent of nobility; nor does Austria stop there, for she has recently sent the order of Francis Joseph to two French artists, one of whom is the dean himself of the Comédie-Française.

Thus monarchies, even those whose aristocratic traditions are world-renowned, have ceased to consider actors as a class set apart in the social world: and France—what do I say! the French Republic persists in regarding them as such; and it is in this classic land of liberty, equality, and fraternity that this heaven-crying inequality is carefully embalmed in the most pious arguments.

Add to this a yet stranger fact: namely, that our repertory is universal; that the theatres of foreign countries feed and flourish upon it; that their actors may be made members of various orders simply for the way in which they interpret our works, and this while the French actor, the creator of those very works, is declared in France *non dignus entrare!*

Another reason constantly alleged has always struck me as utterly absurd, although it is most frequently employed, probably because, like Figaro's precepts, it sounds like a profound piece of thought. It is impossible, it is said, to confer on an actor the red ribbon in question, because he would be obliged to lay it aside at the very time that he exercised the art by which he gained it. Oh ho! But can we yield to logic which would force a man who rescues another from drowning to retain his cross of honor in taking the heroic plunge? And, not to make another odious comparison, although the servants of the house of Molière are sometimes reproached with executing their office with a shade too much solemnity, do not priests of the gospel who have been decorated remove their orders and decorations before they kneel at the altar?

Then what are the real reasons for the supposed inferiority with which certain people desire to brand the actor, the blows across the shoulders, the kicks and cuffs? But this is a mere question of his line of business; and why put under the ban of excommunication a knight like Delaunay, a commander like Maubant, an emperor like Ligier? Is it because these artists discharge their duty in person, and expose themselves to hisses and hoots as well as to applause?

But are they the only ones who do this? I spoke of volleys of onions and eggs just now; but learned professors have felt the same ere now, and M. Renan was once assailed with copper pennies.

And do not orators address themselves directly to the public as well, and do they not employ in their marvelous art —Heaven forgive me, but I was going to say tricks, very nearly akin to our own? I speak not only of political orators, for the pulpit has also its tribunes!

Is it because the actor, in fulfilling the duties of his profession, although exempted from the antique mask, is nevertheless forced by age and long use of paint (forgive the word!) to make a mask of his face? What, such a show of wrath for the red and white and the little pots in which our ladies keep such pretty pomades! Where will you draw the line, if you so sternly proscribe cosmetics and dyes; and are there not a few wigs which will tremble on the heads of our grave judges?

In reality, all the objections, whether serious, specious, or simply ingenious, which have been made to the social elevation of the actor, to his enjoyment of the mere rights of citizenship—all these reasons, I say, may be reduced to a single one, which is purely instinctive, and which I will now attempt to solve.

It is due to the fact that the renunciation by the actor of his own personality, to assume the character of one, ten, or twenty other people, is apparently a renunciation of his own dignity, and a denial of the dignity of mankind.

My words are high-sounding; but if you refuse to assent to them, what charge can you bring against a Talma or a Lekain? It is not because the actor may assume the guise of a Jocrisse that you refuse to yield him the same consideration which you would accord any other artist? for in that case you should, you ought to yield it to him who puts on the imperial purple of Augustus or the soul of the antique Horatius. No, it is merely because he assumes a character which is not his own, and because in ceasing to be himself you feel that he ceases to be a man.

To this objection—the only serious one, in my opinion—I have two answers to make: first, that it is false; second, that were it true, the actor is not responsible for it, and consequently ought not to suffer for it.

Yes, even were it true, the actor would not be responsible for this abdication of his dignity, since it is commanded by his poet-author; and if there be a degradation in the fact, it is not he who should be blamed, but the form itself of the art which necessitates the degradation, and the whole theatre; and you should exempt from your excommunication neither the dramatic author who exposes us poor minors to such corruption nor the manager who lends us his house in which to give ourselves over to vice—in your company, gentlemen.

But I deny that there is degradation, since there is no true abdication of personal dignity. The actor may indeed assume a disguise—I have said so too often to refuse to repeat it now—and it is this assumed character, not his own, which receives the blows and mockery, if need be: but this disguise, which he will doff ere long, he enters into with heart and soul, with all his mind, with all his courage. For on the night of a first performance he is like a soldier under fire; he enters into the character with his personal individuality, directive and creative. It is with this individual *self* that he makes you by turns shiver, weep, or smile, the noblest shudders, the most melting tears, the humanest smiles. He does not abdicate the throne: he reigns supreme. He may surrender to a certain point: he does not resign!

Consequently, his dignity is intact; he is no less a man, and he is an artist.

It seems to me that it would be a worthy action nowadays to lift from the actor, once and for all, the ban pronounced against him by monarchical society, which affected to consider him as a mere instrument of pleasure.

I see only advantages for every one in permitting the actor to resume the position in the French Republic which he held in the Athenian Republic.

And what may that be? Lord high admiral, like Callipides? Well! I don't say that; and whatever may be the inclination of modern artists and men of letters to invest themselves on every occasion with the rights and privileges of the priestly office, I, for one, will never lay claim to a pontificate.

Yet it seems to me that the actor might be profitably employed in matters of education—by means of essays like the present, for instance, by which he might render a real service to art—and that at the periodical festivals held to commemorate our national anniversaries there should be a place which he might worthily occupy. The public recitation of a fine ode or an epic poem could not fail to produce, on a people so gifted as the French, an impression as invigorating and as wholesome as the performance of any choir or orchestra, however melodious. Let my readers recall to mind the success achieved by Rachel with the Marseillaise, and they will better appreciate my meaning. A movement in this direction is already on foot, and I sincerely hope that it may strengthen and increase in extent as time goes on.

When a common emotion unites men, be it patriotic, artistic, or a feeling of religious recognition of some past glory, how effective would be the recitation of some fine poem filled with living thoughts, to rouse the best that there is in humanity, and what profit might not a nation derive from similar solemnities, devoted to the nurture of its native genius!

In rendering to the actor the honor due him, in setting him on an equal footing with his fellows in the eye of the law, we should but spur him on to such noble efforts; we should thus contribute to that elevation of art so often discussed in recent times, and to be effected simultaneously with the elevation of morals and manners.

I can hear the reader jestingly exclaim, "You are in the trade, M. Josse!" Yes, I am, and I am pleading for my house; but what else has been the custom of the world for these many ages past? And could I be expected to underrate the importance—I may say the necessity—of what some may call accomplishments, and many might call useless? Ah, me! The body requires the necessities of life, but it is the superfluous for which the spirit cries aloud.

I recall a charming poem by that excellent, delicate, and profound author, Sully-Prudhomme. The subject is the revolt of the flowers. They are seized with a fit of the spleen. Man, the world, the frightful monotony of fate, sadden and annoy them, and they decide to give over blossoming. All the roses disappear. There are no more lilies, to the grief of the young girls who love them; no more violets—such an injury to the month of May! no more poppies—and how forlorn the wheatfields look! In short, there is an end of the spring. But what is the use of having any flowers? say the philosophers. 'Tis but another bit of frivolity; that's all. Yes, but in this frivolity lies the grace of the year, the charm of life. All has faded; color and perfume, delicacy and beauty, are gone! Then what will become of the women? and of love? and consequently of pleasure and joy? It's of no use to talk about it, every one feels bored; envy and malice spread abroad; evil passions spring into life once more. Give us back the flowers; we must have flowers! And I fairly believe there would have been a regular revolution, barricades and all, if the tender heart of the rose had not been melted by the universal distress.

Well, without pushing the comparison too far, just fancy all the actors and actresses striking work, like Sully-Prud-homme's flowers! I ask you, on your word of honor can you deny that there would be a somewhat similar reversal of the order of nature? Would it be long before Paris, the Paris now so bright and so gay, become utterly uninhabitable? Why, people would drop dead in the streets from sheer *ennui!* If it lasted for any length of time there would certainly be a general return to a savage state of existence.

Ah! it was once said that if there were a dearth of straw-berries, Paris would rise in revolt. Gentlemen, during the Siege there was a terrible dearth, not only of strawberries, but of a great many other good things, and Paris did not rise in revolt in consequence. Her citizens waged a holy warfare, suffered bravely; but there were actors who took the place of strawberries.

Was it a trifling thing, then, during those days of gloom and depression, to keep up those performances by the Comédie-Française and elsewhere, when the inspired words of the poets dropped warm from our hearts into the public heart? And those recitations from Victor Hugo's "Chati-ments," of moving and consoling memory, what of them? and of so many others, whither your actors, for lack of other laurels, brought you the laurel leaves of art, which never fade upon the radiant brow of France? Ah! how every bosom beat! What transports! What unity! Were it but for the memory of those hours, I assure you, I fail to see how any-one can say that the actor is a useless and inferior being. And here let me pause; for nothing can be better fitted to impress me with the conviction—a proud one, perhaps, but correct, I think—that we actors are entitled to hold honorable rank, not only in the art whose soldiers and followers we are, but also in the annals of our country.

Reflections on Acting

by

TALMA

With an Introduction by Sir Henry Irving
and a review by H. C. Fleeming Jenkin

Introduction

Few things can be said about the stage at any time which will not excite controversy; but I think one of the few is that the influence of the drama to-day is wider than it ever was. There is a vast increase of playgoers; the intellectual interest in the stage is steadily growing; and there is a general conviction that the actor is placed in a position of trust which he cannot worthily fill without a strong sense of responsibility. Dramatic artists, as a rule, speak for themselves. Their work is constantly before the public, and it is judged on its merits. None the less is there a want of a permanent embodiment of the principles of our art; a kind of vade mecum of the actor's calling, written by one of themselves, and by an artist universally recognised as a competent expositor. Such a work, in my opinion, is Talma's essay on the actor's art, the following translation of which was originally published in *The Theatre* of 1877 at my suggestion.

No one can read Talma's subtle yet simple description of the qualities and the course of study essential to the actor without a conviction that acting is one of the most fascinating of the arts. To the actor the whole field of human nature is open. Whether in the ideal world of the stage or in the actual world of social intercourse, his mind is continually accumulating impressions which become a part of his artistic being. This experience is common to the students of other arts; but the actor has this advantage, that all he learns is embodied in his own personality, not translated through some medium like the painter's canvas or the novelist's page. At the same time this purely personal art is subjected to the most severe tests. It is easier to detect a flaw in an actor's impersonation than an improbability in a book. The man enacts the character before many—a false intonation jars immediately upon the ear, an unnatural look or gesture is promptly convicted by the eye. The co-operation of sensibility and intelligence of which Talma speaks has thus to be conducted under the most exacting conditions. There must be no suggestion of effort. The essence of acting is its apparent

42

spontaneity. Perfect illusion is attained when every effect seems to be an accident. If the declamation is too measured, the sense of truth is at once impaired; if, on the other hand, it falls only the shadow of a shade below the level of appropriate expression, the auditor's sympathy is instantly checked. "The union of grandeur without pomp, and nature without triviality" is of all artistic ideals the most difficult to attain; and with this goal before him no actor can feel that his art is a plaything.

The end of all acting is "to hold the mirror up to Nature." Different actors have different methods, but that is their common purpose, which can be accomplished only by the closest study and observation. Acting, like every other art, has a mechanism. No painter, however great his imaginative power, can succeed in pure ignorance of the technicalities of his art; and no actor can make much progress till he has mastered a certain mechanism which is within the scope of patient intelligence. Beyond that is the sphere in which a magnetic personality exercises a power of sympathy which is irresistible and indefinable. That is great acting; but though it is inborn and cannot be taught, it can be brought forth only when the actor is master of the methods of his craft.

I am conscious that no words of mine can add any weight to the lessons which are set forth with such earnestness and brilliance in Talma's pages; but I venture to emphasise them by two golden rules. Let the student remember, first, that every sentence expresses a new thought, and therefore frequently demands a change of intonation; secondly, that the thought precedes the word. "The actor should have the art of thinking before he speaks." Of course there are passages in which thought and language are borne along by the stream of emotion, and completely intermingled. But more often it will be found that the most natural, the most seemingly accidental effects are obtained when the working of the mind is visible before the tongue gives it words.

HENRY IRVING

March 1883

Reflections on Acting

I have no pretension to be an author; all my studies have been directed towards my calling, the object of which is to afford at once pleasure and instruction. Tragedy and Comedy, the one by the portraiture of virtue and crime, the other by the exposure of vice or folly, interest us, or make us laugh, while they correct and instruct. Associated with great authors, actors are to them more than translators. A translator adds nothing to the ideas of the author he translates. The actor, putting himself faithfully in the place of the personage he represents, should perfect the idea of the author of whom he is the interpreter. One of the greatest misfortunes of our art is that it dies, as it were, with us, while all other artists leave behind them monuments of their works. The talent of the actor, when he has quitted the stage, exists no longer, except in the recollection of those who have seen and heard him. This consideration should impart additional weight to the writings, the reflections, and the lessons which great actors have left; and these writings may become still more useful if they are commented upon and discussed by actors who obtain celebrity in our day. Doubtless it is this motive which has induced the editors of the *Mémoires Dramatiques* to request me to add to the notice of Lekain some reflections on his talent and on the art which he illustrated.

Lekain had no master. Every actor ought to be his own tutor. If he has not in himself the necessary faculties for expressing the passions and painting characters, all the lessons in the world cannot give them to him. Genius is not acquired. This faculty of creating is born with us. But if the actor possesses it, the counsel of persons of taste may then guide him; and as there is in the art of reciting verse a part in some degree mechanical, the lessons of an actor profoundly schooled in his art may save him much study and time.

Lekain, from the commencement of his career, met with great success. His *début* lasted seventeen months. One day, after he had performed at Court, Louis XV said: "This man has made me weep—I, who never weep!" This illustrious

44

suffrage procured his admission to the Comédie-Française. Before appearing with it he had acquired some reputation at private theatres. It was in one of these that Voltaire first saw and noticed him, and there commenced his connection with that great man.

The system of declamation then in vogue was a sort of sing-song psalmody which had existed from the very birth of the theatre. Lekain—subjected, in spite of himself, to the influence of example—felt the necessity of breaking his shackles and the pedantic rules by which the theatre was bound. He dared to utter for the first time on the stage the true accents of nature. Filled with a strong and profound sensibility and a burning and communicative energy, his action, at first impassioned and irregular, pleased the young, who were enchanted by his ardour and the warmth of his delivery, and, above all, were moved by the accents of his profoundly tragic voice. The admirers of the ancient psalmody criticised him severely, nicknaming him "the bull." They did not find in him that pompous declamation, that chiming and measured declamation, in which a profound respect for the caesura and the rhyme made the verses always fall in regular cadence. His march, his movements, his attitudes, his action had not that liveliness, those graces of our fathers, which then constituted a fine actor, and which the Marcels of the age taught to their pupils in initiating them in the beauties of the minute. Lekain, a plain plebeian, a workman in a goldsmith's shop, had not, it is true, been brought up on the laps of queens, as Baron said actors ought to be; but nature, a still more noble instructress, had undertaken the charge of revealing her secrets to him. In time he succeeded in overcoming the bad taste which his inexperience had at first naturally thrown into his acting. He learnt to master its vivacity and regulate its movements. Yet at first he dared not entirely abandon the cadenced song which was then regarded as the ideal of the art of declamation, and which the actor preserved even in the burst of passion.

It was to this false taste that we must attribute the little progress which costume had made in the time of Lekain. There is no doubt that he regarded fidelity in costume as a very important matter. We discover it in the efforts he made to render it less ridiculous than it was at that period. In fact, truth in the dresses, as in the decorations, contributes greatly to theatrical illusion, and transports the spectator to the age and the country in which the personages represented lived. This fidelity, too, furnishes the actor with the means of giving a peculiar physiognomy to each of his characters.

But a reason still more cogent makes me consider as highly culpable the actors who neglect this part of their art. The theatre ought to offer to youth in some measure a course of living history; and does not this negligence give him entirely false notions of the habits and manners of the personages whom the tragedy resuscitates? I remember well that in my early years, on reading history, my imagination always represented to itself the princes and the heroes whom I had seen at the theatre. I figured to myself Bayard elegantly dressed in a chamois-coloured coat, without a beard, and powdered and frizzled like a *petit maître* of the eighteenth century. Caesar I pictured to myself highly buttoned up in a fine white satin coat, his long, flowing locks fastened with rosettes of ribbon. If in those days an actor occasionally approximated to the antique dress, the simplicity of it was lost in a profusion of ridiculous embroidery, and I fancied that silks and velvets were as common at Athens and Rome as at Paris and London. Statues, monuments, and ancient manuscripts adorned with miniatures existed then as well as now; but they were not consulted. It was the time of the Bouchers and the Van Loos, who took care not to follow the example of Raphael and Poussin in the arrangements of their draperies. It was only when David appeared that painters and sculptors, especially the younger of them, occupied themselves, under his inspiration, with these researches. Connected with most of them, and feeling the utility this study might have for the theatre, I applied myself to it with no common zeal; in my own way I became a painter. I had many obstacles and prejudices to overcome, but success at last crowned my efforts, and without fearing an accusation of presumption I may say that my example has had a great influence over all the theatres of Europe. Lekain could not have surmounted so many difficulties; the time had not come. Would he have dared to risk naked arms, the antique sandals, hair without powder, long draperies, and woolen stuffs? Such a toilet would have been regarded as very offensive, not to say indecent. Lekain did all that was possible; he advanced the first step, and what he dared to do emboldened us to do still more.

Actors ought at all times to take nature for a model, to make it the constant object of their studies. Lekain felt that the brilliant colours of poetry served only to give more grandeur and majesty to the beauties of nature. He was not ignorant that persons deeply affected by the stronger passions, or overwhelmed with great grief, or violently agitated by great political interests, have a more elevated and ideal language; yet this language is still that of nature. It is, therefore, this nature—noble, animated, aggrandised, but at the same time simple—which ought to be the constant object of the studies of the actor, as well as of the poet. I have frequently heard persons of authority state that tragedy is not in nature, and this idea has been repeated without reflection until it has become a kind of maxim. The world, occupied with other objects, has not sufficiently studied all the workings of the passions. It judges too lightly, and indifferent authors and actors, who pay but little attention to their art, serve to accredit this error. But let us examine any of the impassioned or political characters of Corneille and Racine. How often their language is at once simple and elevated! How pathetic and natural is Voltaire when he is inspired by a passion! It is not the negligence and carelessness of a vulgar conversation that we find in the beautiful scenes of those great poets. It is the simple language, the aggrandised but exact expression, of nature itself. Let us examine from every point of view the exposition and *dénouement* of Rotrou's *Venceslas,* the fifth act of *Rodogune* and *Cinna,* the part of Horatius, the scenes of Agamemnon and Achilles, the parts of Joad, Œdipe, the two Brutuses, César, the parts of Phèdre, Andromaque, Hermione, &c. I defy any person to give them a finer or more natural form of expression. Take away the rhyme, and all these personages would have expressed themselves in the same manner as in real life. It is the same with some actors who have adorned the French stage, as Lekain, Mlle. Dumesnil, Molé, and Monvel. It was only by a faithful imitation of truth and nature that they succeeded in creating those powerful emotions in an enlightened nation which still exist in the recollection of those who heard them. It must, however, be confessed that, amongst the great actors of all countries, only a few have sought after this truth. Molière, and Shakespeare before him, had given excellent lessons to their brethren, the one in his *Impromptu de Versailles* and the other in *Hamlet.* How comes it, then, that in spite of the advice of these two great masters and, no doubt, of that of many of their contemporaries, the false system of pompous declamation had been established in almost all the theatres of Europe, and proclaimed as the sole type of theatrical imitation? It is because truth in all art is what is most difficult to find and seize. The statue of Minerva exists in the block of marble, but the chisel of Phidias alone can discover it. This faculty has been given to very few actors; and mediocrity, being in the majority, has laid down the law.

I may here be permitted to make an observation which has been suggested to me by the great event of the Revolution, for its violent crises, of which I was a witness, have often served me as a study. The man of the world and the man of the people, so opposite in their language, frequently express the great agitations of the mind in the same way. The one forgets his social manners, the other quits his vulgar fancies. The former descends to nature, the latter remounts to it. Each puts off the artificial man to become natural and true. The accent of each will be the same in the violence of the same passions or the same sorrows. Picture to yourself a mother intently looking on the empty cradle of a child she had just lost; a sort of stupidity in the features, a few tears flowing down her cheeks at distant intervals, piercing cries and convulsive sobs bursting forth from time to time—these will represent the sorrow of a woman of the people the same as that of a duchess. Suppose, again, a man of the people and a man of the court to have both fallen into a violent fit of jealousy or vengeance; these two men, so different in their habits, will be the same in their frenzy; they will present in their fury the same expression; their looks, their features, their actions, their attitudes, their movements will assume all at once a terrible, grand, and solemn character, worthy in both of the pencil of the painter and the study of the actor. And, perhaps, even the delirium of passion may inspire the one as well as the other with one of those words—one of those sublime expressions—which the poet would conceive. The great movements of the soul elevate man to an ideal nature, in whatever rank fate may have placed him. The Revolution, which brought so many passions into play, has had popular orators who have astonished all by sublime traits of untutored eloquence and by an expression and accent which Lekain would not have been ashamed of.

Lekain felt that the art of declamation did not consist in reciting verse with more or less emphasis, but that this art might be made to impart a sort of reality to the fictions of the stage. To attain this end it is necessary that the actor should have received from nature an extreme sensibility and a profound intelligence, and Lekain possessed these qualifications in an eminent degree. Indeed, the strong impressions which actors create on the stage are the result only of the alliance of these two essential faculties. I must explain what I mean by this. To my mind, sensibility is not only that faculty which an actor possesses of being moved himself, and of affecting his being so far as to imprint on his features, and especially on his voice, that expression and those accents of sorrow which awake all the sympathies of the art and ex-tort tears from auditors. I include in it the effect which it produces, the imagination of which it is the source, not that imagination which consists in having reminiscences, so that the object seems actually present (this, properly speaking, is only memory), but that imagination which, creative, active, and powerful, consists in collecting in one single fictitious object the qualities of several real objects, which associates the actor with the inspirations of the poet, transports him back to the past, and enables him to look on at the lives of historical personages or the impassioned figures created by genius—which reveals to him, as though by magic, their physiognomy, their heroic stature, their language, their habits, all the shades of their character, all the movements of their soul, and even their singularities. I also call sensibility that faculty of exaltation which agitates an actor, takes possession of his senses, shakes even his very soul, and enables him to enter into the most tragic situations and the most terrible of the passions as if they were his own. The intelligence that accompanies sensibility judges the impressions which the latter has made us feel; it selects, arranges them, and subjects them to calculation. If sensibility furnishes the objects, the intelligence brings them into play. It aids us to direct the employment of our physical and intellectual forces, to judge between the relations and connections which connect the poet and the situation or the character of the personages, and sometimes to add the shades that are wanting, or that language cannot express; to complete, in fine, their expression by action and physiognomy.

It may be conceived that such a person must have received from nature a peculiar organisation for sensibility, that common property of our being. Everyone possesses it in a greater or less degree. But in the man whom nature has destined to paint the passions in their greatest excesses, to give them all their violence, and show them in all their delirium, one may perceive that it must have a much greater energy; and, as all our emotions are intimately connected with our nerves, the nervous system in the actor must be so mobile and plastic as to be moved by the inspirations of the poet as easily as the Aeolian harp sounds with the least breath of air that touches it.

If the actor is not endowed with a sensibility at least equal to that of any of his audience he can move them but very little. It is only by an excess of sensibility that he can succeed in producing deep impressions and move even the coldest souls. The power that raises must be greater than the power raised. This faculty ought ever to exist in the actor—I will not say greater or stronger than in the poet who conceived the movement of the soul reproduced on the stage, but more lively, more rapid, and more powerful. The poet or the painter can wait for the moment of inspiration to write or to paint. In the actor, on the contrary, it must be commanded at any moment, at his will. That it may be sudden, lively, and prompt, he must possess an excess of sensibility. Nay, more, his intelligence must always be on the watch and, acting in concert with his sensibility, regulate its movement and effects; for he cannot, like the painter and the poet, efface what he does.

Therefore, between two persons destined for the stage, one possessing the extreme sensibility I have defined, and the other a profound intelligence, I would without question prefer the former. He might fall into some errors, but his sensibility would inspire him with those sublime movements which seize upon the spectator and carry delight to the heart. The superior intelligence of the other would render him cold and regular. The one would go beyond your expectations and your ideas; the other would only accomplish them. Your mind would be deeply stirred by the inspired actor; your judgment alone would be satisfied by the intelligent actor. The inspired actor will so associate you with the emotions he feels that he will not leave you even the liberty of judgment; the other, by his prudent and irreproachable acting, will leave your faculties at liberty to reason on the matter at your ease. The former will be the personage himself, the latter only an actor who represents that personage. Inspiration in the one will frequently supply the place of intelligence; in the other the combinations of intelligence will supply only feebly the absence of inspiration. To form a great actor, like Lekain, the union of sensibility and intelligence is required.

The actor who possesses this double gift adopts a course of study peculiar to himself. In the first place, by repeated exercises he enters deeply into the emotions, and his speech acquires the accent proper to the situation, of the personage he has to represent. This done, he goes to the theatre not only to give theatrical effect to his studies, but also to yield himself to the spontaneous flashes of his sensibility and all the emotions which it involuntarily produces in him. What does he then do? In order that his inspirations may not be lost, his memory, in the silence of repose, recalls the accent of his voice, the expression of his features, his action—in a word, the spontaneous workings of his mind, which he had suffered to have free course, and, in effect, everything which in the moments of his exaltation contributed to the effect he had produced. His intelligence then passes all these means in review, connecting them and fixing them in his memory, to re-employ them at pleasure in succeeding representations. These impressions are often so evanescent that on retiring behind the scenes he must repeat to himself what he had been playing rather than what he had to play. By this kind of labour the intelligence accumulates and preserves all the creations of sensibility. It is by this means that at the end of twenty years (it requires at least this length of time) a person destined to display fine talent may at length present to the public a series of characters acted almost to perfection. Such was the course which Lekain constantly took, and which must be taken by everyone who has the ambition to excel on the stage. The whole of his life was devoted to this kind of study, and it was only during the last five or six years of his life, between 1772 or 1773 and 1778, that he reaped his fruit. It was then that his fertile sensibility raised him to the tragic situations he had to paint, and his intelligence enabled him to display all the treasures he had amassed. It was then that his acting was fixed on such bases, and was so subservient to his will, that the same combinations and the same effect presented themselves without study. Accent, inflections, action, attitudes, looks, all were reproduced at every representation with the same exactness, the same vigour; and if there was any difference between one representation and another, it was always in favour of the last.

Sensibility and intelligence, therefore, are the principal faculties necessary to an actor. Yet these alone will not suffice. Apart from memory, which is his indispensable instrument, and statures and features adapted to the character he has to play, he must have a voice that can be modulated with ease, and at the same time be powerful and expressive. I need scarcely add that a good education, the study of history—not so much the events as the manners of the people, and the particular character of historical personages—and even drawing, ought to add grace and strength to the gifts of nature.

It will be well understood that I here speak only of tragedy. Without entering into the question whether it is more difficult to play tragedy or comedy, I will say that to arrive at perfection in either, the same moral and physical faculties are required, only I think the tragedian ought to possess more power and sensibility. The comedian does not require the same energy; the imagination in him has less scope. He represents beings whom he sees every day—beings of his own class. Indeed, with very few exceptions his task is confined to the representations of folly and ridicule and

to painting passions in his own sphere of life, which, consequently, are more moderate than those which come within
the domain of tragedy. It is, if I may so express it, his own
nature which, in his imitations, speaks and acts; whereas the
tragic actor must quit the circle in which he is accustomed
to live, and plunge into the regions where the genius of the
poet has placed and clothed in ideal forms the beings conceived by him or furnished by history. He must preserve
these personages in their grand proportions, but at the same
time he must subject their elevated language to natural
accents and true expression; and it is this union of grandeur
without pomp, and nature without triviality—this union of
the ideal and the true—which is so difficult to attain in
tragedy. I shall, perhaps, be told that a tragic actor has a
much greater liberty in the choice of his means of offering
to the public objects whose types do not exist in society,
while the same public can easily decide whether the comedian
furnishes an exact copy of his model. I would reply that the
passions are of all ages. Society may weaken their energy,
but they do not the less exist in the soul, and every spectator
is a competent judge from his own feelings. With regard to
the great historical characters, the enlightened public can
easily judge of the truth of the imitation. It will therefore
appear from what I have laid down that the moral faculties
ought to have more force and intensity in the tragic than in
the comic actor.

As to the physical qualities, it is evident that the pliability
of the features and the expression of the physiognomy ought
to be stronger, the voice more full, more sonorous, and more
profoundly articulate, in the tragic actor, who stands in need
of certain combinations and more than ordinary powers to
perform from the beginning to the end with the same energy
a part in which the author has frequently collected in a
narrow compass, and in the space of two hours, all the
movements, all the agitations, which an impassioned being
can feel only in the course of a long life. I repeat, however,
that not fewer qualities, though of a different kind, are
required in a great comedian than in a great tragic actor;
each has need of being initiated into the mysteries of nature,
the inclinations, the weaknesses, the extravagances of the
human heart.

When we consider all the qualities necessary to form an
excellent tragic actor, all the gifts which nature should have
bestowed upon him, can we be surprised that they are so
rare? Amongst the majority of those who go on the stage,

one has penetration, but his soul is cold as ice. Another possesses sensibility, but intelligence is wanting. One possesses both these requisites, but in so slight a degree that it is as if he did not possess them at all; his acting is characterised neither by energy, expression, nor confidence, and is without colour; sometimes he speaks in a loud and sometimes in a low key, quickly or slowly, as if by chance. Another has received from nature all these gifts, but his voice is harsh, dry, and monotonous, and totally incapable of expressing the passions; he weeps without drawing tears from others; he is affected and his audience is unmoved. One has a sonorous and touching voice, but his features are disagreeable; his stature and form have nothing heroic in them. In short, the requisites for a really great actor are so many, and so seldom united in the same person, that we ought not to be surprised at finding them appear at such long intervals.

It must be confessed that Lekain had some faults; but in literature and in the arts of imitation genius is rated in proportion to the beauties it creates. Its imperfections form no part of its fame, and would be forgotten if they were not allied to noble aspirations. Nature had refused to Lekain some of the advantages which the stage demands. His features had nothing noble in them; his physiognomy was common, his figure short. But his exquisite sensibility, the movement of an ardent and impassioned soul, the faculty he possessed of plunging entirely into the situation of the personage he represented, the intelligence, so delicately fine, which enabled him to perceive and produce all the shades of the character he had to paint—these embellished his irregular features and gave him an inexpressible charm. His voice was naturally heavy, and by no means flexible. It was to some extent what is called a veiled voice, but that very veil imparted to it, defective as it was in some respects, vibrations which went to the bottom of the hearer's soul. However, by dint of application, he contrived to overcome its stiffness, to enrich it with all the accents of passion, and to render it amenable to all the delicate inflections of sentiment. He had, in fact, studied his voice as one studies an instrument. He knew all its qualities and all its defects. He passed lightly over the harsh to give fuller effect to the vibrations of the harmonious chords. His voice, on which he essayed every accent, became a rich-keyed instrument from which he could draw forth at pleasure every sound he stood in need of. And such is the power of a voice thus formed by nature attuned by art, that it affects even the foreigner who does not understand the words. Frenchmen who are totally unacquainted with English have been affected even to tears by the accents of the touching voice of Miss O'Neil.

At the commencement of his career, Lekain, like all young actors, gave way to boisterous cries and violent movement, believing that in this way he triumphed over difficulties. In time, however, he felt that of all monotonies that of the lungs was the most insupportable; that tragedy must be spoken, not howled; that a continual explosion fatigues without appealing; and that only when it is rare and unexpected can it astonish and move. He felt, in fine, that the auditor, shocked by the ranting on the stage, forgets the personage represented and pities or condemns the actor. Thus Lekain, often fatigued in long and arduous scenes, took care to conceal from the public the violence of his efforts, and at the very moment when his powers were nearly exhausted they seemed to possess all their strength and vigor.

Lekain has been reproached for having been heavy in his recitation. This defect was natural. He was slow, calm, and reflective. Besides, Voltaire, whose actor he peculiarly was, would not perhaps have readily consented to sacrifice the pomp and harmony of his verse to a more natural tone. He wished him to be energetic, and as he had decked out tragedy a little the actor was obliged to follow in the track of the poet. Again, in the days of Lekain, a period so brilliant from the genius of its writers and philosophers, all the arts of imitation had fallen into a false and mannered taste, and Lekain perhaps thought himself sufficiently rich in all his gifts and attainments to make a slight concession to the bad taste of his days. Yet his style, at first slow and cadenced, by degrees became animated, and from the moment he gained the high region of passion he astonished by his sublimity.

Notwithstanding the bad taste alluded to, there existed in society at that time, and among the friends of Voltaire, a great number of persons whose ideas in matters of art were more correct, and their advice was of great service to Lekain. Voltaire, also, though he was a very indifferent actor, even when he played in his own pieces, possessed a good theatrical knowledge of the stage; this he communicated to Lekain, who profited by it. During one of the actor's visits to Ferney Voltaire made him totally change his manner of playing Genghis-Khan in *The Orphan of China*. On his return to Paris it was the first character he played. The audience, astonished at the change, was for a long time undecided whether to praise or blame the performance. They could not but think that the actor was indisposed. There was nothing of the turbulence or the trickery which had previously procured him so much applause in the same part. It was only after the fall of the curtain that the audience felt that Lekain was right. Public opinion was formed instantaneously, and by an electrical movement it manifested itself in long and loud applause. "What's the matter?" asked Lekain of Rougeot, a servant of the theatre. "It's applause, monsieur; they are at length of your way of thinking."

Experience had taught Lekain that all the silly combinations of mediocrity, the contrast of sounds, ranting and raving might evoke great applause and many bravos; but it conferred no reputation. The lovers of noise and vociferation fancy their souls are wooed, while only their ears are stunned. There is a certain number of artists, connoisseurs, and intelligent persons who are sensible only of what is true and conformable to nature. These persons do not like much noise, and it is upon their opinion that an actor's reputation depends. Lekain despised those plaudits which torment and often distract an actor. He resolved to study only that part of the public which was worth pleasing. He rejected all the charlatanism of his art, and produced a true effect; he always discarded the claptraps which so many others seek to discover. He was consequently one of the actors the least appreciated in his day, but he was the most admired by competent judges, and he rendered tragedy more familiar without depriving it of its majestic proportions.

He knew how to regulate all his movements and all his actions. He regarded this as a very essential part of his art. For action is language in another form. If it is violent or hurried, the carriage ceases to be noble. Thus, while other actors were theatrical kings only, in him the dignity did not appear to be the result of effort, but the simple effect of habit. He did not raise his shoulders or swell his voice to give an order. He knew that men in power had no need of such efforts to make themselves obeyed, and that in the sphere they occupy all their words have weight and all their movements authority. Lekain displayed superior intelligence and great ability in the varied styles of his recitation, which was slow or rapid as circumstances required; and his pauses were always full of deep significance. There are, in fact, certain circumstances in which it is necessary to solicit oneself before we confide to the tongue the emotions of the soul or the calculations of the mind. The actor, therefore, must have the art of thinking before he speaks, and by introducing pauses he appears to meditate upon what he is about to say. But his physiognomy must correspond also with the suspensions of his voice. His attitudes and features must indicate that during these moments of silence his soul is deeply engaged; without this his pauses will seem rather to be the result of defective memory than a secret of his art.

There are also situations in which a person strongly moved feels too acutely to wait the slow combination of words. The sentiment that overpowers him escapes in mute action before the voice is able to give it utterance. The gesture, the attitude, and the look ought, then, to precede the words, as the flash of the lightning precedes the thunder. The display adds greatly to the expression, as it discovers a mind so profoundly imbued that, impatient to manifest itself, it has chosen the more rapid signs. These artifices contribute what is properly called byplay, a most essential part of the theatrical art, and most difficult to acquire, retain, and regulate well. It is by this means that the actor gives to his speech an air of truth and takes from it all appearance of measured speaking.

There are also situations in which a person transported by the violence of feeling finds at once all the expression he wishes. The words come to his lips as rapidly as the thoughts to his mind; they are born with them and succeed one another without interruption. The mind of the actor, then, ought to be hurried and rapid; he must even conceal from the audience the effort he makes to prolong his breath. This effort he must make, since the slightest interruption or the slightest pause would destroy the illusion, because the mind would seem to participate in this pause. Besides, passion does not follow the rules of grammar; it pays but little respect to colons and semi-colons and full stops, which it displaces without any ceremony.

Lekain had a long illness a few years before his death, and it was to this illness that he owed the perfect development and refining of his talents. This may appear strange, but it is literally true. There are violent crises and certain disorders in the animal economy which often excite the nervous system and give the imagination an inconceivable impetus. The body suffers, but the mind is active. Persons stricken down by illness have astonished us by the vivacity of their ideas; others remember things completely forgotten; others seem to pierce the veil which hangs between them and the future. Perhaps Chénier was not wrong in saying that "Heaven gives prophetic accents to the dying."

When the illness passes away something of the excess of sensibility always remains imprinted on the nervous system; the emotions are more profound, and all our sensations acquire more delicacy. It would seem as if these shocks purified and renewed our being; and this was the effect which his illness had upon Lekain. The inaction to which he had been reduced became of service to him; his rest was that of labour. Genius does not always require exercise, and, like the gold mine, it forms and perfects itself in silence and repose.

He reappeared on the stage after a long absence. The audience, instead of having to show indulgence to a man enfeebled by suffering, saw him, as it were, ascend from the tomb with a more perfect intelligence, seemingly clothed with a purer, more perfect existence. It was then that he rejected what his intelligence disapproved. There were no more cries, no more efforts of the lungs, no more of those ordinary griefs, no more of those vulgar tears, which lessen and degrade the personage. His voice, at once pleasant and sonorous, had acquired new accents and vibrations which found responsive chords in every heart; his tears were heroic and penetrating; his acting—full, profound, pathetic, and terrible—roused and moved even the most insensible of his hearers.

It was also at this latter period of his life that, having acquired a greater knowledge of the passions, and having himself perhaps witnessed deep anguish, he was the better able to paint it; and if he frequently, to express great sorrow, suffered his melancholy and dolorous voice to escape through sobs and tears, often, too, in the highest degree of moral suffering his voice changed; it became veiled and uttered only inarticulate sounds of woe. His eyes appeared dull with sorrow, and shed no tears, which seemed to be chased back on the heart. Admirable artifice! drawn from nature, and more calculated to move the soul than tears themselves; for in real life, while we pity those who weep, we feel, at least, that tears are a relief to them; but how much more is our pity excited at the sight of the unfortunate being whom the excess of deep despair deprives of voice to express his suffering and of tears to relieve him.

Lekain was the creature of passion; he never loved but to madness; and, it is said, he hated in the same manner. He whose soul is not susceptible to the extremes of passion will never rise to excellence as an actor. In the expression of the passions there are many shades which cannot be divined and which the actor cannot paint until he has felt them himself. The observations which he has made on his own nature serve at once for his study and example; he interrogates himself on the impressions his soul has felt, on the expression they imprinted upon his features, on the accents of his voice in the various states of feeling. He meditates on these, and clothes the fictitious passions with these real forms. I scarcely know how to confess that, in my own person, in any circumstance of my life in which I experienced deep sorrow the passion of the theatre was so strong in me that, although oppressed with real sorrow, and disregarding the tears I shed, I made, in spite of myself, a rapid and fugitive observation on the alteration of my voice and on a certain spasmodic vibration which it contracted as I wept; and—I say it not without some shame—I even thought of making use of this on the stage, and, indeed, this experiment on myself has often been of service to me.

The contrarieties, the sorrows, and melancholy reflections which an actor may apply to the personage he represents, in exciting his sensibility, place him in the degree of agitation necessary for the development of his faculties. Lekain thus found, in his own passions, display for his talents. As to the odious characters and vile passions, of which the type was not in him—for no man was more honourable than Lekain—he painted them by analogy. In fact, amongst the irregular passions which disgrace humanity there are some which possess points of contact with those which ennoble it. Thus, the sentiment of a lofty emulation enables us to divine what envy may feel; the just resentment of wrongs shows us in miniature the excess of hatred and vengeance. Reserve and prudence enable us to paint dissimulation. The desires, the torments, and the jealousies of love enable us to conceive all its frensies and initiate us into the secret of its crimes.

These combinations, these comparisons, are the result of a rapid and imperceptible labour of sensibility, united with intelligence, which secretly operates on the actor as on the poet, and which reveals to them what is foreign to their own nature—the viler passions of guilty and corrupted minds. Thus Milton, a man of austere probity and so full of the divine power, created the personage of Satan. Corneille, the simplest and the worthiest of men, created Phocas and Felix; Racine, Nero and Narcissus. Voltaire has painted the effects of fanaticism with a frightful truth; and Ducis, whose taste was simple, and whose life was religious, painted in Albufar, in traits of fire, all the transports of incestuous love.

These terminate my hasty reflections on Lekain and our art. I have thrown them together without order; but I hope, in the quietude of silence and repose, to resume the subject and give, for the use of my successors, the result of a long experience in a career devoted entirely to the advancement of the beautiful art I love so deeply.

Review

Mr. Irving, in his preface to this remarkable essay, calls it a kind of vade mecum of the actor's calling, written by one of themselves, and by an artist universally recognised as a competent expositor; "a permanent embodiment of the principles of our art." We may then start with every confidence that we have here a true explanation of the manner in which a great actor works. Let us listen to his words. "Every actor," says Talma, "ought to be his own tutor. If he has not in himself the necessary faculties for expressing the passions and painting characters, all the lessons in the world cannot give them to him. The faculty of creating is born with us; but if the actor possesses it the counsel of persons of taste may then guide him; and as there is in the art of reciting verse a part in some degree mechanical, the lessons of an actor profoundly schooled in his art may save him much study and time." Here, we take it, is the truth, the whole truth, and nothing but the truth as to dramatic teaching. A man can be taught to speak and move well and suitably; then, if he has genius, he may in twenty years teach himself to act, and during the process he may be much helped by the counsel of persons of taste. And how is he to know whether he has the necessary genius? Talma anwsers, "sensibility" and "intelligence" are the two faculties pre-eminently required, but under the general heading of sensibility he includes much. He puts almost contemptuously on one side "the faculty which an actor possesses of being moved himself and of affecting his being so far as to imprint on his features, and especially on his voice, that expression and those accents of sorrow which awake sympathy and extort tears." No doubt the actor must have this kind of sensibility; but to this extent sensibility is not rare. It may sometimes be recognised in amateurs acting for the first time; and we take it that no moderately successful actor, even on a second-rate provincial stage, ever wanted sensibility to this extent. Let us call it, for the purpose of future reference, sensibility in the first degree, and then pass to what Talma further requires and still calls sensibility—namely, that imagination which enables the actor to look on the lives of historical personages, or the impassioned figures created by genius, which reveals to him as though by magic their physiognomy, their heroic stature, their language, their habits, all the shades of their character, all the movements of their soul, and even their singularities. We begin to feel that sensibility in the second degree is more difficult of attainment, and here it is well to remark that Talma does not place this faculty under the heading of "intelligence." He does not tell the actor that he must understand his author. This insight which he so justly acquires is to be a matter of feeling. The revelation comes by magic, not logic. Fanny Kemble says, in perfect accord with Talma, perception rather than reflection reaches the aim proposed. It is the absence of this sensibility in the second degree that makes many ordinary fairly good actors so insufferably bad in great parts. Probably they understand the words they speak and have a vague notion of what the person they represent may be supposed to feel, but they have no insight into heroic thought or feeling; and, says Talma, "if the actor is not endowed with a sensibility at least equal to that of any of his audience, he can move them but very little." Too often our actors have less of this sensibility than many of those who hear them. Why then, it may be asked, do not audience and actors change places? Because the sensitive hearers lack sensibility in the third degree—for Talma has not done with this word yet. He includes in this term "the faculty of exaltation which agitates an actor, takes possession of his senses, shakes even his very soul, and enables him to enter into the most tragic situations and the most terrible of the passions as if they were his own."

Now, not one of the audience, who condemn the second-rate actor in a great part because they have more sensibility than he has, will be found capable of the kind of exaltation here described. We think that here Talma has confused or blended two very different faculties under one name. To feel and to express were one to the great actor, but the vast majority of mankind is, we think, denied the gift of expressing emotion. And here it seems to us that Talma misses the very point which distinguishes the actor from other artists. All artists must have this sensibility he demands, but the form which each naturally employs to express his emotion determines whether he shall be author, painter, musician, or actor. Under the influence of this "exaltation" the actor finds the tone, the look, the gesture required to express the feeling with which he is inspired, and this gift is, to some extent, possessed by all actors who can earn their bread. This is the faculty which is trained by stage practice. And here we may again refer for support to *Notes on Some of Shakespeare's Plays*, by F. A. Kemble. Speaking with the authority of tradition in a great family, she says: "There is a specific comprehension of effect and the means of producing it, which in some persons is a distinct capacity, and this forms what actors call the study of their profession." And although Talma mixed up expression and feeling when endeavouring in a brief way to write an analytical account of his own art, he takes precisely this view of study. Here is his method. "The actor who possesses this double gift [sensibility and intelligence] adopts a course of study peculiar to himself. In the first place, by repeated exercises he enters deeply into the emotions, and his speech acquires the accent proper to the situation, of the personage he has to represent. This done, he goes to the theatre not only to give theatrical effect to his studies, but also to yield himself to the spontaneous flashes of his sensibility and all the emotions which it voluntarily produces in him. What does he then do? In order that his inspirations may not be lost, his memory, in the silence of repose, recalls the accent of his voice, the expression of his features, his action—in a word, the spontaneous workings of his mind, which he had suffered to have free course, and, in effect, everything which in the moments of his exaltation contributed to the effect he had produced. His intelligence then passes all these means in review, connecting them and fixing them in his memory, to re-employ them at pleasure in succeeding representations." This passage expresses better than anything we have ever read what the actor's study really should be. After a certain amount of preparation, he yields in a state of exaltation to impulse; suggestions crowd upon him; tones, cries, gestures, expressions, actions are created. The exaltation is extreme, and these moments when he is alone and the god works in him may be those of keenest pleasure. But this state is succeeded by a calm and critical mood, in which the true artist chooses, rejects, and groups the partial effects obtained so as to produce one great and consistent whole. In this work he will be greatly aided if he has a sympathetic friend of sound judgment—Talma's "person of taste"—whose counsel he may take. Those who know what this study means are driven almost to distraction when they hear an actor—perhaps a great actor—complimented on being able to remember the words of his part. But, on the other hand, it must be almost as galling when a great actor is told that he really understands his author's meaning. One great charm in this essay by Talma lies in the total absence of this contemptible worship of the human understanding—a very good thing in its way, though one of but small importance in mere art. To Talma intelligence meant a sound critical faculty, not logical, but perceptive, enabling its possessor to keep what was good in art and reject that which was less good. We find in this essay a clear solution of the question continually asked, whether the actor really feels what he is acting. Talma, as we understand him, only felt the emotion once in its full intensity—that is to say, at the moment of creation during the solitary rehearsal. Subsequently the effect was produced by the aid of memory; but the body is so constituted that if by the aid of memory we perfectly reproduce a tone or cry, that tone or cry brings back simultaneously a close reproduction of the feeling by which it was first created. Thus to act a great part a man must be capable of real greatness. As Talma says: "He will never rise to excellence as an actor whose soul is not susceptible of the extremes of passion." And yet the representation night after night of these great feelings may come to be almost mechanical, or rather the feelings of the actor can be almost mechanically reawakened by the excellence of his own art. Thus in describing Lekain at his best period, when his art was ripe, he says: "Accent, inflections, actions, attitudes, looks, all were reproduced at every representation with the same exactness, the same vigour; and if there was any difference between one representation and another, it was always in favour of the last." Spontaneity is an admirable gift, but you cannot be spontaneous a second time. Spontaneous movements are right and necessary at the moment of creation, but are wholly out of place before an audience.

Talma likes good scenery and correct dresses, but one feels that if he were alive now, he might say, *Faut de la vertu, pas trop n'en faut*. His remarks on truth and nature are true and natural. He points out, taught by the scenes he had witnessed during the Reign of Terror, that "the man of the world and the man of the people, so opposite in their language, frequently express the great agitations of the mind in the same way," and that "the great movements of the soul elevate man to an ideal nature in whatever rank fate may have placed him." While, however, he recommends the observation of passion in others, it is clear that he never condescended to mimicry. Some talent for mimicry is very common among actors, and is indeed a useful accomplishment, especially in the lower walks of the profession; but no man can ever hope to play Coriolanus by mimicking some statesman.

Talma's chief observations were made upon himself. He attended to his own tones, his own face, when in real grief; he is half ashamed and half proud of having done so. We imagine that all artists are alike on this point, and that in this fact lies a certain compensation for the exact keenness of their feelings. They suffer more than any other men, and get more good from suffering. Talma observed that an emotion truly expressed moved an audience which did not understand the words. Most people would attribute this to gesture; but he, rightly as we think, considered the effect as due to the voice, and as an instance he speaks of Miss O'Neil moving Frenchmen who did not understand her to tears. The point is a curious one, for we have observed that a foreigner can judge artistic truth in acting with fair success when he is wholly incapable of appreciating any little niceties of accent or elocution. Thus too we allow foreigners to act on our stage who cannot speak one word so as to be acceptable to our ears in English. Yet their tones will bring tears almost as readily as if they spoke with English tongues. We believe that this admits of explanation; but the theory would demand too much space to be developed here. Let all those who are interested in acting read Talma's essay; and then, if they wish for a little amusement, they may turn to *The Actor's Art*, by Mr. Gustave Garcia. Talma tells his readers what a great actor must learn; Mr. Garcia explains what small actors can be taught and do learn.

H. C. FLEEMING JENKIN

Mrs. Siddons as Lady Macbeth and as Queen Katharine

by

H. C. FLEEMING JENKIN

With an Introduction by Brander Matthews

Introduction

1. Sarah Siddons

In the history of no art are there more instances of the transmitting of great ability from father to son, and from son to grandson, than in the history of the art of acting. In political life and in literature it is not uncommon to see a son follow in his father's footsteps; but on the stage it is far more frequent. Instances abound, and there is no need to do more here than to set down the names of Edmund and Charles Kean, of Junius Brutus and Edwin Booth, and of Charles and Charles James Mathews; of the Jeffersons there have been five generations on the stage. This is perhaps because there is no profession in which inherited faculty and early training count more for success than they do in the histrionic. In no family has this inherited faculty and this early training given to the world more and greater artists than in the family of the Kembles; and there is no more glorious name in histrionic annals than that of Sarah Siddons. As Henderson, the actor, said of her when she was on the threshold of her career, she was an actress who had never had an equal, nor would she ever have a superior.

Sarah Kemble was born July 5, 1755, at Brecknock, in South Wales. Her father was Roger Kemble, a strolling manager and actor; he was a man of high character and good breeding. His wife once said to Boaden, "there sits, unconscious of our remarks, the only *gentleman* Falstaff that I have ever seen." Mrs. Kemble was a daughter of Ward, the actor and manager who in 1746 gave a benefit in the Town Hall of Stratford for the purpose of restoring Shakespeare's monument. It was from her mother, apparently, that Mrs. Siddons inherited her beauty. As a child she appeared on the stage with the other members of the family. Her father sought to give all his children the advantage of a good education, and Sarah Kemble was as carefully instructed as their circumstances would allow; she was more especially trained in music. "When she was about seventeen," Campbell records,

"Mr. Siddons, who was still an actor in her father's company, paid his first attentions to her; and it was soon perceived that they were acceptable." But if acceptable to the young lady, they were not to her parents. Mr. Siddons thought he was to be jilted in favor of a neighboring squire, and he took the audience into his confidence one night, by a song of his own composing, in which he called himself Colin and bewailed the fickleness of Phyllis; his allusions were so personal and direct that when he came off the stage the manager's wife boxed his ears. With the daughter he soon made it up; and she agreed to marry him whenever her parents would consent. It was probably to separate the lovers that Mr. Kemble for a while placed his daughter in a private family, apparently as a companion or reader. She soon returned to the stage, and to Mr. Siddons; and at Coventry, November 26, 1773, they were married. Mr. Siddons was a useful actor, ready to play any part at shortest notice, and likely to render it at least acceptably; but he was not a genius, and his wife was. He made her a devoted husband, and the marriage was happy in all respects.

Two years later, when she was twenty, she was engaged by Garrick, and as Portia she made her first appearance at Drury Lane Theatre, December 29, 1775. Portia was as unsuitable a character for Mrs. Siddons as Shylock was for King, who acted with her; she made no hit in the part. Garrick was then giving his farewell performances; and when, in May 1776, he revived *The Suspicious Husband* to play Ranger, he cast her as Mrs. Strictland—with a line to herself in the bills. She had other parts of no great value, and she played Lady Anne to his Richard III. Then Garrick retired, and Sheridan, Linley, and Ford succeeded him. Plainly enough, Garrick had not seen—as indeed, how should he?— what she was capable of; he seems not to have recommended her especially to the new manager; and in the summer, while she was acting at Birmingham, she received an official letter from the prompter of Drury Lane, acquainting her that her services would be no longer required. "It was a stunning and cruel blow," she wrote years afterward in the autobiographic fragment which Campbell used; "it was very near destroying me. My blighted prospects, indeed, induced a state of mind that preyed upon my health, and for a year and a half I was supposed to be hastening to a decline."

For six years Mrs. Siddons remained in the provinces, playing chiefly at York and at Bath, both theatrical towns of high repute, and her reputation increased constantly. Boaden records that she even ventured to appear as Hamlet,

just as Charlotte Cushman acted both Romeo and Wolsey—
an effort more curious than valuable. She strove steadily to
perfect herself in her art, and she had her reward. In time
there came an offer of a three years' engagement, from the
new managers of Drury Lane, and for the sake of her children, so she says, she accepted it. She took leave of her
friends at Bath, in a poetical address of her own composing
quite as personal as the song of Mr. Siddons of ten years
before. She had promised to produce three reasons for leaving Bath, and she kept her word, bringing forward her three
children—

> These are the moles that heave me from your side,
> Where I was rooted, where I could have died.

Mrs. Siddons reappeared at Drury Lane Theatre, October
10, 1782, as Isabella in Southerne's *Fatal Marriage*. During
her absence her powers had matured, and her success was
instant and indisputable. In the next three weeks she repeated the part eight times; and on October 30 she appeared
in *The Grecian Daughter*. Then she was seen as Jane Shore,
and as Belvidere (in *Venice Preserved*). In these she sustained and deepened the impression she had made as Isabella;
they were all pathetic and tear-compelling characters, and
never before had their tragic force been so well revealed.
She became the social, as well as the theatrical, celebrity of
the hour. She acted eighty nights in that season, and fifty-
three in the next, appearing in a greater variety of plays,
including two of Shakspeare's, *Measure for Measure* and *King
John*, in which she was Isabella and Constance. During this
second season Sir Joshua Reynolds painted her as the Tragic
Muse. "When I attended him for the first sitting," she wrote
(Campbell, i. 242), "after more gratifying encomiums than
I can now repeat, he took me by the hand, saying 'Ascend
your undisputed throne, and graciously bestow upon me some
good idea of the Tragic Muse.' I walked up the steps, and
instantly seated myself in the attitude in which the Tragic
Muse now appears. This idea satisfied him so well, that
without one moment's hesitation he determined not to alter
it." When the picture was finished he told her that the colors
would remain unfaded as long as the canvas would keep them
together, gallantly adding, "And, to confirm my opinion, here
is my name; for I have resolved to go down to posterity on
the hem of your garment." (It is to be noted that Sir Joshua
seldom signed his pictures.) When Garrick's *Jubilee* was revived, which was a sort of pageant or procession of the whole
company, in the costumes of the chief Shakespearean char-

acters—not wholly unlike the *cérémonie* still seen on set occasions at the Théâtre Français—Mrs. Siddons was drawn in a car as the Tragic Muse.

In the succeeding seasons she appeared as Lady Macbeth, as Queen Katharine, and as Volumnia to the Coriolanus of John Kemble. In the winter of 1789-90 she withdrew from Drury Lane and acted only occasionally in the provinces. While she was in Birmingham, she was asked to buy a stucco bust of herself; it could not have been a striking likeness, as the shopman did not recognize her. The actress could not help thinking she could do better; and from that time on she busied herself with sculpture, as Mélingue and Mme. Sarah Bernhardt have done in our day, and as Mr. Jefferson amused himself with painting. In the Dyce Library at South Kensington there is her own bust of herself. No doubt the study of sculpture was of use to her, although her attitudes had always been statuesque. She told Lord Lansdowne, so Moore records, "that the first thing that suggested to her the mode of expressing intensity of feeling, was the position of some of the Egyptian statues, with the arms close down by the side, and the hands clenched." Campbell was with her when she first visited the Louvre and saw the Apollo Belvedere; she remained a long time before the statue and said at last, "What a great idea it gives us of God, to think that he has made a human being capable of fashioning so divine a form!" She played Hermione in *A Winter's Tale*, March 25, 1802, and in the great scene, as Campbell says, "looked the statue, even to literal illusion; and, whilst its drapery hid her lower limbs, it showed a beauty of head, neck, shoulders and arms, that Praxiteles might have studied." Boaden declares that upon "the magical words, pronounced by Pauline, 'Music, awake her: strike!' the sudden action of the head, absolutely *startled*, as though such a miracle had really vivified the marble."

In 1803 John Kemble bought one sixth of Covent Garden theatre, and Mrs. Siddons and Charles Kemble joined him. She acted at Covent Garden every season until 1812, when, on June 29, she took her farewell in a poetic address written by her nephew, Horace Twiss. She had been acting in London, at the head of the profession, for thirty years. At intervals she was seen again on the stage at benefit performances; between 1813 and 1819 she acted perhaps twenty times in London and Edinburgh. These occasions were probably a welcome relief to the monotony of her retirement. Fanny Kemble declared that "the vapid vacuity of the last years of my aunt Siddons' life, had made a profound impression upon me

—her apparent deafness and indifference to everything, which I attributed (unjustly, perhaps) less to her advanced age and impaired powers than to what I supposed the withering and drying influence of the overstimulating atmosphere of emotion, excitement, and admiration in which she had passed her life" (*Records of a Girlhood*, p. 223). She died May 31, 1831, in London, at the age of seventy-six.

Mrs. Siddons was probably the greatest actress the world has ever seen. Her voice was rich and warm and free from the weakness which kept John Kemble constantly on his guard; Erskine said that he had studied her cadences and intonation, and that to the harmony of her periods and pronunciation he was indebted for his best displays. Boaden declares that there never was a better stage figure than hers. She was strong, supple, graceful and easy in her person. Her face was "so thoroughly harmonized when quiescent and so expressive when impassioned that most people think her more beautiful than she is." Although she had humor in private life, she failed to reveal it on the stage; her comedy was not mirthful. And she seems to have been a little lacking in variety. But these trifles were all that detracted from her perfection. In youth she gave a pathos to the young and lovely heroines of tragedy that they had never known before; and in the maturity of her powers she arose to the severe majesty of the highest histrionic genius. She filled exactly Talma's ideal of tragic acting—"the union of grandeur without pomp, and nature without triviality." Of her Lady Macbeth, her greatest part, we are fortunate in having her own analysis (see Campbell's *Life of Mrs. Siddons*, Vol. ii, p. 10); but Fanny Kemble anticipated Fleeming Jenkin in declaring that Mrs. Siddons' "analysis of the part of Lady Macbeth was to be found *alone* in her representation of it—of the magnificence of which the essay which she has left upon the character gives not the faintest idea." Fanny Kemble also dismisses her aunt's analysis of Queen Katharine as equally "feeble" and "superficial." It may be noted that the essay written on Othello by Salvini, the most superb of later impersonations of the part, is quite as negligible.

"Next to the pleasure of running a man down," said Byron, "the critics like nothing so much as the vanity of writing him up; but once up, and fixed there, he is a mark for their arrows ever afterwards." It is perhaps the highest possible testimony to Mrs. Siddons' merits as an artist, and to her character as a woman, that the only fault found with her was that she was a little grasping in money matters. The same accusation was brought against Rachel and Charlotte Cushman; and in no case, probably, had it any more basis than the charge of parsimony often urged against Garrick. Her life was written by Thomas Campbell, and he dedicated it to Samuel Rogers, beginning his dedicatory letter with the assertion: "I have often heard you say, that rare as it was to meet with so gifted a genius as that of Mrs. Siddons, it was almost equally so to meet in human nature with so much candid and benignant singleness of mind as belonged to her personal character." The longer one labors over the abundant records of her life, the more emphatically is one inclined to echo this saying of one poet written down by another.

ii. H. C. Fleeming Jenkin

The fundamental principles of the art of acting are less widely apprehended than those of any other of the arts; and it is rare indeed to find a clear understanding of these principles in the conversations or in the compositions of anyone not actively engaged in the practical work of the theatre, as an author, as an actor, or as a stage manager. Even among the professionals of the playhouse, capable of applying these principles more or less satisfactorily in their regular routine, there are very few who are gifted with the critical faculty and the literary ability that would enable them to deduce and to declare those laws of the art of acting which they are competent to apply instinctively. They may know what ought to be done, without being able to proclaim the theory underlying the intuitive belief in obedience to which they work. If this comprehensive understanding of the basic laws of acting is very infrequent among professionals of acknowledged distinction, there is occasion for surprise that we should find it possessed by an amateur, an outsider like Fleeming Jenkin, by vocation an engineer and by avocation an untiring investigator into the principles of several of the arts, notably that of the playwright and that of the player. His possession of this comprehensive understanding of acting is disclosed in these two papers on Mrs. Siddons as an actress in Shakespeare's tragedies; and it is proclaimed in the memoir of him written by his intimate friend, Robert Louis Stevenson.

Henry Charles Fleeming Jenkin was born in 1833 and he died in 1885. His mother was the author of two or three novels, of which *Who breaks, pays* is the least forgotten. Educated partly in his native Scotland and partly in Italy, he served an apprenticeship in engineering; and in 1859 he became associated with Lord Kelvin in the development of the telegraph cable and in the advance of electric science. In

1865 he was appointed professor of engineering at University College in London; and in 1868 he accepted the same professorship at the University of Edinburgh. He contributed abundantly to the literature of his profession; and he invented a system of conveying goods by electric devices, in which he was aided by Gordon Wigan (son of Alfred Wigan, the actor). But he did not allow his profession, keenly as he was interested in it, to absorb all his abounding energy. He wrote a play on the story of patient Griselda; he worked out a theory of English versification; he analyzed several Greek tragedies; he investigated Greek costume; he discussed the atomic theory of Lucretius and the *Origin of Species* of Darwin; and he stage-managed frequent private theatricals. His various activities are revealed in the two volumes of his literary and scientific papers collected after his death.

The first of these volumes contained the memoir prepared at the request of his widow by his former pupil, Stevenson, himself the child of a long family of engineers. Stevenson had earlier commemorated the brilliant conversational powers of his friend by presenting him as Cockshot in the pair of sparkling essays entitled "Talk and Talkers." Perhaps one of those who came to know Fleeming Jenkin in the last years of his life and to appreciate his many-sided intelligence, his alert wit, and his unfailing keenness, may be permitted here to suggest that Fleeming Jenkin was not altogether fortunate in his biographer, in spite of Stevenson's loyalty to his dead friend and in spite of his manifest desire to show this friend for what he was. Perhaps a narrative by a less expert pen would have presented a larger figure, or at least a figure less obscured by the personality of the biographer himself. It would not be quite fair to suggest that there is any hint of patronizing in Stevenson's attitude, and yet it is not unjust to say that he seems at times to be a little condescending; and we have his own assertion that the pleasures of condescension are strangely one-sided.

I did not know Fleeming Jenkin intimately, but I had the pleasure of meeting him frequently at luncheon during several successive summers; and I can recall my surprised delight in his scintillating discourse the first time I met him in the dingy smoking room of the Savile Club in 1881. We had fallen into talk over our coffee, without any formal introduction, as is the kindly custom of the Savillians; and I remember the eagerness with which I slipped into the adjoining room to inquire from Andrew Lang the name of the brilliant conversationalist with whom I had unwittingly forgathered. As I grew to know him better I came to have a high regard, not only for the marvelous range of his interests and of his attainments, but also for the man himself, for his character, for his integrity and his sincerity.

Our topics were many and various, and the art of acting was only one of them. Yet this tended to recur frequently, since his associate Gordon Wigan had inherited a knowledge of its principles inferior only to Fleeming Jenkin's own; and often we had for a fourth in our discussions Walter Herries Pollock, the son of the editor of Macready's *Reminiscences,* then serving as the dramatic critic of the *Saturday Review.*

Stevenson is absolutely in accord with the fact when he tells us that Fleeming Jenkin "was all his life a lover of the play and all that belonged to it. Dramatic literature he knew fully. He was one of the not very numerous people who can read a play; a knack, the fruit of much knowledge and some imagination, comparable to that of reading-score." Stevenson's own innocence in regard to the drama is revealed in his next remark: "Few men better understood the artificial principles on which a play is good or bad, few more unaffectedly enjoyed a piece of any merit of construction." The word *artificial* here is curiously ill-chosen, as the principles on which a play is good or bad are no more "artificial" than those on which a picture, a statue, or a novel is good or bad. "Acting," so Stevenson continued, "had always, since Rachel and the 'Marseillaise,' a particular power on him. 'If I do not cry at the play,' he used to say, 'I want my money back.' "

This is significant in that it tends to explain the emphasis Fleeming Jenkin placed on the supreme importance of the emotional appeal in a play. This he dwelt upon more than once in the incidental remarks upon playwriting which illuminate the two papers on Mrs. Siddons; and here his attitude is just the opposite of that which the ill-informed critic of the drama from a purely literary standpoint is likely to take— oblivious of the fact that Jenkin's attitude is that from which Aristotle always considered the effectiveness of a tragic story. Like Aristotle, Fleeming Jenkin had had a severe training in scientific modes of thought; and perhaps it is not fanciful to find in this schooling an explanation of their ability to pierce to the center whenever they undertook an inquiry into the laws which govern artistic achievement.

Keen as Fleeming Jenkin was in his analysis of the problems of playmaking, he was quite as clear in his disentangling of the principles of acting; and in this pair of papers on Mrs. Siddons he had a most excellent text. She was the greatest tragic actress ever seen on our English-speaking stage; and she was at her best in the mightiest of Shakespeare's tragic women. It is a commonplace that the actor leaves only a name behind him, since his work necessarily dies when he does; and that succeeding generations must take his reputation on trust, since the only witnesses who might be called in rebuttal are all dead. In the future the phonograph may preserve for us the voice of an honored performer and thus supply material for opinion about the quality of his tones and the justice of his readings. At best, these will be but specimen bricks, and we shall still lack the larger outlines of the performance as a whole. Yet there is phenomenal value in such a record as that which Bell made in the theatre itself, and while he was actually under the spell of Mrs. Siddons' enchantment. In these notes we are told how she stood and how she looked, what gestures she made and what pauses she employed to give her words time to sink in. And these notes —brief yet adequate for their purpose, in which Bell sets down what he saw and what he heard and what he was made to feel—Fleeming Jenkin interprets for us, making us sharers in the pleasure of the performance and appreciators of at least a few of its manifold merits.

It was fortunate for all of us who are interested in the arts of the theatre that Bell was moved to make these notes and that they were preserved almost by accident; and it was doubly fortunate that they fell at last into the hands of Fleeming Jenkin, than whom no one was better qualified to appreciate their abiding importance. It is greatly to be desired that observers as competent and as careful as Bell may be moved to make a like record of the best performances of the best actors of our time; but perhaps it is too much to hope that these contemporary documents may be interpreted to later students of the stage by a critic as gifted as Fleeming Jenkin. Critics of his insight and attainments come as spies and not in battalions.

BRANDER MATTHEWS

August 1915

Mrs. Siddons as Lady Macbeth and as Queen Katharine

When any great work of art perishes from among us, we not only grieve, but we rebel against the decree of fate. The wars, the traffic, the mechanical arts of old, nay even the men and women, wither into an oblivion which is not painful but kindly. We sigh and smile and acquiesce—better so, for here was nothing fitted to endure for ever.

They had their time, as we have ours, and who would wish that the strife, the bustle, the men of to-day should last for ever? But the destruction of any beautiful thing, whether it be the work of art or nature, fills us, on the contrary, with sickening regret. The temple, statue, picture gone imply a loss of joy to uncounted generations. We suffer real pain when we think of lost tragedies by Sophocles, and our whole classical system of education is a protest that though kingdoms, peoples, tongues may die, their works of beauty shall endure.

If this be our feeling as to the more durable works of art, what shall we say of those triumphs which by their very nature last no longer than the action which creates them— the triumphs of the orator, the singer, or the actor? There is an anodyne in the words "must be so," "inevitable," and there is even some absurdity in longing for the impossible. This anodyne and our sense of humour temper the unhappiness we feel when, after hearing some great performance, we leave the theatre and think, "Well, this great thing has been, and all that is now left of it is the feeble print upon my brain, the little thrill which memory will send along my nerves, mine and my neighbour's; as we live longer the print and thrill must grow feebler, and when we pass away the impress of the great artist will vanish from the world." The regret that a great art should in its nature be transitory explains the lively interest which many feel in reading anecdotes or descriptions of a great actor, and it is this feeling which prompts the publication of the following notes on Mrs. Siddons' acting made by an eye-witness of ability and true artistic feeling.

The public of to-day are perhaps hardly aware of the height to which the art of acting may rise. Yet those who have been familiar with the creations of Rachel and Salvini will not only credit the assertion that the genius of Mrs. Siddons in representing the characters of Murphy, Lillo, Southerne, and Otway was greatly superior to that of the writers, but that, even when representing Shakespeare, she supplied much which enriched the conceptions of the poet. To-day we often speak of an actor as the mere interpreter of Shakespeare. We are apt to imagine that there is some one Hamlet or Lady Macbeth, a creature of Shakespeare's brain, an *eidolon* which the actor must of necessity endeavour to represent, his success being measured by the approach which he makes to this unattainable ideal. Those, however, who have seen the acting of the last thirty years in Paris will know that this view of the actor's province is far from true when he interprets even the best modern authors. They know that an actor, when he receives the manuscript, has to create his part in the sense of conceiving a complete human being who, under the given circumstances, employs the words which the author has supplied. They know that no critic could, by reading a play, evolve a portrait of the man whom an original actor will represent as the embodiment of some new part. They know that each new actor of real merit re-creates the persons of the older drama, sending traditions to the winds and producing a new person on the stage using the old words, but with marvellous differences of manner, voice, gesture, and intention. They know that there is not merely one good way of representing a great part, but as many ways as there are great actors. Each actor is bound so to fashion his conception that his own physical attributes and mental powers will lend themselves to its execution; and thus the great parts on the French stage have bound up with them a long series of portraits each representing the creation of a separate actor—all the creations good and to be judged of on their own merits, not by reference simply to the mind of the author.

In small parts, and in the lower walks of the art, the English public will admit this truth readily. No one can suppose that the writer of *Rip Van Winkle* conceived his man with the tones and gestures which we find so admirable in Mr. Jefferson; but the majesty of Shakespeare's name overawes us when we hear that a Mrs. Siddons created a part which Shakespeare wrote—when we are told that an actor's first business is not to think how Shakespeare conceived his character as standing or looking, but how he, the actor, can make

a real human being stand and look while speaking Shakespeare's words. Yet the words of the part do not by themselves supply the actor with one-hundredth part of the actions
he has to perform. Every single word has to be spoken with
just intonation and emphasis, while not a single intonation
or emphasis is indicated by the printed copy. The actor must
find the expression of face, the attitude of body, the action
of the limbs, the pauses, the hurries—the life, in fact. There
is no logical process by which all these things can be evolved
out of the mere words of a part. The actor must go direct to
nature and his own heart for the tones and action by which
he is to move his audience; these his author cannot give him,
and in creating these, if he be a great actor, his art may be
supremely great.

The distinction between the mechanical arts and what are
commonly called the fine arts lies in the creation or invention required by the artist as compared with the skill or
dexterity which are alone required by the craftsman. The
one copies or executes; the other creates, invents, or *finds*
the treasure which he gives to the world. Arts are great or
small as the thing created is noble or petty; the artist is true
or false as he possesses more or less of this creative power,
for the exercise of which he in all cases requires skill more
or less mechanical, which technical skill is often called "art,"
as if there were no other. This technical skill can be taught
and must be learnt by every artist. The poetic creative power
can never be taught, though in a sense it is learnt from every
sight, sound, and feeling; but this greater art is learnt unconsciously, and few have the power to learn the lesson.

Judged by this canon, the art of the actor may claim high
rank whenever its scope is the presentment of the highest human types. To truly great actors the words they have to speak
are but opportunities of creating these types—opportunities
in the sense that a beautiful model, a fine landscape, are
opportunities to the painter. In these he finds his picture, in
those the actor finds his person; but the dramatist does less
for the actor than nature for the painter. It is the involuntary
unconscious perception of this truth which makes men accord
a generous recognition to artists such as Mrs. Siddons while
treating, not without justice, the rank and file of the profession as mere skilled workmen.

It is probable, nay certain, that in writing the words to be
uttered by each character, a great author has vividly present
to his mind an ideal man or woman speaking these with natural and effective tones and gestures—perhaps in Shakespeare's case, though not in others, the best tones and gestures

possible; perhaps, however, with tones and gestures so old-fashioned that they would not move us now. What is certain is that we have no means of discovering these; indeed, he could not himself have imparted them to a fellow-actor. Moreover, when writing the words of *Macbeth,* he cannot have had present to his mind all the gestures and expressions of Lady Macbeth as she listened. Yet this by-play of the great actress was such that the audience, looking at her, forgot to listen to Macbeth. Corneille never thought of how Camille would listen to the account of the death of her lover in *Les Horaces,* or, if he thought of it, his conception must have been a mere sketch as compared with the long and marvellous scene which Rachel, playing the part, showed to the astonished audience.

In truth, the spectators do not know the marvellous study which a great actor applies to every word of a speech. Some think that the study consists in finding out what the author meant the hero to say or express by given words. Sometimes this demands study; more often with great writers it is as plain as can be, requiring no study. When the meaning is understood, next comes the consideration of the feeling which the speech implies or requires in the speaker. The conception of this is far more difficult than the simple interpretation of the words, and will alter with each new actor; not differing *toto coelo,* but differing in shade, colour, and intensity. Any one of us can understand the reasoning in "To be or not to be." Very few of us can form any vivid conception of the state of Hamlet's mind, sentence by sentence, word by word, as he utters them. Of the few who can form any conception beyond a mere colourless, shadeless, pointless impression of gloom or bitterness, each one must of necessity form a distinct and new conception. In order that such a speech may sway a house, it must represent a series of emotions, each intense, natural, and noble—each succeeding the other in a natural sequence. After the speech has been understood and the feelings to which it corresponds conceived, comes a task of ineffable difficulty—that of finding tones, look, and action which shall represent those feelings. The author gives an outline, which the actor must fill up with colour, light and shade, so as to show a concrete fact; and no two actors can or ought to do this in one and the same way. Let any reader who doubts this—who thinks, for instance, that there is some one Hamlet, Shakespeare's Hamlet, who could only speak the speech in one attitude, with one set of tones—open the book and in the solitude of his chamber try first to find out the emotions which Shakespeare meant his Hamlet to feel, and then try to express those emotions in tones which would indicate them to others. If honest and clever, he will find out after half an hour's study how little the author has done for the actor, how much the actor is called upon to do for the author.

These views will find their illustration in the remarkable notes by Professor G. J. Bell on Mrs. Siddons' acting, which are now published for the first time, having been kindly placed at the disposal of the writer by his surviving son, Mr. John Bell, of the Calcutta bar. Written apparently on the spot and during the red-hot glow of appreciation, they bring the great actress before us in a way which no laboured criticism or description could do. They show how noble an art she practised, and might almost inspire some young and generous mind with the power once more to create heroic men and women on the stage.

Professor G. J. Bell, brother of the great surgeon Sir Charles Bell, was Professor of Scottish Law in the University of Edinburgh and author of *Commentaries on the Law of Scotland,* a standard work still in high repute. He was well known by his friends to be a man of fine taste and keen sensibility, as is indeed proved by these notes. They were made in 1809, or about that time, and are contained in three volumes, lettered "Siddons," which of themselves prove the great interest taken in Mrs. Siddons' acting. They contain acting editions of the plays in which she appeared, edited by Mrs. Inchbald. Professor Bell was himself in the habit of reading aloud, and, besides critical remarks, he has noted in many places the rise or fall of Mrs. Siddons' voice, putting a mark ´ for a rise, and ` for a fall. The words on which the emphasis fell, italicised below, are underlined. The following is an introductory note on *Macbeth:*

Of Lady Macbeth there is not a great deal in this play, but the wonderful genius of Mrs. Siddons makes it the whole. She makes it tell the whole story of the ambitious project, the disappointment, the remorse, the sickness and despair of guilty ambition, the attainment of whose object is no cure for the wounds of the spirit. Macbeth in Kemble's hand is only a co-operating part. I can conceive Garrick to have sunk Lady Macbeth as much as Mrs. Siddons does Macbeth, yet when you see Mrs. Siddons play this part you scarcely can believe that any acting could make her part subordinate. Her turbulent and inhuman strength of spirit does all. She turns Macbeth to her purpose, makes him her mere instrument, guides, directs, and inspires the

whole plot. Like Macbeth's evil genius she hurries him on
in the mad career of ambition and cruelty from which his
nature would have shrunk. The flagging of her spirit, the
melancholy and dismal blank beginning to steal upon her, is
one of the finest lessons of the drama. The moral is complete in the despair of Macbeth, the fond regret of both
for that state of innocence from which their wild ambition
has hurried them to their undoing.

The writer of this note, obviously, like Milton, considered
a tragedy the moralest of poems, as indeed it is; but special
attention may be paid to two points. First, Mrs. Siddons did
not herself conceive Shakespeare's Lady Macbeth as turbulent and with inhuman strength; she represented her as a
woman of this type because this conception suited her physical
powers and appearance. But in her own memoranda, published
in her life by Campbell, she speaks thus of Lady Macbeth's
beauty:

> According to my notion it is of that character which I
> believe is generally allowed to be most captivating to the
> other sex—fair, feminine, nay perhaps even fragile—
>
> > Fair as the forms that, wove in fancy's loom,
> > Float in light visions round the poet's head.
>
> Such a combination only, respectable in energy and strength
> of mind, and captivating in feminine loveliness, could have
> composed a charm of such potency as to fascinate the mind
> of a hero so dauntless, a character so amiable, so honour-
> able as Macbeth.

There is something to be said for Mrs. Siddons' argument
that an overbearing woman could never have guided Macbeth; but this point is for the moment of secondary interest,
compared with the light which her remark throws on the
statement made above, that there is not one conception which
alone the actor must form of a given part. Here we have a
great actress forming two distinct conceptions: for no one can
believe that if Mrs. Siddons had been able to appear the fair
and fragile beauty she conceived, she would have used a single
gesture or one inflection similar to those employed when she
was representing turbulent inhuman strength.

The second point of interest in Professor Bell's note is, that
the melancholy and dismal blank beginning to steal on Lady
Macbeth is more the creation of Siddons than of Shakespeare. There is nothing in the text to contradict it, but

little to indicate it. This will become more apparent when we reach the detailed notes.

A second notice in another copy of *Macbeth* appears as follows:

> Mrs. Siddons is not before an audience. Her mind wrought up in high conception of her part, her eye never wandering, never for a moment idle, passion and sentiment continually betraying themselves. Her words are the accompaniments of her thoughts, scarcely necessary, you would imagine, to the expression, but highly raising it, and giving the full force of poetical effect.

What a tribute! Shakespeare's words hardly necessary! And this was written by a man who idolized Shakespeare.

Professor Bell elsewhere remarks:

> A just observation that is unhappy when the part of Lady Macbeth is in the hands of a Siddons, and Macbeth an inferior actor. She then becomes not the affectionate aider of her husband's ambition, but the fell monster who tempts him to transgress, making him the mere instrument of her wild and uncontrollable ambition.

The notes on this play will now be given, only so much of each scene being quoted as is necessary to render the notes intelligible. The text of Shakespeare is given as found in the edition annotated by Professor Bell.

ACT I

SCENE 5—*Macbeth's Castle at Inverness*
Enter LADY MACBETH,[1] *reading a letter.*

Lady. "They met me in the day of success: and I have learned by the *perfectest* report, they have *more* in them than mortal knowledge. When I burned in desire to question them further, they made themselves air, into which they vanished. Whiles I stood rapt in the *wonder of* it, came missives from the king, who all-hailed me 'Thane of Cawdor;' by which title, before, these weird sisters saluted me, and referred me to the coming on of time´, with 'Hail, king that shalt be!' This have I thought good to deliver thee, my dearest partner of greatness, that thou mightest not lose the dues of rejoicing, by being ignorant of what greatness is promised thee. Lay it to thy heart, and farewell."

[1] Mrs. Siddons.

Glamis thou art, and Cawdor, *and shalt be*[2]
What thou art promised:[3] yet do I fear thy nature;
It is too full o' the milk of human kindness
To catch the nearest way: thou wouldst be great:
Art not without ambition, but without
The *illness* should attend it:[4] what thou wouldst highly,
That wouldst thou holily`; wouldst not *play* false,
And yet wouldst wrongly win: thou'd'st have, great Glamis,
That which cries "Thus thou must do, if thou have it;"
And that which rather thou dost fear to do
Than wishest should be undone. Hie thee hither,
That I may pour *my*[5] spirits in thine ear;
And chastise with the valour of my tongue
All that impedes thee from the golden round
Which *fate*[6] and metaphysical aid doth seem
To have thee crown'd withal.

Enter SEYTON.

                              What is your tidings?
Seyton. The king comes here to-night.
Lady.   *Thou'rt mad to say it;*[7]
[8]Is not thy master with him? who, were't so,
Would have inform'd for preparation.[8]

Seyton. So please you, it is true: our thane is coming;
One of my fellows had the speed of him,
Who, almost dead for breath, had scarcely more
Than would make up his message.
Lady.   Give him tending;
He brings great news.

                              [*Exit* SEYTON.

[2] Exalted prophetic tone, as if the whole future were present
to her soul.

[3] A slight tincture of contempt throughout.

[4] Here and in the night scenes it is plain that he had imparted
to her his ambitious thoughts and wishes.

[5] Starts into higher animation.

[6] The whole of this following scene a picture of this highest
working of the soul. Kemble plays it not well, yet some things
good. Much of the effect depends on the fire which she strikes
into him, and which the player must make out.

[7] Loud.

[8] Soft, as if correcting herself, and under the tone of reasoning
concealing sentiments almost disclosed.

[9]The raven himself is hoarse
That croaks the *fatal* entrance of Duncan
Under my battlements. [10]Come, all you spirits
That tend on mortal thoughts, unsex me here,
And fill me from the crown to the toe top-full
Of direst cruelty! make thick my blood;
Stop up the access and passage to remorse,
That no compunctious visitings of nature
Shake my fell purpose, nor keep pace between
The effect and it! [10] [11]Come to my woman's breasts,
And take my milk for gall, you murdering ministers,
Wherever in your sightless substances
You wait on nature's mischief! Come, thick night,
And pall thee in the dunnest smoke of hell,
That my keen knife see not the wound it makes,
Nor heaven peep through the blanket of the dark,
To cry "Hold, hold!" [11]

Enter MACBETH.

[12]Great Glamis! worthy Cawdor!
Greater than both, by *the all-hail hereafter!*
Thy letters have transported me beyond
This ignorant present, and I feel now
The future in the instant.
   Macbeth.   My dearest love,
Duncan comes here to-night.
   Lady.[13]   And when goes hence?
   Macbeth. To-morrow, as he purposes.
   Lady.   O, never ˇ . . .
(never) Shall sun that morrow see ˇ! [14]

[9] After a long pause when the messenger has retired. Indicates her fell purpose settled and about to be accomplished.

[10] In a low voice—a whisper of horrid determination.

[11] Voice quite supernatural, as in a horrible dream. Chilled with horror by the slow hollow whisper of this wonderful creature.

[12] Loud, triumphant, and wild in her air.

[13] High purpose working in her mind.

[14] O, neverˇ. A long pause, turned from him, her eye steadfast. Strong dwelling emphasis on "never," with deep downward inflection, "never shall sun that morrow see!" Low, very slow sustained voice, her eye and her mind occupied steadfastly in the contemplation of her horrible purpose, pronunciation almost syllabic, not unvaried. Her self-collected solemn energy, her fixed posture, her determined eye and full deep voice of fixed resolve never should be forgot, cannot be conceived nor described.

[16]Your face, my thane, is as a book where men
May read strange matters. To beguile the time,
Look like the time,[15] bear welcome in your eye,
Your hand, your tongue: look like the innocent flower,
[16]*But be the serpent under't.* He that's coming
Must be provided for: and you shall put
This night's great business into my dispatch;
[17]Which shall to all our nights and days to come
Give solely sovereign sway and masterdom.[17]

   Macbeth. We will speak further.

   Lady.   Only look up clear;
[18]To alter favour ever is to fear:
Leave all the rest to me.[18]   *[Exeunt.*

Does not the reader feel that in these close personal observations is to be found a far better conception of what the
genius of Siddons could do than is given in the long lives by
Campbell and Boaden? Mrs. Siddons appears to have repeated
the word "never" before "shall sun that morrow see." This
appears not only from note (14), but from a manuscript in-
sertion of a second "never" after the pause indicated above.
The next notes are on the sixth scene, where Lady Macbeth
addresses Duncan.

   Lady.   [19]All our service
In every point twice done and then done double
Were poor and single business, to contend
Against those honours deep and broad, wherewith
Your majesty loads our house: for those of old,
And the late dignities heap'd up to them,
We rest your hermits.[19]

At her exit comes this note:

   Bows gracefully to the king, when she gives him the *pas*
in entering. Then graciously and sweetly to the nobles
before she follows the king.

[15] Observing the effect of what she has said on him, now first
turning her eye upon his face.

[16] Very slow, severe and cruel expression, her gesture impressive.

[17] Voice changes to assurance and gratulation.

[18] Leading him out, cajoling him, her hand on his shoulder clap-
ping him. This vulgar—gives a mean conception of Macbeth, unlike the high mental working by which he is turned to her ambitious purpose.

[19] Dignified and simple. Beautifully spoken; quite musical in her
tones and in the pronunciation, soothing and satisfying the ear.

On Macbeth's speech, Scene 7, beginning

If it were done, when 'tis done, then 'twere well
It were done quickly,

there is the following:

Kemble speaks this, as if he had never seen his sister, like a *speech* to be recited. None of that hesitation and working of the mind which in Mrs. Siddons seems to inspire the words as the natural expression of the emotion. After the entrance of Lady Macbeth the notes continue:

Lady. He has almost supp'd: why have you left the chamber? [20]
Macbeth. Hath he ask'd for me?
Lady.   *Know* you not he has?
Macbeth. We will proceed no further in this business:
[21]He hath honour'd me of late; and I have bought
Golden opinions from all sorts of people,[21]
Which would be worn now in their newest gloss,
Not cast aside so soon.
Lady.   [22]Was the hope drunk
Wherein you dressed yourself? hath it slept since?
And wakes it now, to look so green and pale
At what it did so freely? [23] From this time
Such I account thy love. Art thou afeard
To be the same in thine own act and valour
As thou art in desire? Wouldst thou have that
Which thou esteem'st the ornament of life,
And live a coward in thine own esteem,
Letting "I dare not" wait upon "I would,"
Like the poor cat i' the adage?
Macbeth.   [24]Prithee, peace:
I dare do all that may become a man;
Who dares do more is none.[24]
Lady.   What beast was it then
That made you break this enterprise to me?

[20] Eager whisper of anger and surprise.
[21] Here again Mrs. Siddons appears with all her inimitable expression of emotion. The sudden change from animated hope and surprise to disappointment, depression, contempt, and rekindling resentment, is beyond any powers but hers.
[22] Very cold, distant, and contemptuous.
[23] Determined air and voice. Then a tone of cold contemptuous reasoning.
[24] Kemble speaks this well.

When you durst do it, then you were a man;
And, to be more than what you were, you would
Be so much more than man. Nor time nor place
Did then adhere, and yet you would make both:
They have made themselves, and that their fitness now
Does unmake you.[25] [26]I have given suck, and know
How tender 'tis to love the babe that milks me:
I would, while it was smiling in my face,
Have plucked my nipple from his boneless gums
And dashed the brains out, had I but so sworn as *you*
Have done to this.

    Macbeth.   If we should fail?

    Lady.   [27]We fail˅!
But screw your courage to the sticking-place,
And we'll *not* fail.[27] When Duncan is asleep—
Whereto the rather shall his day's hard journey
Soundly invite him—his two chamberlains
Will I with wine and wassail so convince
That memory, the warder of the brain,
Shall be a fume, and the receipt of reason
A limbec only;[28] when in swinish sleep
Their drenched natures lie as in a death,
What cannot you and I perform upon
The *unguarded Duncan*˄? *what* not put upon
His spongy officers, who shall bear the guilt
Of our great quell?

    Macbeth.   Bring forth men-children only;
For thy undaunted mettle should compose

---

[25] Cold, still, and distant; slow with remarkable distinctness and great earnestness.

[26] She has been at a distant part of the stage. She now comes close to him—an entire change of manner, looks for some time in his face, then speaks.

[27] *We fail*˅. Not surprise, strong downward inflection, bowing with her hands down, the palm upward. Then voice of strong assurance, "When Duncan," &c. This spoken near to him, and in a low earnest whisper of discovery she discloses her plan.

[28] Pauses as if trying the effect on him. Then renews her plan more earnestly, low still, but with increasing confidence. Throughout this scene she feels her way, observes the wavering of his mind; suits her earnestness and whole manner to it. With contempt, affection, reason, the conviction of her well-concerted plan, the assurance of success which her wonderful tones inspire, she turns him to her purpose with an art in which the player shares largely in the poet's praise.

Nothing but males. Will it not be received,
When we have marked with blood those sleepy two
Of his own chamber and used their very daggers,
That they have done't?
' *Lady*.   Who *dares* receive it other,[29]
As we shall make our griefs and clamour roar
Upon his death?
      Macbeth.   I am settled, and bend up
Each corporal agent to this terrible feat.
Away, and mock the time with fairest show:
False face must hide what the false heart doth know.
                                                         [*Exeunt*.

The next note refers to Macbeth's dagger scene, and is
very interesting, although referring more immediately to
Kemble than to his sister. Professor Bell says:

> There is much stage trick and very cold in this scene of
> Kemble—walks across the stage, his eyes on the ground,
> starts at the sight of the servant, whom he forgets for the
> purpose, renews his walk, throws up his face, sick, sighs,
> then a start theatric and then the dagger. Why can't he
> learn from his sister?
>
> Charles Bell thinks (and justly) that he should stand or
> sit musing, his eye fixed on vacancy, then a more piercing
> look to seem to see what still is in the mind's eye only,
> characterised by the bewildered look which accompanies the
> want of a fixed object of vision; yet the eye should not
> roll or start. N. B.: Mrs. Siddons in reading *Hamlet*
> showed how inimitably she could by a mere look, while
> sitting in a chair, paint to the spectators a horrible shadow
> in her mind.

At the point where Macbeth says "there's no such thing,"
Professor Bell continues:

> Kemble here hides his eyes with his hand, then fearfully
> looks up, and peeping first over then under his hand, as if
> for an insect whose buzzing had disturbed him, he removes
> his hand, looks more abroad, and then recovers—very poor
> —the recovery should be by an effort of the mind. It is
> not the absence of a physical corporeal dagger, but the
> returning tone of a disordered fancy. A change in the look,
> the clearing of a bewildered imagination, a more steadfast

---

[29] Pause. Look of great confidence, much dignity of mien. In
"dares" great and imperial dignity.

and natural aspect, the hand drawn across the eyes or forehead, with something of a bitter smile.

These remarks illustrate well what was said before as to the nature of an actor's study. Professor Bell had reached the second stage, and knew well what the actor should feel. The third stage, how to show it, can only be acted, not described. With the entrance of Lady Macbeth the notes become detailed.

Scene 2

Enter Lady Macbeth.

Lady.[30] That which hath made them drunk hath made me bold;
What hath quenched them hath given me fire. *Hark! Peace!*[31]
It was the owl that shrieked, the fatal bellman,
Which gives the stern'st good-night. *He is about it:*[32]
The doors are open, and the surfeited grooms
Do mock their charge with snores: I have drugg'd their possets,
That death and nature do contend about them,
Whether they live or die.
   Macbeth. [*Within*]   Who's there? what, ho!
   Lady. [33]Alack, I am afraid they have awaked,
And 'tis not done. The attempt and not the deed
Confounds us. Hark! I laid their daggers ready;
He could not miss them. Had he not resembled
My father as he slept, I had done't.[34]—*My husband!*

Enter Macbeth.

   Macbeth. [35]I have done the deed. Didst thou not hear a noise?
   Lady. I heard the owl scream and the crickets cry.
Did not you speak? [34]
   Macbeth.   When? [35]

[30] With a ghastly horrid smile.
[31] Hsh! Hsh! Whisper.
[32] Breathes with difficulty, hearkens towards the door. Whisper horrible.
[33] The finest agony; tossing of the arms.
[34] Agonised suspense, as if speechless with uncertainty whether discovered.
[35] Macbeth speaks all this like some horrid secret—a whisper in the dark.

Lady.   Now.
Macbeth.   As I descended? [36]
Lady. Ay.
Macbeth. Hark!
Who lies i' the second chamber?
Lady.   Donalbain.
Macbeth. This is a sorry sight.

                            [*Looking on his hands.*
Lady. A foolish thought, to say a sorry sight.
Macbeth. [37]There's one did laugh in his sleep, and one cried "Murder!"
That they did wake each other: I stood and heard them:
But they did say their prayers, and address'd them
Again to sleep.
Lady. There are two lodged together.
Macbeth. One cried "God bless us!" and "Amen" the other;
As they had seen me with these hangman's hands:
Listening their fear, I could not say "Amen,"
When they did say "God bless us!"
Lady. Consider it not so deeply.
Macbeth. But wherefore could not I pronounce "Amen"?
I had most need of blessing, and "Amen"
Stuck in my throat.
Lady.   These deeds must not be thought
After these ways; *so, it will make us mad.*[37]
Macbeth. [38]Methought I heard a voice cry "Sleep no more!"
                            . . . to all the house
"Glamis hath murder'd sleep, and therefore Cawdor
Shall sleep no more; Macbeth shall sleep no more." [38]
Lady. Who was it that thus cried? Why, worthy thane,
[39]You do unbend your noble strength, to think
So brainsickly of things. Go get some water,
And wash this filthy witness from your hand.[39]

[36] Very well spoken; horrid whisper.

[37] Mrs. Siddons here displays her wonderful power and knowledge of nature. As if her inhuman strength of spirit overcome by the contagion of his remorse and terror. Her arms about her neck and bosom, shuddering.

[38] Her horror changes to agony and alarm at his derangement, uncertain what to do; calling up the resources of her spirit.

[39] She comes near him, attempts to call back his wandering thoughts to ideas of common life. Strong emphasis on *who*. Speaks forcibly into his ear, looks at him steadfastly. "Why, worthy thane," &c.: fine remonstrance, tone fit to work on his mind.

[40]*Why did you bring these daggers from the place?*
They must lie there: go carry them, and smear
The sleepy grooms with blood.
　　Macbeth.　　　　　　　　　I'll go no more:
I am afraid to think what I have done;
Look on't again I dare not.
　　Lady.　　　　　　　　　Infirm of purpose!
[41]Give me the daggers: the sleeping and the dead
Are but as pictures: 'tis the eye of childhood
That fears a painted devil.[41] *If he do bleed,*[42]
I'll gild the faces of the grooms withal;
For it must seem their guilt.
　　　　　　　　　　　　　[*Exit. Knocking within.*
　　Macbeth.　　　　　　　　　Whence is that knocking?
How is't with me, when every noise appals me?
What hands are here? ha! they pluck out mine eyes.
Will all great Neptune's ocean wash this blood
Clean from my hand? No; this my hand will rather
The multitudinous seas incarnadine,
Making the green one red.

Re-enter LADY MACBETH.

　　Lady. [43]My *hands* are of your color; but I shame
To wear a *heart* so white. [*Knocking within.*] I hear a
　　knocking
At the south entry; retire we to our chamber:
A little water clears us of this deed:
How easy is it, then! Your constancy
Hath left you unattended. [*Knocking within.*] Hark, more
　　knocking.
Get on your nightgown, lest occasion call us
And show us to be watchers. Be not lost
So poorly in your thoughts.
　　Macbeth. To know my deed, 'twere best not know myself.
　　　　　　　　　　　　　[*Knocking within.*
Wake Duncan with this knocking! Oh, would thou couldst! [43]

　　　　　　　　　　　　　　　　　　　[*Exeunt.*

[40] Now only at leisure to observe the daggers.

[41] Seizing the daggers very contemptuously.

[42] As stealing out she turns towards him stooping, and with the finger pointed to him with malignant energy says, "If he do bleed," &c.

[43] Contempt. Kemble plays well here; stands motionless; his bloody hands near his face; his eye fixed, agony in his brow; quite rooted to the spot. She at first directs him with an assured and

The notes are resumed where Lady Macbeth enters as queen.

ACT III

Scene 2—*The Palace*

Enter Lady Macbeth, *as Queen, and* Seyton.

Lady. [44]Is Banquo gone from court?
Seyton. Ay, madam, but returns again to-night.
Lady. Say to the king, I would attend his leisure
For a few words.
   Seyton.   Madam, I will.   [*Exit.*
   Lady.   [45]Nought's had, all's spent,
Where our desire is got without content:
'Tis safer to be that which we destroy
Than by destruction dwell in doubtful joy.[45]

Enter Macbeth.

[46]How now, my lord! why do you keep alone,
Of sorriest fancies your companions making;
Using those thoughts which should indeed have died
With them they think on? Things without all remedy
Should be without regard: what's done is done.[46]
   Macbeth. We have scotch'd the snake, not kill'd it:
She'll close and be herself, whilst our poor malice
Remains in danger of her former tooth.
But let the frame of things disjoint, both the worlds suffer,
Ere we will eat our meal in fear, and sleep
In the affliction of these terrible dreams
That shake us nightly; better be with the dead,
Whom we, to gain our place, have sent to peace,
Than on the torture of the mind to lie
In restless ecstasy. Duncan is in his grave;

---

confident air. Then alarm steals on her, increasing to agony lest
his reason be quite gone and discovery be inevitable. Strikes him
on the shoulder, pulls him from his fixed posture, forces him away,
he talking as he goes.
  [44] Great dignity and solemnity of voice; nothing of the joy of
gratified ambition.
  [45] Very mournful.
  [46] Still her accents very plaintive. This is one of the passages
in which her intense love of her husband should animate every
word. It should not be contemptuous reproach, but deep sorrow
and sympathy with his melancholy.

176190

After life's fitful fever he sleeps well;
Treason has done his worst: nor steel, nor poison,
Malice domestic, foreign levy, nothing,
Can touch him further.
    Lady.   Come on;
Gentle my lord, sleek o'er your rugged looks;
Be bright and jovial [47] among your guests tonight.
    Macbeth. O, full of scorpions is my mind, dear wife!
Thou know'st that Banquo, and his Fleance, live.
    Lady. [48]But in them nature's copy's not eterne.

There are no further remarks on this scene.
In Scene 4, where at the banquet Macbeth speaks to the
murderers, the remark is written: "During all this a growing
uneasiness in her; at last she rises and speaks." Full notes are
resumed towards the end of the scene, as follows:

                              [*The Ghost of* BANQUO *enters,*
                                and sits in MACBETH'S *place.*
    Macbeth. Here had we now our country's honour roof'd,
Were the graced person of our Banquo present;
Who may I rather challenge for unkindness
Than pity for mischance!
    Ross.   His absence, sir,
Lays blame upon his promise. Please 't your highness
To grace us with your royal company.
    Macbeth. [49]The table's full.
    Lennox. Here is a place reserved, sir.
    Macbeth. Where?
    Lennox. Here, my good lord. What is't that moves your
        highness?[49]
    Macbeth. Which of you have done this?
    Lennox. What, my good lord?
    Macbeth. Thou canst not say, I did it: never shake
Thy gory locks at me.
    Ross. Gentlemen, rise: his highness is not well.
    Lady. [50]Sit, worthy friends:—my lord is often thus,
And hath been from his youth: pray you, keep seat;
The fit is momentary; upon a thought
He will again be well: if you much note him,
You shall offend him, and extend his passion;

[47] Mournful: a forced cheerfulness breaking through it.
[48] A flash of her former spirit and energy.
[49] Her secret uneasiness very fine. Suppressed, but agitating her
whole frame.
[50] Descends.

Feed, and regard him not. *Are you a man?* [51]
  Macbeth. Ay, and a bold one, that dare look on that
Which might appal the devil.
  Lady. [52]O, proper stuff!
This is the very painting of your fear:
This is the air-drawn dagger, which, you said,
Led you to Duncan. O, these flaws and starts
(Impostors to true fear) would well become
A woman's story, at a winter's fire,[52]
Authorized by her grandam. Shame itself!
[53]Why do you make such faces? When all's done,
You look but on a stool.[53]
  Macbeth. Prithee, see there! behold! look! lo! how say
    you?
Why, what care I? If thou canst nod, speak too.
If charnel-houses and our graves must send
Those that we bury back, our monuments
Shall be the maws of kites.

                                [Ghost vanishes.
  Lady.   What, quite unmann'd in folly?
  Macbeth. If I stand here, I saw him.
  Lady.   *Fie, for shame!* [54]

Re-enter Ghost.

  Macbeth. [55]Avaunt! and quit my sight! let the earth hide
    thee!
Thy bones are marrowless, thy blood is cold;
Thou hast no speculation in those eyes
Which thou dost glare with.
  Lady.[56]   Think of this, good peers,
But as a thing of custom: 'tis no other;
Only it spoils the pleasure of the time.
  Macbeth. [57]What man dare, I dare:

---

[51] Comes up to him and catches his hand. Voice suppressed.
[52] Peevish and scornful.
[53] In his ear, as if to bring him back to objects of common life.
Her anxiety makes you creep with apprehension: uncertain how
to act. Her emotion keeps you breathless.
[54] Returns to her seat; this whispered.
[55] Her secret agony again agitates her.
[56] Rises and speaks sweetly to the company.
[57] Macready plays this well. Even Kemble chid and scolded the
ghost out! and rose in vehemence and courage as he went on.
Macready began in the vehemence of despair, but, overcome by
terror as he continued to gaze on the apparition, dropped his
voice lower and lower till he became tremulous and inarticulate,

Approach thou like the rugged Russian bear,
The arm'd rhinoceros, or the Hyrcan tiger;
Take any shape but that, and my firm nerves
Shall never tremble: or be alive again,
And dare me to the desert with thy sword;
If trembling I inhibit, then protest me
The baby of a girl. Hence, horrible shadow!
Unreal mockery, hence! [57]

[Ghost vanishes.

                 Why, so: being gone,
I am a man again.
    Lady. You have displaced the mirth, broke the good meet-
      ing,
With most admired disorder.
    Macbeth.   Can such things be,
And overcome us like a summer's cloud,
Without our special wonder? You make me strange
Even to the disposition that I owe,
When now I think you can behold such sights,
And keep the natural ruby of your cheeks,
When mine is blanch'd with fear.
    Ross.   What sights, my lord?
    Lady. [58]I pray you, speak not; he grows worse and worse;
Question enrages him. At once, good night:
Stand not upon the order of your going,
But go at once.
    Lennox.   Good night; and better health
Attend his majesty!
    Lady.   A kind good night to all!

[Exeunt all but MACBETH
and LADY MACBETH.

    Macbeth. It will have blood: they say blood will have
      blood:
Stones have been known to move and trees to speak;
Augurs and understood relations have
By maggot-pies and choughs and rooks brought forth
The secret'st man of blood. What is the night?
    Lady. [59]Almost at odds with morning, which is which.

---

and at last uttering a subdued cry of mortal agony and horror,
he suddenly cast his mantle over his face, and sank back almost
lifeless on his seat.

[58] Descends in great eagerness; voice almost choked with anxiety
to prevent their questioning; alarm, hurry, rapid and convulsive
as if afraid he should tell of the murder of Duncan.

[59] Very sorrowful. Quite exhausted.

Macbeth. How say'st thou, that Macduff denies his person
At our great bidding?
   Lady.   Did you send to him, sir?
   Macbeth. I hear it by the way, but I will send:
There's not a one of them but in his house
I keep a servant fee'd. I will to-morrow,
And betimes I will, unto the weird sisters:
More shall they speak, for now I am bent to know,
By the worst means, the worst. For mine own good
All causes shall give way: I am in blood
Stepp'd in so far that, should I wade no more,
Returning were as tedious as go o'er.
   Lady. [60] You lack the season of all natures, sleep.
   Macbeth. Come, we'll to sleep. My strange and self-abuse
Is the initiate fear that wants hard use:
We are yet but young in deed.

                                    [Exeunt.

It is curious to see by these last two notes, as by the
introductory remarks, that Mrs. Siddons conveyed by her
demeanour the impression of being already almost broken
down, and quite as much in need of sleep as Macbeth. This
preparation for the sleeping scene is a very fine idea, and
hardly seems to be suggested in the insignificant remarks
given by Shakespeare to Lady Macbeth at the close of this
scene. We now come to the fifth act.

Gentlewoman. Lo you, here she comes!
This is her very guise; and, upon my life, fast asleep. Observe her; stand close.

        Enter LADY MACBETH, *with a taper.*[61]

   Physician. How came she by that light?
   Gentlewoman. Why, it stood by her: she has light by her
continually; 'tis her command.
   Physician. You see her eyes are open.
   Gentlewoman. Ay, but their sense is shut.
   Physician. What is it she does now?
Look, how she rubs her hands.

[60] Feeble now, and as if preparing for her last sickness and final
doom.
[61] I should like her to enter less suddenly. A slower and more
interrupted step more natural. She advances rapidly to the table,
sets down the light and rubs her hand, making the action of lift-
ing up water in one hand at intervals.

Gentlewoman. It is an accustomed action with her, to seem
thus washing her hands: I have known her continue in this
a quarter of an hour.

Lady. Yet here's a *spot.*

Physician. Hark! she speaks.

Lady. Out, damned spot! out, I say!—*One:*[62] *two:* why,
then 'tis time to do't.[63]—Hell is murky!—Fie, my lord, fie!
a soldier, and afeard? What need we fear who knows it, when
none can call our power to account?—Yet who would have
thought the old man to have so much blood in him?

Physician. Do you mark that?

Lady. *The thane of Fife had a wife:*[64] where is she now?—
What, will these hands ne'er[65] be clean?—No more o' that,
my lord, *no more o' that:*[66] you mar all *with this* starting.

Physician. Go to, go to; you have known what you should
not.

Gentlewoman. She has spoke what she should not, I am
sure of that: heaven knows what she has known.

Lady. Here's the smell of the blood still: all the perfumes
of Arabia will not sweeten this little hand. *Oh, oh, oh!* [67]

Physician. What a sigh is there! The heart is sorely charged.

This is the last of these notes by which we have been able
to follow the great actress from the exalted prophetic tone of
her entrance to the sigh of imbecility at the end.

No other part played by Mrs. Siddons was annotated by
Professor Bell in the thorough manner adopted by him when
witnessing her Lady Macbeth and Queen Katharine. He left,
however, some notes on her Mrs. Beverley and Lady Randolph,
concerning which a few words may be said before speaking
of Shakespeare's play.

Home's *Douglas,* though known to all by name, is so little
read that a sketch of the plot is necessary to make Professor
Bell's remarks intelligible to the general reader. Lady Randolph was secretly married in early youth to one of a family
at feud with her own, a Douglas, who was killed in battle
three weeks after the marriage. The widow bore a son, but
this infant, whose birth had been concealed, disappeared with
his nurse, and his mother believes him to be dead. He, young

---

[62] Listening eagerly.

[63] A strange unnatural whisper.

[64] Very melancholy tone.

[65] Melancholy peevishness.

[66] Eager whisper.

[67] This not a sigh. A convulsive shudder—very horrible. A tone
of imbecility audible in the sigh.

Norval of the Grampian Hills, was however saved, and has been brought up in ignorance of his birth. Lady Randolph did not inform her second husband, Lord Randolph, of her first marriage, and explained her continual melancholy by attributing it to grief for the death of a brother. At the period when the play begins, young Norval is fortunate enough to save the life of his stepfather, Lord Randolph, who introduces him to his unknown mother and promotes him to an honourable command. In the course of the play the mother recognises her son and makes herself known to him. The intimacy which results enables a villain, Glenalvon, so to poison the mind of Lord Randolph with jealousy as to cause him to attempt the youth's life. Young Norval or Douglas, while defending himself against Lord Randolph, is wounded to death by the villain, and dies in his mother's presence. She, in despair, commits suicide. In accordance with the taste of the day, neither combat nor suicide takes place before the audience.

Although much of the sentiment in this play is expressed in language which nowadays provokes a smile, an actress may find great scope for her art in presenting the feelings of the mother, who gradually acquires the certainty that her child still lives and is the gallant youth who has already shown himself worthy of her love.

Professor Bell's notes, while sufficient to convince us that Mrs. Siddons could express great tenderness and strong affection, no less than the sterner emotions with which her name is more commonly connected, lack the precision by which, in writing of Shakespeare's plays, he enables us in some measure to understand the means she employed. Referring to the wish expressed by the lady that every soldier of the two opposing armies might return in "peace and safety to his pleasant home," he writes:

> The most musical sound I ever heard, and on the conclusion a melancholy recollection seemed to fill her whole soul of the strength of that wish in former times, and of its first disappointment.

Again, where Lady Randolph addresses Sincerity as the first of virtues, the note says:

> Fine apostrophe. Her fine eyes raised in tears to heaven, her hands stretched out and elevated.

At the close of the well-known speech beginning, "My name is Norval," the following remark is appended:

The idea of her own child seems to have been growing, and at this point overwhelms her and fills her eyes with tears. Beautiful acting of this sweet feeling throughout these speeches. The interest she takes in the youth—her manifest retrospection.

The byplay of Lady Randolph throughout the long speeches of her husband and son was obviously the center of interest to the spectator, and ended in what is called—

A great and affecting burst of affection and interest, as if she had already almost identified him with her son, or adopted him to supply the loss.

Answering Norval, who assures her that he will never be unworthy of the favour shown him, Lady Randolph says:

I will be sworn thou wilt not. Thou shalt be *my knight.*

The words printed in italics were underlined by Professor Bell.

Lady Randolph explains to her confidante that while Norval spoke she thought that, had the son of Douglas lived, he might have resembled this young gallant stranger.

Professor Bell writes:

It is this she has been acting during the preceding scene.

There are no further notes on this play, nothing to guide us as to the manner in which Mrs. Siddons said the famous "Was he alive?" when a certain old man describes the finding of her infant son, who turns out to be Norval.

When we read Home's *Douglas* we may feel a certain interest in our ancestors who liked it, but Moore's *Gamester* awakens a feeling of loathing which extends even to the audience that can endure the degrading spectacle. The character of Lady Randolph is far from noble; this woman, who deceives her parents and husband, who lost her child and held her tongue, who has maundered through life for twenty years nursing her melancholy and despising all good things present, because they are not better things past, belongs to no heroic type. We cannot admire her indifference to the excellent husband who after twenty years of married life still sues in vain for

Decent affection and complacent kindness.

But Lady Randolph's well-bred coldness is preferable to Mrs. Beverley's form of love. Says Mrs. Beverley: "All may be well yet. When he has nothing to lose, I shall fetter him in these arms again; and *then* what is it to be poor?" Professor Bell adds:

> Such a speech as this the wonderful voice of Mrs. Siddons and her speaking eye make very affecting.

Surely no one but a Mrs. Siddons could do so.

An old servant offers to sacrifice his little fortune to the much-loved gamester, who has been out all night for the first time: he proposes to go to him and if possible to bring him home. Mrs. Beverley says, "Do so, then; but take care how you upbraid him—I have never upbraided him." There is a note here:

> Follows him to the door; then laying her hand on his arm detains him with an earnest look, and then speaks solemnly.

The lady uses much the same language to her husband's sister Charlotte, and Professor Bell notes:

> She repeats an injunction she had given to Jarvis, more familiarly but with equal earnestness, with more sorrow and less of dignity; then crossing the stage to go out, she bows kindly to Charlotte; then, with her finger up and a fine look of determination, leaves her.

In a subsequent scene the husband has come home, and his honest friend Jewson tries to open his eyes to the machinations of the villain Stukeley by telling what a bad boy he had been at school. Mrs. Siddons, who listens, is described thus:

> She stands with riveted attention. She is behind at a little distance. The earnest and piercing look of her eyes, the simplicity of her attitude, is perfect nature.

The gamester replies to his honest friend: "You are too busy, sir." Mrs. Beverley rejoins: "No, not too busy; mistaken, perhaps—that had been milder." The note on this runs:

> Comes up to Beverley with a hasty anxiety and hurried voice, alarm and kind reproach in her look and manner.

The notes on *The Gamester* end here.

We are nowadays happily delivered from the false sentiment which required the ideal woman to love the more, the more she was ill-treated. We are rather in danger of shutting our eyes to the real beauty of patient Grisyld, the original of many copies, mostly like Mrs. Beverley's caricatures. Chaucer's Grisyld fawns unpleasantly, but in the story of Griselda as Boccaccio tells it we find a very noble woman who thought herself of so small account in this great world that she claimed nothing, while she held herself bound in all things to do her best. Her goodness is above all strong, whereas Mrs. Beverley is above all weak; her husband ruins, cheats, insults her, and she simply dotes on him all the time with slavish animal affection. No play can, however, be successful which has not some merit, and it is easy to recognise that in the conduct of the plot Moore shows skill, in so far as each scene reveals a deeper and deeper misery.

In Queen Katharine, Shakespeare has shown to what extent a woman of heroic mould might continue to love a husband who had mortally wronged her, and how fully the same woman could be just to a fallen enemy. Katharine, unlike Mrs. Beverley, is both good and strong.

Professor Bell wrote as follows on the fly-leaf of *King Henry the Eighth:*

> Mrs. Siddons' Queen Katharine is a perfect picture of a great, dignified, somewhat impatient spirit, conscious of rectitude, and adorned with every generous and every domestic virtue.
>
> Her dignified contempt of Wolsey when comparing her own royal descent, her place and title as queen, her spotless honour, with the mean arts and machinations by which this man was driving her into the toils and breaking in upon her happiness; her high spirit and impatient temper; the energies of a strong and virtuous mind guarding the King at all hazards from popular discontent and defending her own fame with eloquence and dignity; her energy subdued, but her queen-like dignity unimpaired by sickness; and the candour and goodness of her heart in her dying conversation concerning her great enemy—all this, beautifully painted by Mrs. Siddons, making this one of the finest female characters in the English drama.

Our notes begin with the entrance of the Queen. The text, as before, is that of Mrs. Inchbald. The words on which the emphasis fell are underlined in the notes and are here printed in italics. An acute accent marks a word on which the voice was raised in pitch; a grave accent marks a word on which the voice fell.

ACT I

Scene 2

Enter the Queen, *ushered by* Guildford, *who places a cushion on which she kneels. The* King *rises, takes her up, and places her by him.*

King. Rise.

Queen. Nay, we must longer kneel; I am a suitor.

King. Arise, and take place by us:—half your suit
Never name to us; you have half our power;
The other moiety, ere you ask, is given;
Repeat your will, and take it[68]

    Queen.   *Thank your Majesty.*
That you would love yourself, and, in that love,
Not unconsider'd leave your honour, nor
The dignity of your office, is the point
Of my petition.

    King.   Lady mine, proceed.

    Queen. I am solicited, not by a few,
And those of true condition, that your subjects
Are in great grievance: there have been commissions
Sent down among them, which have flaw'd the heart
Of all their loyalties:—wherein, although,
My good lord cardinal, they vent reproaches
Most bitterly‸ on you⸍, as putter-on
Of these exactions, yet the king our master
(*Whose honour heaven shield from soil!* [69]) even he escapes
    not
Language unmannerly, yea, such which breaks
The sides of loyalty, and almost appears
In loud rebellion.

    Nor.   Not almost appears—
It doth appear; for, upon these taxations,
The clothiers all, not able to maintain
The many to them 'longing, have put off
The spinsters, carders, fullers, weavers, who,
Unfit for other life, compell'd by hunger,
And lack of other means, in desperate manner
Daring the event to the teeth, are all in uproar,

    [68] Rises and sits by him. Then, in a composed and dignified tone, addresses him, very articulate and very earnest.

    [69] Tenderly and religiously.

And danger serves among them.

King. Taxation!
Wherein? and what taxation?—my lord cardinal,
You that are blam'd for it alike with us,
Know you of this taxation?

Wol. Please you, sir,
I know but of a single part in aught
Pertains to the state; and front but in that file
Where others tell steps with me.

Queen. No, my lord,
You *know* no more than others:[70] but you frame
Things that are known alike, which are not wholesome
To those which would not know them, and yet must
Perforce be their acquaintance. These exactions
Whereof my sovereign would have note, they are
Most pestilent to the hearing; and to bear them
The back is sacrifice to the load. They say
They are devis'd by you; or else you suffer
Too hard an exclamation.

King. Still exaction!
The nature of it? In what kind, let's know,
Is this exaction?

Queen. [71]I am much too venturous
In tempting of your patience; but am bolden'd
Under your promis'd pardon.[71] [72]The subjects' grief
Comes through commissions, which compel from each
The sixth part of his substance, to be levied
Without delay; and the pretence for this
Is nam'd, your wars in France:[72] this makes bold mouths:
Tongues spit their duties out, and cold hearts freeze
Allegiance in them; their curses now
Live where their prayers did; and it's come to pass,
This tractable obedience is a slave
To each incensed will.[73] I would your highness
Would give it quick consideration.

King. By my life,
This is against our pleasure.

The notes cease until the surveyor of the Duke of Buckingham enters, to whom Wolsey speaks:

[70] Mildly, but very decidedly, accusing him
[71] Gracious apology.
[72] Very articulate and clear.
[73] Very earnest.

Wol. Stand forth; and with bold spirit relate what you,
Most like a careful subject, have collected
Out of the Duke of Buckingham.
  King.   Speak freely.
  Surv. First, it was usual with him—every day
It would infect his speech—that if the king
Should without issue die, he'd carry it so
To make the sceptre his: these very words
I have heard him utter to his son-in-law,
Lord Aberga'ny; to whom by oath he menac'd
Revenge upon the cardinal.[74]
  Wol.   Please your highness, note
This dangerous conception in this point.
Not friended by his wish, to your high person
His will is most malignant; and it stretches
Beyond you, to your friends.
  Queen.   [75]My learn'd lord cardinal,
Deliver all with *charity*.[75]
  King.   Speak on:
How grounded he his title to the crown,
Upon our fail? to this point hast thou heard him
At any time speak aught?

The Surveyor continues to give his evidence, stating that a
Chartreux friar had phophesied to the Duke that he should
govern England. Then the Queen intervenes:

  Queen.[76]   If I know you well,
You were the duke's surveyor, and lost your office
On the complaint o' the tenants;[77] *take good heed*
You charge not in your spleen a noble person,
And spoil your nobler soul: I say, take heed.[77]
  King.   Go forward.

The Surveyor continues his evidence and states that Buckingham had said that if he had been committed to the Tower
he would have put a knife into the King; on which the King
exclaims:

[74] She hears all this with a dignified, judge-like aspect, often
darting a keen look of inquiry at the witness and the Cardinal.

[75] A grand sustained voice. The emphasis on *"charity"* strong.

[76] A very penetrating look. Looks very steadfastly and seriously
in his face for some time, then speaks.

[77] The second part of this speech very severe tone of remonstrance. Grand swell on *"and spoil your nobler soul,"* "I say," &c.,
very emphatic.

King.   A giant traitor!
Wol. Now, madam, may his highness live in freedom,
And this man out of prison?
Queen.   God mend *all!* [78]

The scene shortly ends. Mrs. Siddons in this scene evidently
brought into strong relief the intellect and power of the
Queen as well as her rectitude. In the fourth scene of the
second act the Queen enters, called into the court at Black-
friars. The clerk of the court says, "Katharine, queen of
England, come into the court." Again Guildford precedes the
Queen with a cushion, and again she kneels.

ACT II

SCENE 4

Queen. [79]Sir, I desire you do me right and justice,
And to bestow your pity on me; for
I am a most poor woman, and a stranger,
Born out of your dominions; having here
No judge indifferent, nor no more assurance
Of equal friendship and proceeding.[79] [*She rises.*] [80]Alas, sir,
In what have I offended you? what cause
Hath my behaviour given to your displeasure,
That thus you should proceed to put me off,
And take your good grace from me? [80] [81]Heaven witness,
I have been to you a *true and humble* wife,
At all times to your will conformable.[81]

                                  [82]Sir, call to mind
That I have been your wife, in this obedience,
Upward of twenty years, and have been blest
With many children by you: if, in the course
And process of this time, you can report,
And *prove it too,* against mine honour aught,
My bond to wedlock, or my love and duty,
Against your sacred person ⌐, in God's name,
Turn me away; ⌐and let the foul'st contempt

[78] A long emphasis, intimating that the Cardinal and his designs
were known to her.
[79] A most sweet and gracious prelude, yet no departure from her
dignity.
[80] Remonstrance, dignified, without any bitterness.
[81] Earnest protestation.
[82] Dignified confidence in her own innocence.

Shut door upon me, and so give *me* up
To the sharpest kind of justice.[82] [83]Please you, sir,
The king, your father, was reputed for
A prince⌐ most prudent⌐, of an excellent
And *unmatch'd* wit and judgment ⌐: Ferdinand,
My father, king of Spain, was reckon'd one
The wisest prince, that *there* had reign'd by many
A year before: it is not to be question'd
That they had gather'd a wise council to them
Of *every* realm, that did debate this business,
Who *deem'd our marriage lawful:* wherefore I humbly
Beseech you, sir, to spare me, till I may
Be by my friends in Spain advis'd; whose counsel
I will implore; if not, i' the name of God,
Your pleasure be fulfill'd!

    Wol.   [84]You have here, lady
(And of your choice), these reverend fathers; men
Of singular integrity and learning,
Yea, the elect of the land, who are assembled
To plead your cause: it shall be therefore bootless,
That longer you desire the court; as well
For your own quiet, as to rectify
What is unsettled in the king.

    Cam.   [85]His grace
Hath spoken well and justly: therefore, madam,
It's fit this royal session do proceed;
And that, without delay, their arguments
Be now produc'd and heard. [[86]CAMPEIUS *rises.*]

    Queen.   Lord Cardinal,
To you I speak.

    Wol.   Your pleasure, madam?

    Queen.   Sir,
I am about to weep; but, thinking that
We are a queen [87](*or long have dream'd so*),[87] certain

---

[83] Pause. A new division of the discourse. The argument beautifully spoken, very distinct.

[84] This response taken by her with great impatience, very indignant at his interference.

[85] Surprise and grief when the legate speaks thus.

[86] When Campeius comes to her she turns from him impatiently; then makes a sweet bow of apology, but dignified. Then to Wolsey, turned and looking *from* him, with her hand pointing back to him, in a voice of thunder, "to *you* I speak." This too loud perhaps; you must recollect her insulted dignity and impatience of spirit before fully sympathising with it.

[87] Great contempt in this parenthesis.

The *daughter of a king,*[88] my drops of tears
I'll turn to sparks of fire.
    Wol.   Be patient yet.
    Queen. [89]*I will, when you are humble;* nay, *before,*
Or God will punish me.[89] [90]I do believe,
Induc'd by potent circumstances, that
You are mine enemy; and make my challenge.
You shall not be my judge: for it is you
Have blown this coal betwixt my lord and me,
Which God's dew quench! [90]—[91]*Therefore,* I say, again,
I utterly abhor, yea, from my soul
Refuse you for my judge:[91] whom, yet once more,
[92]I hold my most malicious foe, and think *not*
At all a friend to truth.[92]
    Wol.   [93]I do profess
You speak not like yourself; who ever yet
Have stood to charity, and display'd the effects
Of disposition gentle, and of wisdom
O'ertopping woman's power. Madam, you do me wrong:
I have no spleen against you; nor injustice
For you or any: how far I have proceeded,
Or how far further shall, is warranted
By a commission from the consistory,
Yea, the whole consistory of Rome. You charge me
That I have blown this coal: I do deny it:
The king is present: if it be known to him
That I gainsay my deed, how many he wound,
And worthily, my falsehood! yea, as much
As you have done my truth. If he know
That I am free of your report, he knows
I am not of your wrong. Therefore in him
It lies to cure me: and the cure is, to
Remove these thoughts from you; the which before
His highness shall speak in, I do beseech
You, gracious madam, to unthink your speaking,
And to say no more.
    Queen.[94]   My lord, my lord,
I am a single woman, much too weak

[88] Very dignified.

[89] Great contempt. Her voice swelled, but monotonous.

[90] Very distinct articulate charge against him.

[91] Great swell.

[92] "I hold," &c., very pointed. *"Not at all,"* &c., syllabic and most impressive.

[93] Great impatience and contempt during this speech of Wolsey.

[94] Breaking impatiently through his speech.

To oppose your cunning. [95]You're *meek* and humble-*mouth'd;*
You sign your place and calling, in full seeming
With meekness and humility; but your *heart*
Is cramm'd with arrogancy, spleen, and pride.[95]
You have, by fortune and his highness' favours,
Gone slightly o'er low steps, and now are mounted
Where powers are your retainers; and your words,
Domestics to you, serve your will, as 't please
Yourself pronounce their office. I must tell you,
You tender more your person's honour than
Your high profession spiritual: that again
I do refuse you for my judge; and here,
Before you all, appeal unto the pope,
To bring my whole cause 'fore his holiness,
And to be judg'd by him.
  [*She curtsies to the* KING, *and offers to depart.*]
    Cam.   The queen is obstinate,
Stubborn to justice, apt to accuse it, and
Disdainful to be tried by 't; 'tis not well
She's going away.
    King.   Call her again.
    Crier. Katharine, queen of England, come into the court.
    Grief. Madam, you are called back.
    Queen. [96]What need you note it? pray you, keep your way:
When you are call'd, return.[96]—[97]Now the Lord help,
They vex me past my patience! [97]—Pray you, pass on:
[98]I will not tarry: [98]no, nor ever more,
Upon this business, my appearance make
In any of their courts.
                    [*Exeunt* GUILDFORD *and the* QUEEN.

Professor Bell was as good a hearer as actor or actress need
hope for.

The scene in the fourth act where Katharine is discovered
sick unto death is prefaced with these remarks:

Mrs. Siddons in this scene admirable in simplicity and
pathos. No affectation, not a more complete deception in
dramatic art than this of the sickness of Katharine. The
voice subdued to softness, humility, and sweet calmness.
The soul too much exhausted to endure or risk great emo-

[95] Contempt. Contrast strong between "mouthed" and "heart."
[96] Very impatient, angry, and loud.
[97] Peevish expression.
[98] Strong determination.

tion. The flash of indignation of her former spirit very fine at Guildford's interruption.

Unfortunately there is only one more remark; it is appended to Katharine's verdict on Wolsey, which in Mrs. Inchbald's edition runs as follows:

Queen. So may he rest; his faults lie gently on him!
Yet thus far, Cromwell, give me leave to speak him,
And yet with charity.—He was a man
Of an unbounded stomach, ever ranking
Himself with princes.
His promises were, as he then was, mighty;
But his performance, as he is now, nothing.
Of his own body he was ill, and gave
The clergy ill example.

Professor Bell says of this:
"Beautifully spoken, with some mixture of energy; but the subdued voice throughout.

"Probably the writer was too much affected by this scene to be able to make minute critical observations."

Of Mrs. Siddons' readings Professor Bell says:

Mrs. Siddons in her readings was like the tragic muse. She sat on a chair raised on a small platform, and the look and posture which always presents itself to me is that with which she contemplates the figure of Hamlet's ghost. Her eyes elevated, her head a little drawn back and inclined upwards, her fine countenance filled with reverential awe and horror, and the chilling whisper scarcely audible but horrific. Sir Joshua Reynolds' picture of Mrs. Siddons as the tragic muse gives a perfect conception of the general effect of her look and figure in these readings.

In her readings the under parts, which in acting are given offensively by some vile player, were read with a beauty and grace of utterance which was like the effect of very fine musical recitative, while the higher parts were the grand and moving airs. It was like a fine composition in painting; the general groundwork simple, the parts for effect raised and touched by a master's hand.

In the higher parts it was like the finest acting. The looks, the tones. the rapid hurry of the tumultuous emotions, the chilling whisper of horror, the scream of high-wrought passion, were given less strongly, but as affecting as on the stage.

The comic touches were light and pretty, but she has no comic power.

The graceful and sweet parts were quite enchanting. The mellow subdued voice of sorrow, to give variety, she kept much in whisper—very audible notwithstanding. *Her* whisper is more audible and intelligible than the loudest ranting of an ordinary player.

She read *Hamlet* and *The Merchant of Venice*. *Lear,* I think, should be read by her, not acted.

There is special mention of her manner when reading Hamlet's speech beginning

> Angels and ministers of grace defend us.

Mrs. Siddons in reading gave, by her look of reverential awe and chilling whisper of horror, more fully the idea of a ghost's presence than any spectral illusion on the stage.

This was a whispered speech throughout, growing in energy and confidence as other ideas took the place of the first startle of horror and dismay. Kean speaks too loudly and boldly, not enough as in the withering presence of a supernatural being. The first line should be a whisper of horror, with a long pause before venturing to address the phantom.

It is believed that Sir Charles Bell made notes similar in character to those now published; but if so the books have been mislaid. There is a curious passage in a letter from him to his brother, dated the 10th of June, 1809, in which he says:

Jeffrey saw my *Shakspere* and liked it much, and talked to Mrs. Siddons about it. I said I intended some time to take a good play and make it so *in fancy*. He said he should like to do so too. He saw your pencillings in the margin; not knowing whether you would like it, and not knowing what they were, I told him they were all mine; so perhaps his liking this kind of thing was owing to you. Do not forget to pursue it.

This appropriation by one man of another's work reads oddly, though it is an indication of the absolute confidence of one brother in the other. We may all feel glad that Professor G. J. Bell did pursue the plan, and wish he had pursued it further.

In reading of Mrs. Siddons one cannot but regret that her genius should have been employed in representing a Mrs. Beverley or even a Lady Randolph. It is a standing reproach to our literature that outside the roll of Shakespeare's char-acters a great actor can hardly find a great part. When we reflect that West and Haydon have been followed at no distant time by Millais, Leighton, Burne-Jones, and Watts, we cannot but hope that in a sister art a similar revival may occur. The time seems ripe, for the novel is in decadence, and coming writers must win distinction in a new field. A man who has sufficient talent to make a good novel would probably succeed in writing a good play if he went to work in the right way; but the art of the playwright has not been studied by our leading authors for many generations. This art is that of selecting proper subjects for stage representation and giving them such a form as will enable the actors to move their audience. The success of a play in stirring an audience depends less than is usually supposed on style, on the delineation of character, or even on the invention of an ingenious and probable plot. Plays succeed which are glaringly defective in all these respects; for instance, *The Lady of Lyons*. The one necessary condition for success is that the scene represented shall move the audience; the emotion may be sad or merry, noble or ignoble, but emotion there must be. If this element be wanting, no depth of thought, no beauty of language, no variety of incidents will save the play. The skilled playwright knows what scenes will stir the hearers, and how best to frame each scene and the whole play with this purpose. If with this knowledge he possesses originality of conception and beauty of style, his plays become part of the literature of his country; without these higher qualities he remains a mere playwright, but we go to see his plays, built up as they are of old worn-out materials. The playwright is familiar with the materials used in his art; he knows the stage well on both sides of the footlights; he mixes with actors, managers, stage-managers, scene-painters, and stage-carpenters. From Aeschylus downwards, all great dramatists have had this practical knowledge of the instruments at their command. A drama should be written for the stage, as a song should be written to be sung. The author must subconsciously —if such a word may be used—have the stage always in mind: the exits, the entrances, the time required to cross the stage, the positions of the actors, their very attitudes and dress. No author provides more admirably for all these stage exigencies than Shakespeare, as anyone may see who will consider his inimitable contrivances for removing dead bodies from the stage. There is no doubt a danger that those who become familiar with stage-machinery may content themselves with remodelling the old puppets, rearranging stock incidents, and repatching old rags to produce good guaranteed old stage effects; but a man of real talent would not be mis-led by the Mr. Worldly Wiseman of the stage.

We may learn much from French practice as to the frame-work of a drama. A great part of the success which is cer-tainly achieved by modern French plays depends on the art shown in their construction. M. E. Legouvé, who is a skilful playwright, tells us frankly how a Frenchman proceeds. First, he chooses or conceives the situation which is to be the crisis of the play: from this he works backwards, considering how that situation is to be brought about, and what characters will be necessary for the purpose. His first act is devoted wholly to informing the audience of the relations between the characters at the beginning of the piece; his second act develops the plot; in his third act the plot thickens; his fourth act contains the crisis for which the play is written, and his fifth act gives the solution of the knot which has been tied in the fourth act.

These rules seem rather barren, but we shall see their sig-nificance if we consider what other courses may be followed.

A writer may begin by inventing an ingenious or interest-ing plot, or by choosing some historical period which he will dramatise, or by conceiving some marked characters whose feelings and thoughts he will expound. M. Legouvé tells us that none of these is the French method; that for the French author the motive of the play is essentially one situation; that his characters are chosen so as to make this situation tell, and that his plot is a matter for after-consideration, devised so as to reveal the characters of the persons and lead up to the crisis. Shakespeare did not work in this way, but in this one matter of construction it may be worth while to listen to maxims derived from the study of plays which in all other respects are greatly inferior to his. Moreover, these maxims are ultimately derived from the practice of Sophocles, no mean master.

The French, following the Greeks in this, look on a play as a representation of feelings rather than of actions. The incidents which occasion the feelings, and the actions they lead to, are alike kept in the background in French as in Greek plays. Rapid action in a play does not, in France, mean a rapid succession of events, but a rapid development of feel-ing in the persons of the drama. A scene in which the emo-tion represented is monotonous will be dull even if crammed with incidents.

The author who is penetrated with the belief that the aim of the drama is to produce emotion will be indifferent to beauty of language or of metaphor, to profound philosophy and to brilliant sayings, except when these help to move the audience. He will know that obscurity of language or of thought is fatal to his purpose. The knot, crisis, or motive of his play will be chosen by him to exhibit, not a striking event, but strong feelings. He will so contrive the story leading to the crisis as to exhibit a gradually culminating series of emotions, produced by incidents arranged so as powerfully to affect the personages of the drama, and through them the audience. The direct action of incidents on the audience is of importance only in that low form of art which aims at stirring the vulgar feeling of curiosity and the vulgar love of gaping.

The most telling play is that in which the feelings naturally exhibited by the persons of the drama are strongest. The greatest play is that which shows the feelings of the noblest men and women. This, in the opinion of Plato and Aristotle, is the object of the drama in its higher form.

Plato, in the *Laws*, after saying that no freeborn man or woman should learn comic songs, grotesque dances, or burlesques, but that it might be well to have these things presented by slaves and hired strangers, in order better to understand by contrast that which is truly beautiful, speaks thus, referring to his ideal city: "If any serious poets, such as write tragedies, should ask us, 'Shall we, O strangers, come to your city and bring our poetry and act it? How stand your laws in this respect?' what answer ought we to give to these divine men? For myself I should reply thus: 'Oh, most excellent of strangers, we are ourselves, to the utmost of our power, poets of a tragedy the most beautiful and the best; for the whole of our polity consists in an imitation of a life the most beautiful and best, which we may say is in reality the truest tragedy.'" We here see that Plato thought the object of tragedy was to represent the noblest kind of life, and only rejected the imitation as unnecessary where this life itself was to be seen.

Aristotle defined what he meant by a tragedy with greater fulness. He points out that a certain magnitude is necessary in the event represented; that the spectator as he follows the action feels pity and a kind of awe which may be termed fear or terror, and that he comes away from the spectacle chastened and purified. The first part of his definition requires that the action shall be heroic, or such as represents the thoughts, deeds, and feelings of great men. By the last part of his definition he, like Plato, required that the action should have moral beauty. This does not imply that a play should be didactic, or deal only with the actions of well-behaved persons. The teaching of the dramatist is as the teaching of nature. See these heroes in their strength and their weakness, live with them, and you will learn from them. The function of the tragic poet, from Aeschylus to Shakespeare, has been to show us the intense life of heroic men and women at the moment of their trial.

But not all heroic or beautiful actions can be made the subjects of a tragedy. Aristotle points out that the action must be such as will stir certain moral emotions—pity and fear, he calls them; but the English words very imperfectly describe the feelings roused by a great tragedy. Those feelings give keen pleasure, whereas pity and fear are painful. Sympathy may be a better word; the pleasure is to live a little while greatly with the great ones of the world, to feel their feelings, to experience their passions, to dare, to love, to hate with them, so that for a little while we too are great; but words fail to describe emotions to those who have not felt them. If it be suggested that the sensation experienced while watching a tragedy is rather a feeling *with* the persons of the drama than a feeling *for* them; that when Othello cries out, "O the pity of it!" we feel as he feels and what he feels, and are very far indeed from entertaining a pleasant and comfortable pity *for* him; that the strange pleasure depends on our recognition in ourselves of the power to feel as Othello feels, to suffer as he suffers, even to sin as he sins—this suggestion may awaken a memory of what the emotion was in those who have known it but can explain nothing to others.

The higher and lower forms of the drama differ simply in respect of the character of the feelings awakened. The highest may be our highest moral emotions; the lowest, the lowest animal passions. Either moral or immoral the stage must be, and always has been, for its very existence depends on its action upon this part of our nature.

The morality of a play depends on no exclusion of crime, no enumeration of maxims, no system of rewards or punishments; it flows from the heart of the author and is tested by its action on the audience.

It is in moral grandeur that Shakespeare, Aeschylus, and Sophocles stand absolutely pre-eminent. It is to this that Racine and Corneille owe their hold on men. It is by this that *The Misanthrope* claims high rank. It is in this that the modern French stage chiefly fails.

The French dramatic authors of the Second Empire have succeeded in producing living plays because, besides being skilled playwrights, they do in their works appeal to real and strong feelings. A certain moral poverty alone prevents the school from taking a very high rank. The authors have usually meant well; and if the verdict must be that their moral ideal is always poor and often false, this conclusion is forced upon us by the words and actions rather of their good than of their bad people. Even Victor Hugo's verse cannot make us believe that Ruy Blas is not a poor creature.

Our own writers show no similar moral ineptitude, and since they have created scores of types which in freshness, truth, power, and interest surpass the men and women of French authors, we are driven to the conclusion that if the English do not write great plays it is rather because they do not know how than that they lack power. Our best authors, when they attempt the drama, seem to be misled by a desire to appeal rather to the intellect or to the aesthetic sense of their hearers than to their moral emotions. If they were to mix with actors on familiar terms they would soon learn the playwright's art; for the actor knows what will succeed on the stage. An actor calls a part well written when the words and situations are such as enable him powerfully to express strong feelings. He will, if permitted, cut out every line which does not help him in this, his art, and for stage purposes he is right. Charm of style, beauty of metre, wisdom of thought, novelty of character, ingenuity of plot, poetry of conception, all these things may be added to a play with much advantage; but they will not insure success either singly or all together. A play which does not move an audience, as neither intellectual nor artistic pleasure ever can move them, must fail upon the stage.

Professor Bell's notes show what he felt when a Siddons acted a Katharine. He was a man of hard intellect, whose dry legal labours still guide shrewd lawyers. He was a man of learning and taste; but when seeing a great actress in a great play, no ingenious theories, no verbal emendations, no philosophical reflections, no analytical remarks occur to him. He records his emotion, and, as far as he can, how that emotion was produced. He may be taken as representing an ideal audience—that which does not comment, but responds to author and to actor.

The Illusion of the
First Time in Acting

by

WILLIAM GILLETTE

With an Introduction by George Arliss

Introduction

The art of acting is so intimately connected with what is known as "personality" that it is an exceedingly dangerous experiment to attempt to set down in writing any assertion of what methods should be adopted in the making of a good actor and what should be avoided as a preventive measure against becoming a bad one.

There are actors who know every move on the board, whose technique is beyond reproach, who are endowed with those advantages of voice and appearance generally regarded as being "exactly suited to the stage," and who are yet very bad actors indeed. And there are others who are painfully devoid of any visible fitness for their calling, who defy—or rather fail to observe—almost every known canon of stage-technique, and who yet succeed in giving the greatest delight to their audiences. The actor of this type is, as a rule, physically and mentally incapable of adopting the acknowledged methods; he "gets across the footlights" without any real knowledge of "how it's done"—by ways that baffle even the expert; he is carried to success almost entirely by what for the moment I will call his personality; he manufactures his methods from material close at hand and seldom borrows or profits by the experience of others. Such an exponent of the art is generally spoken of by his professional brethren as "a very bad actor, but the people like him."

But is he a bad actor merely because he adopts his own methods and knows nothing about the art of other people? Well, I think perhaps he is. Although he amuses me, I'm afraid he is a bad actor. But he is not as bad as he would be if that other type, who really knows the rules, took him in hand and tried to make him a good actor. Then he would be atrocious. As a matter of fact, he is an actor who can play only one kind of part. But he plays that better than any good actor living. Therefore the public, for whom the theatre is run, gets the advantage. His reign lasts just as long as there are plays which require that type. If his part is a prominent one and he makes a very great success, so much the worse for him. He is then placed in an exalted position from which he is bound to fall when the authors have worn themselves out in their frantic endeavour to hold him there; and he will automatically pass from the public ken, destined merely to bob up now and then in a small part that lends itself to his "personality"—and destined to become a disappointed man for the rest of his life.

This actor would never know such bitter disappointment if we could have the ideal condition of stock and repertory companies; he would then find his proper place—which would possibly be that of a valuable "small part" actor for certain "bits." Under present conditions he goes along, possibly for five or six years, in a false position—a bad actor disguised by a mere fluke as a good one. In reality his success is merely an adventure. But he doesn't know that. How should he? He is in the position of Christopher Sly—flattered and deceived. But unlike Sly, he is never again able to realize that he is not really a king dethroned by a fickle and ignorant people; and his life is soured for all time. The mere theatre-goers may very naturally argue that, as the theatre is run for their amusement, and as they pay for its support, they would much prefer to have the "types" selected for each play. Thus they are quite content to have the bad actor in the one part in which he shines, and to allow him to go into oblivion as soon as possible afterwards. There would be something in this argument if the success of plays generally depended mainly on the proper selection of types. But I am convinced that the success of a season's plays, so far as their success shall be swayed by the acting, depends upon the greatest number of actors and actresses who know their business.

I have used the word "personality" because it is difficult to find another word to express the different degrees of that much discussed attribute of the actor who is remembered. The personality of the bad actor I have been considering should have a name of its own; it is in reality more of the nature of a deformity. It is generally quite distinct from the personality that helps an actor along to a distinguished position which he is then able to hold. And, after all, what is this personality that actors are sometimes asked to stifle and at other times counselled to cultivate? Surely it is the Man Himself as he has grown up in his own particular environment. Whether he gets the something that we like about him from his father, or his mother, or his grandfather doesn't matter. But he certainly hasn't placed it there himself—and he just as certainly cannot remove it. It is inextricably a part of the individual. It is as the egg which is added to enrich the salad in the making. It is part of him as he speaks and lives and has his being. It is that which has made us notice him on the stage. He didn't put it there in order to be noticed; he didn't even know he had it, till we told him so. If personality were merely a particular movement of the eyelid peculiar to the individual, or if it were only the repetition of some unnecessary gesture, it might with some effort be eliminated. But it is so much more. I do not think it fair to an actor to say that he "fits a part to his personality." In studying a part, should he meet with a scene in which he feels he should strike a certain note that he realizes he is physically incapable of reaching, if he then adopts another method which will bring the scene within his range—this is not pandering to his personality; it is merely using legitimately the tools of his trade. Your voice is part of your personality, and so is your nose, and so are your eyes and your mouth; so the way you open your mouth and your eyes, and the way you close them again, and the way your head is put on your shoulders, and the way you move those shoulders to which your head is loosely attached.

Now, how is an actor to set about stifling his personality? It will be at once conceded, at any rate by those of experience in acting, that it is an undoubted mistake to attempt to alter one's voice throughout an entire performance. So personality cannot be stifled that way. The mouth may be covered by a large moustache; but in parting with that mouth you are giving up a very eloquent lieutenant that might be most useful during the action of the play. We can let the nose stand, because it is possible that that assists your personality less than any other feature—although it has its uses. But what about the eyes, and the head that is on *your* shoulders and nobody else's? If they are to be swathed in disguises, you become a lay figure and not a human being at all. No, you must give it up! The only way for you to stifle your personality is to cease to be a person.

On the other hand, how are you going to foster your personality? I confess that I haven't the remotest idea. You may play nothing but footmen, or nothing but gardeners, or nothing but gay husbands in French farces, who can all be played one way—but that isn't fostering your personality, that is merely limiting your sphere of experience. There are a great many people on the stage who have peculiarities; but I do not remember any one having been accused by an audience of possessing personality who had not great sincerity. It is the fact that the actor is feeling and living the life of the man he is impersonating that compels his features and his body to have free play, and so the real flesh-and-blood man is seen.

The individuality of the actor cannot be stifled if the actor himself is feeling and living his part. It may be charged then that personality is a bar to varied characterization. I think not. Let us suppose that it takes one hundred attributes to make a personality plus a characterization. Now, it requires only ten of these to assimilate the character of an old *roué:* the other ninety are required to make him a vital human creature. One of the ten is used to keep the limbs a trifle stiff, another to give a slight limp perhaps, No. 3 to infuse a little deadness into the eyes, No. 4 to soften the voice, No. 5 to take care of a slower delivery, and so on. But out of the remaining ninety flow all the other springs of life that belong to the actor and are always playing and being drawn upon and governed by his imagination. Peculiarities and mannerisms may sometimes attach themselves to personality, but they must in no wise be regarded as the whole thing. They may perhaps be units in the hundred, but they are not what make an actor attractive to an audience.

Mr. Gillette's situation is, I believe, unique in the English-speaking world, inasmuch as he is not only an author of established reputation but has maintained as an actor a position of great distinction for more years than I feel at liberty to mention without his special permission. And so I feel that his paper on "The Illusion of the First Time," written as it is with a thorough knowledge of both ends of the game, and set forth with that expert pen which has helped (whatever he may say to the contrary) to give him his position as a dramatist, is a very valuable contribution to the literature of the stage.

The Illusion of the First Time is without doubt of the utmost importance to the full appreciation of any stage performance. Even the professional equilibrist feels this when he makes two ineffectual efforts to perform his *chef d'oeuvre* and then victoriously accomplishes it with that extraordinary assumption of pride and relief that fills our hearts with gladness—when he could have done it quite easily the first time.

But the illusion is, for the actor, not quite so difficult to maintain as might be supposed. The lay members of society (by lay members I mean those who ask an actor if he will dine with them at eight o'clock on Monday night), if they think about it at all, suppose that the actor speaks a given number of words every night, for a thousand nights if necessary, without any further inspiration than that which is allowed him by the author and that which reaches him in the form of handclapping from the lay members themselves.

Of course, if this were so, the length of the working life

of an actor could be figured out mathematically, just as the length of the life of a London 'bus horse used to be worked out in advance in the general offices of the Omnibus Company. I believe the life of the 'bus horse came out at three years. I should not give an actor quite so long. I think he would be taken to a lunatic asylum towards the end of the second year. But the thousand influences which inspire an actor and help to give each performance something of the elements of a First Time can be fully realized only by the person who has been through it. It is true, there are actors —small part actors—who can go on night after night and speak the same lines and feel no outside influence at all. But then, they don't feel any inside influence either. They are lunatics to start with, or they would never have remained in a calling for which they have not the least aptitude.

But the mental machinery of the actor is even more delicate than the record of a phonograph. That mental needle which acts upon the record of the author's words is influenced by weather, by sudden sounds, by unusual lights, by pains in the back and head, by dinner, by no dinner, by a letter from home, by feeling too well, by not feeling well enough, by no ink in the place where the ink ought to be, by a fear of forgetting, by a sudden awful realization of being stared at by hundreds of pairs of eyes and of not being able to escape. These are only a few of the thousand influences that are entirely apart from the ever varying influence of the pulse of the audience.

But I am not sure that the lay members understand what I mean. I will try to explain. The actor comes on to the stage to play his same part for the 500th time—to go through the "grind" once more, as he often put its (but seldom means it). The audience is dull, the play is dull, and the whole thing seems a bore. Suddenly the electrician (who is always doing something mysterious at the back of the stage) drops a hundred lamps with a crash; it is possibly only two or three, but it sounds like a hundred. The spectators hear it, of course, and commence talking pleasantly to one another about it, and fall to speculating as to what is really the cause. The actor instantly becomes mad with rage; and the next instant he realizes the necessity of regaining the attention of the audience at once, or allowing the first act to go to pieces. So he "acts for all he's worth" for the next ten minutes, and he gradually feels his audience coming back to him. And they become more and more attentive; and the sensation of having brought them back is so pleasant that the actor becomes interested in them personally and feels a certain friendly relationship between them and himself; and for the rest of that performance he gives them the best he has. And something of this kind happens almost every night. The Illusion of the First Time is assisted materially by the fact that the actor is nearly always fighting against some odds. I am speaking now of the time when the play has settled down to a long run. If he is feeling ill, he is anxious that he should not appear so; and he fights against any possible evidence of his pain, mental or physical. If there is an understudy playing, he makes an effort to cover any defect that may thus arise. If there is no ink when there ought to be ink, this is sufficient to break the monotony and to stimulate him to a certain degree of spontaneity.

Then, of course, there is the audience, the great stimulant. One intensely attentive figure in a dull audience, one distinct but invisible chuckle at a pet line, one spontaneous ejaculation expressive of appreciation, will serve to stimulate for a whole evening. Two sneezes, two coughs from the same scoundrel, will put the devil into you and make you swear to yourself that you will keep him quiet or die in the attempt. Then, of course, there is the great concerted influence of an audience, that inspires the actor and lifts him far above himself. This concerted influence is frequently brought about if some petty incident has served to break the monotony of repetition and has aroused in the actor that delightful sensation of spontaneity. These conditions in themselves are not sufficient to prevent an actor from falling into many evil practices which creep in as a result of long familiarity with the author's lines; but they help very considerably.

Mr. Gillette raises an interesting question when he speaks of the necessity of the stage lover adopting an artificial method if he desire to please the dramatic critics. I wonder if the critics are not after all right in their attitude. How many authors *write* a love-scene that is a real love-scene? There must be many—but for the moment I don't recall one. I will even go so far as to sympathize with and forgive the authors for not doing so. I believe that love-scenes in real life are generally spread over a fairly considerable time. They cover several luncheons, and some dinners, possibly an occasional dance, and a number of unexpected meetings in the morning. As a matter of fact, I doubt whether the majority of people who marry for love have ever had a love-scene which, segregated, would be recognized as such. Of course, the author hasn't time for all this—or rather the audience has not. So the lovers have to say it all in words, and in one afternoon—or perhaps in the middle of dinner, or while some mature person is putting on her cloak in the next room. It therefore becomes an artificial love-scene. Now the result of attempting to play an artificial love-scene in a natural way is fatal; it must be played artificially. It is necessary for the actor of these scenes "to stand behind the lady and breathe the love messages down the back of her neck, so that they can both face to the front at the same time." These messages are generally so long that if she turned her back all the time, the audience might easily imagine she was fast asleep —unless she moved her shoulders, in which case it might have some doubt as to whether she was laughing or crying. And if he turned his back to the audience and let her "have the stage," half the people in the house would hear only half he was saying to her, which might be "natural" for the lovers, but it would be very unnatural for the spectators to be there at all, because the only reason they came and paid their money was because they were led to believe they were going to hear it all.

Of course, one can never be really, truly "natural" on the stage. Acting is a bag of tricks. The thing to learn is how to be unnatural, and just how unnatural to be under given conditions. Many plays appear to be natural to the casual audience, but are in reality perfectly artificial from beginning to end. To play these naturally would be equivalent to an artist sticking real leaves on his painted canvas in order to suggest a natural tree. Half the fun and half the art of the actor is to play such pieces artificially while appearing to play them naturally.

Leading actors are continually being blamed for taking the centre of the stage and facing the audience. It is called entirely unnatural. It is. But an actor who gets his living by acting will discover that the leading actor generally has the most to say. As he goes through the country playing in all sorts and sizes of theatres he may find that his manager will come round to him and say: "I have had a number of complaints at the box-office lately that you are rather inaudible in some scenes." If the actor shouts he can ruin any scene. Now, the centre of the stage is the spot that can be seen easiest by everybody in the house, and in some theatres it is the only spot that can be seen from certain portions of the house. Therefore, I say, use it as much as possible. It has to be admitted that the words of a play are quite necessary to the proper interpretation of an author's work. It has also to be admitted that, speaking generally, the face expresses more to the square inch, by at least one hundred per cent, than any other available adjunct in the actor's equipment. Therefore, I say, face the audience as much as possible.

The thing to learn is how to do these things without being found out.

GEORGE ARLISS

April 1915

The Illusion of the
First Time in Acting

I am to talk a brief paper this morning on a phase of what is called Drama, by which is meant a certain well-known variety of stage performance usually but not necessarily taking place in a theatre or some such public building, or even transplanted out into the grass, as it occasionally is in these degenerate days.

If you care at all to know how I feel about having to talk on this subject—which I do not suppose you do, but I'll tell you anyway—I am not as highly elated at the prospect as you might imagine. Were I about to deliver a Monograph on Medicine or Valuable Observations on Settlement Work and that sort of thing, or even if I had been so particularly fortunate as to discover the Bacillus of Poetry and could now report progress toward the concoction of a serum that would exterminate the disease without killing the poet—that is, without quite killing him—I could feel that I was doing some good. But I can't do any good to Drama. Nobody can. Nothing that is said or written or otherwise promulgated on the subject will affect it in the slightest degree. And the reason for this rather discouraging view of the matter is, I am sorry to say, the very simplest in the world as well as the most unassailable, and that is, the Record.

And what is meant by a "Record" is, roughly speaking, a History of Behavior along a certain line—a history of what has been done, of what has taken place, happened, occurred; of what effect has been produced in the particular direction under consideration. We might say that Records are past performances or conditions along a specified line.

And upon these Records or Histories of Behavior, Occurrences, or Conditions depends all that we know or may ever hope to know; for even Experiment and Research are but endeavors to produce or discover Records that have been hidden from our eyes. To know anything, to have any opinion or estimate or knowledge or wisdom worth having, we must take account of Past Performances, or be aware of the results

124

of their consideration by others, perhaps more expert than we. Yet, notwithstanding this perfectly elementary fact of existence, there is a group or class of these Records, many of them relating to matters of the utmost interest and importance, the consideration of which would at least keep people from being so shamelessly duped and fooled as they frequently are, to which no one appears to pay the slightest attention.

This class or group of forgotten or ignored Items of Behavior I have ventured, for my own amusement, to call the Dead Records—meaning thereby that they are *dead to us;* dead so far as having the slightest effect upon human judgment or knowledge or wisdom is concerned, buried out of sight by our carelessness and neglect. And in this interesting but unfortunate group, and evidently gone to its last long rest, reposes the Record of the Effect upon Drama of what has been said and written about it by scholars and thinkers and critics. And if this Record could be roused to life—that is, to consideration but for a moment—it would demonstrate beyond the shadow of a doubt that Drama is perfectly immune from the maneuvers of any germ that may lurk in what people who are supposed to be "Intellectual" may say or write or otherwise put forth regarding it.

The unending torrent of variegated criticism, condemnation, advice, contempt, the floods of space-writing, prophesying, high-brow and low-brow dinner-table and midnight-supper anathematizing that has cascaded down upon Drama for centuries has never failed to roll lightly off, like water from the celebrated back of a duck, not even moistening a feather.

From all of which you will be able to infer without difficulty that it is perfectly hopeless for me to try to do any good to Drama. And I can't do it any harm either. Even that would be something. In fact, nothing at all can be done to it. And as I am cut off in that direction, there seems to be nothing left but to try if, by describing a rather extraordinary and harassing phase of the subject involving certain conditions and requirements from a Workshop point of view, it is possible so to irritate or annoy those who sit helpless before me that I can feel something has been accomplished, even if not precisely what one might wish.

It must be a splendid thing to be able to begin right—to take hold of and wrestle with one's work in life from a firm and reliable standing-ground, and to obtain a comprehensive view of the various recognized divisions, forms, and limitations of that work, so that one may choose with intelligence the most advantageous direction in which to apply one's

efforts. The followers of other occupations, arts, and professions appear to have these advantages to a greater or less
degree, while we who struggle to bring forth attractive
material for the theatre are without them altogether; and not
only without them, but the jumble and confusion in which
we find ourselves is infinitely increased by the inane, con-
tradictory, and ridiculous things that are written and printed
on the subject. Even ordinary names which might be supposed to define the common varieties of stage work are in
a perfectly hopeless muddle. No one that I have ever met or
heard of has appeared to know what Melodrama really is;
we know very well that it is *not* Drama-with-Music, as the
word implies. I have asked people who were supposed to have
quite powerful intellects (of course the cheap ones can tell
you all about it—just as the silliest and most feeble-minded
are those who instantly inform you regarding the vast
mysteries of the universe)—I say I have made inquiries
regarding Melodrama of really intellectual people, and none
of them have appeared to be certain. Then there's plain
Drama, without the Melo—a very loose word applied to any
sort of performance your fancy dictates. And Comedy—some
people tell you it's a funny, amusing, laughable affair, and the
Dictionaries bear them out in this; while others insist that
it is any sort of play, serious or otherwise, which is not
Tragedy or Farce. And there's Farce, which derives itself
from force—to stuff—because it was originally an affair
stuffed full of grotesque antics and absurdities; yet we who
have occasion to appear in Farce at the present day very well
know that unless it is not only written but performed with the
utmost fidelity to life it is a dead and useless thing. In fact,
it must not by any chance *be* Farce! And there is the good
old word "play" that covers any and every kind of Theatrical
Exhibition and a great many other things besides. Therefore,
in what appears—at least to us—to be this hopeless confusion,
we in the workshops find it necessary to make a classification
of Stage Work for our own use. I am not advising anyone
else to make it, but am confessing, and with considerable
trepidation—for these things are supposed to be sacred from
human touch—that *we* do it. Merely to hint to a real Student
of the Drama that such a liberty has been taken would be
like shaking a red bull before a rag. Sacrilege is the name of
this crime.

More or less unconsciously, they end without giving any
names or definitions (I am doing that for you this morning),
we who labor in the shops divide Stage Performances in which

people endeavor to represent others than themselves for the amusement and edification of spectators, into two sections:

1. Drama.
2. Other Things.

That's all. It's so simple that I suppose you'll be annoyed with me for talking about it. Drama—in the dictionary which we make for ourselves—is that form of Play or Stage Representation which expresses what it has to express in Terms of Human Life. Other Things are those which do not. Without doubt those Other Things may be classified in all sorts of interesting and amusing ways, but that is not our department. What we must do is to extricate Drama from among them; and not only that, but we must carefully clear off and brush away any shreds or patches of them that may cling to it. We do not do this because we want to, but because we have to.

For us, then, Drama is composed of—or its object is attained by—simulated life episodes and complications, serious, tragic, humorous, as the case may be; by the interplay of simulated human passion and human character.

Other Things aim to edify, interest, amuse, thrill, delight, or whatever else they may aim to do, by the employment of language, of voice, of motion, of behavior, etc., as they would not be employed in the natural course of human existence. These unlifelike things, though they may be and frequently are stretched upon a framework of Drama, are not Drama; for that framework so decorated and encumbered can never be brought to a semblance or a simulation of life.

Although I have stated, in order to shock no one's sensibilities, that this is our own private and personal classification of Stage Work, I want to whisper to you very confidently that it doesn't happen to be original with us; for the development and specialization of this great Life-Class, *Drama*—or whatever you may please to call it—has been slowly but surely brought about by that section of the Public which has long patronized the better class of theatres. It has had no theories, no philosophy, not even a realization of what it does, but has very well known what it *wants*—yet by its average and united choosing has the character of Stage Work been changed and shaped and molded, ever developing and progressing by the survival of that which was fittest to survive in the curious world of Human Preference.

Be so good as to understand that I am not advocating this classification in the slightest degree, or recommending the use of any name for it. I am merely calling attention to the fact that this Grand Division of Stage Work is here—with us—at the present day; and not only here, but as a *class* of work—as a method or medium for the expressing of what we have to express—is in exceedingly good condition. After years and centuries of development, always in the direction of the humanities, it closely approximates a perfect instrument, capable of producing an unlimited range of effects from the utterly trivial and inconsequent to the absolutely stupendous. These may be poetical with the deep and vital poetry of Life itself, rather than the pleasing arrangement of words, thoughts, and phrases; tragical with the quivering tragedy of humanity—not the mock tragedy of vocal heroics; comical with the absolute comedy of human nature and human character—not the forced antics of clowns or the supernatural witticisms of professional humorists.

The possibilities of the instrument as we have it today are infinite. But those who attempt to use it—the writers and makers and constructors of Drama—are, of course, very finite indeed. They must, as always, range from the multitudes of poor workers—of the cheap and shallow-minded—to the few who are truly admirable. I have an impression that the conditions prevailing in other arts and professions are not entirely dissimilar. Someone has whispered that there are quite a few Paintings in existence which could hardly be said to have the highest character; a considerable quantity of third-, fourth-, and fifth-rate Music—and some of no rate at all; and at least six hundred billion trashy, worthless, or even criminally objectionable Novels. It would not greatly surprise me if we of the theatre—even in these days of splendid decadence—had a shade the best of it. But whether we have or have not, the explanation of whatever decline there may be in Dramatic Work is so perfectly simple that it should put to shame the vast army of writers who make their living by formulating indignant inquiries regarding it. For the highest authority in existence has stated in plain language that the true purpose of the Play is to hold the mirror up to Nature—meaning, of course, human nature; and, this being done at the present day, a child in a kindergarten could see why the reflections in that mirror are of the cheapest, meanest, most vulgar and revolting description. Imagine for one moment what would appear in a mirror that could truthfully reflect, upon being held up to the average Newspaper of today in the United States! But I admit that this is an extreme case.

And now I am going to ask you—but it is one of those questions that orators use with no expectation of an answer

—I am going to inquire if anyone here or anywhere else goes so far as to imagine for an instant that a Drama, a Comedy, a Farce, a Melodrama—or, in one word, a Play—is the manuscript or printed book which is ordinarily handed about as such? And now I will answer myself—as I knew I should all the time. One probably does so imagine unless one has thought about it. Doubtless you all suppose that when a person hands you a play to read he hands you that Play—to read. And I am here with the unpleasant task before me of trying to dislodge this perfectly innocent impression from your minds. The person does nothing of that description. In a fairly similar case he might say, "Here is the Music," putting into your hands some sheets of paper covered with different kinds of dots and things strung along what appears to be a barbed-wire fence. It is hardly necessary to remind you that that is not the Music. If you are in very bad luck it may be a Song that is passed to you, and as you roll it up and put it in your handbag or your inside overcoat pocket, do you really think that is the *Song* you have stuffed in there? If so, how cruel! But no! You are perfectly well aware that it is not the Song which you have in your handbag or music roll, but merely the Directions for a Song. And that Song cannot, does not, and never will exist until the specific vibrations of the atmosphere indicated by those Directions actually take place, and only during the time in which they *are* taking place.

And quite similarly the Music which we imagined in your possession a moment ago was not Music at all, but merely a few sheets of paper on which were written or printed certain Directions for Music; and it will not be Music until those Directions are properly complied with.

And, again quite similarly, the Play which you were supposed to be holding in your hand is not a Play at all, but simply the written or printed Directions for bringing one into being; and that Play will exist only when these Directions for it are being followed out—and not then unless the producers are very careful about it.

Incredible as it may seem, there are people in existence who imagine that they can *read* a Play. It would not surprise me a great deal to hear that there are some present with us this very morning who are in this pitiable condition. Let me relieve it without delay. The feat is impossible. No one on earth can read a Play. You may read the *Directions* for a Play and from these Directions imagine as best you can what the Play would be like; but you could no more read the *Play* than you could read a Fire or an Automobile Accident or a Baseball Game. The Play—if it is Drama—does not even *exist* until it appeals in the form of Simulated Life. Reading a list of the things to be said and done in order to make this appeal is not reading the appeal itself.

And now that all these matters have been amicably adjusted, and you have so quietly and peaceably given up whatever delusion you may have entertained as to being able to read a Play, I should like to have you proceed a step farther in the direction indicated and suppose that a Fortunate Dramatic Author has entered into a contract with a Fortunate Producing Manager for the staging of his work. I refer to the Manager as fortunate because we will assume that the Dramatist's Work appears promising; and I use the same expression in regard to the Author, as it is taken for granted that the Manager with whom he has contracted is of the most desirable description—one of the essentials being that he is what is known as a Commercial Manager.

If you wish me to classify Managers for you—or indeed, whether you wish it or not—I will cheerfully do so. There are precisely two kinds, Commercial Managers and Crazy Managers. The Commercial Managers have from fifty to one hundred and fifty thousand dollars a year rent to pay for their theatres, and, strange as it may seem, their desire is to have the productions they make draw money enough to pay it, together with other large expenses necessary to the operation of a modern playhouse. If you read what is written you will find unending abuse and insult for these men. The followers of any other calling on the face of the earth may be and are commercial with impunity. Artists, Musicians, Opera Singers, Art Dealers, Publishers, Novelists, Dentists, Professors, Doctors, Lawyers, Newspaper and Magazine Men, and all the rest—even Secretaries of State—are madly hunting for money. But *Managers*—Scandalous, Monstrous, and Infamous! And because of a sneaking desire which most of them nourish to produce plays that people will go to see, they are the lowest and most contemptible of all the brutes that live. I am making no reference to the managerial abilities of these men; in that they must vary as do those engaged in any other pursuit, from the multitudinous poor to the very few good. My allusion is solely to this everlasting din about their commercialism; and I pause long enough to propound the inquiry whether other things that proceed from intellects so painfully puerile should receive the slightest attention from sensible people.

Well, then, our Book of Directions is in the hands of one of these Wretches, and, thinking well of it, he is about to assemble the various elements necessary to bring the Drama for which it calls into existence. Being a Commercial Person of the basest description, he greatly desires it to attract the paying public, *and for this reason* he must give it every possible advantage. In consultation with the Author, with his Stage Manager and the heads of his Scenic, Electric, and Property Departments, he proceeds to the work of complying with the requirements of the Book.

So far as painted, manufactured, and mechanical elements are concerned, there is comparatively little trouble. To keep these things precisely as much in the background as they would appear were a similar episode in actual life under observation—*and no more*—is the most pronounced difficulty. But when it comes to the Human Beings required to assume the Characters which the Directions indicate, and not only to assume them but to breathe into them the Breath of Life— and not the *Breath* of Life alone but all other elements and details and items of Life so far as they can be simulated— many and serious discouragements arise.

For in these latter days Life-Elements are required. Not long ago they were not. In these latter days the merest slip from true Life-Simulation is the death or crippling of the Character involved, and it has thereafter to be dragged through the course of the play as a disabled or lifeless thing. Not all plays are sufficiently strong in themselves to carry on this sort of morgue or hospital service for any of their important roles.

The perfectly obvious methods of Character Assassination, such as the sing-song or "reading" intonation, the exaggerated and grotesque use of gesture and facial expression, the stilted and unnatural stride and strut, cause little difficulty. These, with many other inherited blessings from the Palmy Days when there was acting that really amounted to something, may easily be recognized and thrown out.

But the closeness to Life which now prevails has made audiences sensitive to thousands of minor things that would not formerly have affected them. To illustrate my meaning, I am going to speak of two classes of these defects. I always seem to have two classes of everything—but in this case it isn't so. There are plenty more where these two came from. I select these two because they are good full ones, bubbling over with Dramatic Death and Destruction. One I shall call, to distinguish it, "The Neglect of the Illusion of the First Time"; the other, "The Disillusion of Doing It Correctly." There is an interesting lot of them which might be assembled under the heading "The Illusion of Unconsciousness of What

Could Not Be Known"—but there will not be time to talk about it. All these groups, however, are closely related, and the First Time one is fairly representative. And of course I need not tell you that we have no names for these things—no groups—no classification; we merely fight them as a whole—as an army or mob of enemies that strives for the downfall of our Life-Simulation, with poisoned javelins. I have separated a couple of these poisons so that you may see how they work, and incidentally how great little things now are.

Unfortunately for an actor (to save time I mean all known sexes by that), unfortunately for an actor he knows or is supposed to know his part. He is fully aware—especially after several performances—of what he is going to say. The Character he is representing, however, does *not* know what he is going to say; but, if he is a human being, various thoughts occur to him one by one, and he puts such of those thoughts as he decides to into such speech as he happens to be able to command at the time. Now it is a very difficult thing—and even now rather an uncommon thing—for an actor who knows exactly what he is going to say to behave exactly as though he didn't; to let his thoughts (apparently) occur to him as he goes along, even though they are there in his mind already; and (apparently) to search for and find the words by which to express those thoughts, even though these words are at his tongue's very end. That's the terrible thing—at his tongue's very end! Living and breathing creatures do not carry their words in that part of their systems; they have to find them and send them there—with more or less rapidity according to their facility in that respect—as occasion arises. And audiences of today, without knowing the nature of the fatal malady, are fully conscious of the untimely demise of the Character when the actor portraying it apparently fails to do this.

In matters of speech, of pauses, of giving a Character who would think time to think; in behavior of eyes, nose, mouth, teeth, ears, hands, feet, etc., while he does think and while he selects his words to express the thought—this ramifies into a thousand things to be considered in relation to the language or dialogue alone.

This menace of Death from Neglect of the Illusion of the First Time is not confined to matters and methods of speech and mentality, but extends to every part of the presentation, from the most climactic and important action or emotion to the most insignificant item of behavior—a glance of the eye at some unexpected occurrence, the careless picking up of some small object which (supposedly) has not been seen or handled before. Take the simple matter of entering a room to which, according to the plot or story, the Character coming in is supposed to be a stranger; unless there is vigilance the actor will waft himself blithely across the threshold, conveying the impression that he has at least been born in the house —finding it quite unnecessary to look where he is going and not in the least worth while to watch out for thoughtless pieces of furniture that may, in their ignorance of his approach, have established themselves in his path. And the different scenes with the different people; and the behavior resulting from *their* behavior; and the love-scenes, as they are called—these have a little tragedy all their own for the performers involved; for, if an actor plays his part in one of these with the gentle awkwardness and natural embarrassment of one in love for the first time—as the plot supposes him to be—he will have the delight of reading the most withering and caustic ridicule of himself in the next day's papers, indicating in no polite terms that he is an awkward amateur who does not know his business, and that the country will be greatly relieved if he can see his way clear to quitting the stage at once; whereas if he behaves with the careless ease and grace and fluency of the Palmy Day Actor, softly breathing airy and poetic love-messages down the back of the lady's neck as he feelingly stands behind her so that they can both face to the front at the same time, the audience will be perfectly certain that the young man has had at least fifty-seven varieties of love-affairs before and that the plot has been shamelessly lying about him.

The foregoing are a few only of the numberless parts or items in Drama-Presentation which must conform to the Illusion of the First Time. But this is one of the rather unusual cases in which the sum of all the parts does *not* equal the whole. For although every single item from the most important to the least important be succesfully safeguarded, there yet remains the Spirit of the Presentation as a whole. Each successive audience before which it is given must feel —not think or reason about, but *feel*—that it is witnessing, not one of a thousand weary repetitions, but a Life Episode that is being lived just across the magic barrier of the footlights. That is to say, the Whole must have that indescribable Life-Spirit or Effect which produces the Illusion of Happening for the First Time. Worth his weight in something extremely valuable is the Stage Director who can conjure up this rare and precious spirit!

The dangers to dramatic life and limb from the Disillusion of Doing It Correctly are scarcely less than those in the

First Time class, but not so difficult to detect and eliminate. Speaking, breathing, walking, sitting, rising, standing, gesturing—in short behaving correctly, when the character under representation would not naturally or customarily do so—will either kill that character outright or make it very sick indeed. Drama can make its appeal only in the form of Simulated Life as it is Lived—not as various authorities on Grammar, Pronunciation, Etiquette, and Elocution happen to announce at that particular time that it ought to be lived.

But we find it well to go much further than the keeping of studied and unusual correctness *out,* and to put common and to-be-expected errors *in,* when they may be employed appropriately and unobtrusively. To use every possible means and device for giving Drama that which makes it Drama— Life-Simulation—must be the aim of the modern Play-Constructor and Producer. And not alone ordinary errors, but numberless individual habits, traits, peculiarities are of the utmost value for this purpose.

Among these elements of Life and Vitality, but greatly surpassing all others in importance, is the human characteristic or essential quality which passes under the execrated name of Personality. The very word must send an unpleasant shudder through this highly sensitive assembly; for it is supposed to be quite the proper and highly cultured thing to sneer at Personality as an altogether cheap affair and not worthy to be associated for a moment with what is highest in Dramatic Art. Nevertheless, cheap or otherwise, inartistic or otherwise, and whatever it really is or is not, it is the most singularly important factor for infusing the Life-Illusion into modern stage creations that is known to man. Indeed, it is something a great deal more than important, for in these days of Drama's close approximation to Life, it is essential. As no human being exists without Personality of one sort or another, an actor who omits it in his impersonation of a human being omits one of the vital elements of existence.

In all the history of the stage no performer has yet been able to simulate or make us aware of a Personality not his own. Individual tricks, mannerisms, peculiarities of speech and action may be easily accomplished. They are the capital and stock in trade of the Character Comedian and the Lightning Change Artist, and have nothing whatever to do with Personality.

The actors of recent times who have been universally acknowledged to be great have invariably been so because of their successful use of their own strong and compelling Personalities in the roles which they made famous. And when they undertook parts, as they occasionally did, unsuited to their Personalities, they were great no longer and frequently quite the reverse. The elder Salvini's Othello towered so far above all other renditions of the character known to modern times that the others were lost to sight below it. His Gladiator was superb. His Hamlet was an unfortunate occurrence. His personality was marvelous for Othello and the Gladiator, but unsuited to the Dane. Mr. Booth's personality brought him almost adoration in his Hamlet; selections from it served him well in Iago, Richelieu, and one or two other roles; but for Othello it was not all that could be desired. And Henry Irving and Ellen Terry and Modjeska, Janauschek and Joseph Jefferson and Mary Anderson, each and every one of them with marvelous skill transferred their Personalities to the appropriate roles. Even now—once in a while—one may see Rip Van Winkle excellently well played, but without Mr. Jefferson's Personality. There it is in simple arithmetic for you—a case of mere subtraction.

As indicated a moment ago I am only too well aware that the foregoing view of the matter is sadly at variance with what we are told is the Highest Form of the Actor's Art. According to the deep thinkers and writers on matters of the theatre, the really great actor is not one who represents with marvelous power and truth to life the characters within the limited scope of his Personality, but the performer who is able to assume an unlimited number of totally divergent roles. It is not the thing at all to consider a single magnificent performance such as Salvini's Othello, but to discover the Highest Art we must inquire how many kinds of things the man can do. This, you will observe, brings it down to a question of pure stage gymnastics. Watch the actor who can balance the largest number of roles in the air without allowing any of them to spill over. Doubtless an interesting exhibition if you are looking for that form of sport. In another art it would be: "Do not consider this man's paintings, even though masterpieces, for he is only a Landscape Artist. Find the chap who can paint forty different kinds." I have an idea the Theatre-going Public is to be congratulated that none of the great Stage Performers, at any rate of modern times, has entered for any such competition.

The Art of Acting

by

Dion Boucicault

With an Introduction by Otis Skinner

Introduction

A keen student of the theatre has said that to no artist does popular demonstration and approval come so readily and in such abundance as it does to the actor. There is a sound reason for this. The actor's art plays upon the more or less unrestrained emotions of his auditors to a degree not to be compared with that of the appeal of the sculptor, the painter, the poet, the novelist, the architect, or even the sensuous art of the dancer, or the more emotional art of the musician. To be sure, there is close kinship in the enthusiasm evoked by a gifted orator or a celebrated soloist; but even in these instances there is not that complete amalgamation of the artist and his product that we find in the case of the actor.

Canvases may be hidden in rubbish heaps, sculptural masterpieces buried in the dirt of ages, music scores locked in forgotten boxes—and still be perfect works of art: but the work of the actor is never accomplished without his actual presence and the presence of an audience. Nothing in his art is ever alive until that moment of collaboration and contact. An actor may take himself to remote fields and terrify peaceable cattle with lonely histrionic outbursts, or rouse the neighbors of his city apartment with exclamations of grief, joy, rage, exaltation, and laughter; but he is not acting then—he is only getting ready to act. A fencer or a boxer may make the most exhausting preparations in training, and practice ingenious tricks of surprise, attack, and defense, but until he stands face to face with his opponent there is no contest. You never know what the other fellow is going to do, and you never know what the audience is going to do. Sometimes you think you know and prepare your surprises, your sure-fire effects, your man-traps and your spring-guns; but often your audience unmasks your batteries and you are at its mercy.

While art for art's sake is never absent from the player's purpose, his thoughts, or even his prayers (if he says them), it is art for audiences' sake that is his supreme endeavor.

This ideal audience is always the actor's hope. Not necessarily the audience that checks its intelligence in the cloakroom before taking its orchestra, balcony, or gallery seat, but the audience with the tablets of its emotion wiped clean and ready to give itself to the intent and the art of the actor. It is the audience that generally eludes the actor's first nights like an *ignis fatuus*. It is rarely without its prejudices for or against. The professional critic is a bad audience-maker. He takes his seat, examines his weapons, and waits the first sign of weakness to indicate his opportunity for attack. He knows the rules of the game and rarely admits the premises, the purpose, or the virtues of its players if these factors conflict with his preconceived ideas. It is a rare occasion when the first-night audience in a New York theatre is a success. Friends of the author and actor are there to boost, and to applaud in spite of all shortcomings, however obvious; the critics are there to dissect and destroy and to search for pegs on which to hang epigrams and smart phrases for the following morning's criticism. And then there is, Heaven save the mark! the first-nighter. To him the occasion is as the ticker tape in the café to the speculator, the solitaire card game to the man with nothing but time on his hands. He likes to go to this or that club and remark for the edification of all within the sound of his voice, "I've just come from the first night of Haggarty's play at the Gotham." Thereat a few trained cue-givers, knowing what is expected of them, ask languidly, "How was it?" "Rotten," he replies, and orders a Welsh rabbit from the waiter. And she can exult next day (the first-nighter is also feminine) over her less fortunate sisters at lunch, and tell them of the lovely gowns of the leading lady.

Between these groups the true play auditor has very little chance. His opportunity comes later when subsequent performances devoid of the nervous fear and hysteria of the player, doubly anxious to please his friends and placate his foes, yield occasion for the perfect collaboration of audience and actor. The most valuable plays are a framework for the expression of emotion, and until such emotional appeal is adjusted to a nicety, until the actor's house is really put in order, many thoughtful, well-considered plays fail.

It is this confusion, this lack of complete control on the part of the actor before his first night audience, that sometimes gives rise to comparison of the professional player with the amateur—often to the credit of the latter. Pressed on by the excitement of a dramatic performance before an audience blissfully unaware of the laws of cause and effect, blind to the pitfalls that would strike terror to the soul of the skilled artist, the amateur player plunges ahead in a zestful, uncontrolled gallop, much as an unbroken colt tears about a field and evokes admiration for his spirit. In subsequent representations, however, if he is called upon to repeat his impersonation, his spirit will lack the incentive of the adventure and excitement of first performance. His only safety will be to fall back upon method; and as he has no method his work becomes more and more futile until it reaches utter ineffectiveness.

Millions of people can act: those who can make a decent living from acting are few. Millions of people can sing—were born with voices: how many could carry through an opera singer's career, year after year, with the unvarying success of Enrico Caruso? It follows then that no actor can become an artist without constant association with an audience. Not only are audiences the collaborators of the actor, they are his instructors as well. Not actively and consciously do they fill this function, though annals of the stage tell us that the audiences of London and Dublin in David Garrick's and Dr. Johnson's time knew their Shakespeare so well that sometimes an actor who mangled the text, mispronounced a word, or even misplaced an emphasis was hissed or noisily corrected by the pit and gallery. I mean instruction such as a baby gives its mother by its smiles and tears, its inarticulate sounds of pleasure or pain. The baby's instinct is toward what it wants, and the mother learns.

We often miscalculate our effects in study and rehearsal. I recall my experience in *The Honor of the Family,* a play which up to the first entrance of Colonel Bridau was one that rather bored the audience. It was a long series of demonstrations and preparations. Two persons were plotting and conspiring to get away with an old man's money when, at the end of their plotting, Colonel Bridau appears to put these plotters to flight. At the entrance of the Colonel the doors fly open, and, slamming his cane upon the table, he demands in a loud voice to see his uncle. They are amazed at his appearance. He tells them that he is going out to smoke a cigar; that he is coming back in five minutes, and that if at the end of that time he cannot see his uncle, everyone connected with this affair can clear out. This struck me as being a spirited, forceful, and interesting end of an act, but I was not prepared for the reception that bit of acting received. The howls of laughter on my appearance disconcerted me, and immediately on the drop of the curtain the continuation of laughter was something I had not considered possible. I knew that the part was humorous, but not that it was intensely funny. The audience told me that it was a character whose comic possibilities outweighed his serious ones and gave me my lesson as to how to treat Colonel Philippe Bridau.

I had the same experience in the character of Hajj in *Kismet*. The character of Hajj is that of a wily Oriental doting upon his daughter and seeking revenge for the wrong done him by his ancient enemy Jawan. I saw excellent melodrama in the play, but I failed to see the comic characteristics that actually worked out for the audience. I did not know that my bloodthirsty threats were going to provoke laughter, or that I could commit murder to the accompaniment of howls of joy. Before opening the play a New York theatre manager said, "I understand that there are a few murders in this play. Do you think Broadway is going to stand that?" I told him that I thought Broadway would at least accept it, possibly enjoy it. But I was not prepared, when I found my fingers on the throat of my deadly enemy, to hear bursts of uncontrolled mirth, nor for the laughter that arose when my other enemy was flung into the pool and my hand was on his head thrusting him down under the water, while I counted the bubbles that came up—one, two, three—from the expiring man's lips. I was taught then that these two murders were something that had a seriocomic aspect, and the delight of my audience was joined to mine. They were not impressed with the bloodthirsty aspect of these two events. They had entered into the spirit of this tale of a thousand and one years ago. They were enjoying my joy and their heels were clicking together with glee as my heels did. As the play progressed I found unexpected "laughs" creeping into the performance.

There was a speech in the scene where I met my ancient enemy in the darkness of the dungeon. We were both thrust there, condemned to die, undiscovered by each other, but when I became aware of his identity, I raised my hands crying: "Allah, Allah, we shall end our lives side by side. I die content." It was the cry of a revengeful, exultant man. I saw nothing funny about it. One night there was a slight laugh somewhere in the audience, and I was told by that laugh that there was humor in the speech. How could I find it? The audience would have to tell me. In my search I took various readings and finally discovered it in a joyous shout that went in downward leaps like the descent of a staircase. Just why it should have been funny I have never been able to tell. I only know that it was.

It is comedy that the audience teaches more readily, but

instruction in serious emotion comes from them as well. We know when we are over or under in expressing emotion. Our audience is co-operating. A scene may be full of possibilities, but if it is overemphasized the audience doesn't get it, and if it is underemphasized it does not give the audience what it craves.

An accident more often makes than mars a performance. The success of the elder Sothern in *Our American Cousin* is well known to have been made largely by an accident. He took no pains to study the part. On his first appearance he slipped over a misplaced rug, and the audience laughed. Later on, he sneezed and the audience laughed again, and from his first-aid instruction he continued to sneeze and to stumble and to stammer Lord Dundreary into lasting fame.

Happy accident is not a thing that can be transferred. The story is told of Edmund Kean that Mrs. David Garrick came to him and said: "Davy used to do a wonderful thing in the closet scene in *Hamlet,* and you don't do it. He overturned a chair when he saw the ghost." Kean tried it; when he saw the ghost he rose, put his heel under the leg of the chair, and overturned it. But every particle of merit in the action was ruined because of his self-consciousness. He couldn't do it as David did it.

Joseph Jefferson, than whom I think no actor ever better understood his art, tells the story of his association with William J. Florence. He had played Bob Acres many times. It was a favorite performance. When he became associated with his distinguished fellow actor he felt he should give way somewhat. The duel scene was always provocative of great laughter. "But," he said, "when William came, I felt I ought to do something to eliminate myself from the scene, that he might have an opportunity as Sir Lucius O'Trigger, so I didn't do anything. If they could not laugh at me, they would laugh at William. But, by George! they laughed at me more than ever." The unexpected brought him to a realization that the more he tried the less he was comical, and the less he tried, the more comical he became—a fact he had no means of discovering for himself without the instruction from his audience.

Mrs. Drew, at the time of this Jefferson-Florence combination, went to him in distress one night, saying, "Mr. Jefferson, I don't know why they don't laugh at that speech of mine as they used to. What is the matter?" "It is very simple," said he. "You think you are funny. You know it is a comic speech, but you show the audience that you know it is funny. That is the reason you have lost the laugh."

If anything untoward comes before an audience, it is apt to excite mirth. I had a terrible moment in one of Augustin Daly's plays. I came on the scene with my young wife in the usual accouterments of a man who has been to the opera. I started to take off my overcoat and revealed a huge area of white shirt on my right shoulder. Then I tried the other side with the same result. My coatsleeves were locked in the sleeves of the outer topcoat. As adroitly as I could I kept on with the dialogue, but the audience by this time discerned my predicament and smiled. I knew that it was a contest between myself and the audience. The laugh grew louder. I cut the Gordian knot by taking off both coats. I stood in my shirt sleeves. Before I could continue the scene I had to separate the two coats. In the process the sleeves of the under coat turned wrong side out and showed the satin lining. Then, having unturned the coatsleeves, I resumed my habit. The audience rewarded me with friendly applause.

I recall the first night at the Lyceum Theatre in London of Henry Irving in *The Corsican Brothers*. Mr. Irving (it was before the days of his knighthood) was a man of pronounced peculiarities, of strange, uncontrollable vocal characteristics, and he had a halting gait. He took the parts of Fabian and Louis—a dual rôle. One is killed in a duel, and the deed is revealed to his brother. On this night Mr. Irving was more than usually Irvingesque. When he saw the vision, his hands went up in the air, and his exclamation was something like "Louis, a-h-h-a-h-h-a—h!" A wave of laughter swept over the audience. It was not expected, and the performance nearly went on the rocks. But of course Irving was artist enough to save it.

The name of Irving recalls his controversy with Coquelin as to how much the actor should put of himself and his own emotions into the character. It is an old dispute with right on both sides, but it seems to me the contention of the French actor was the one which more nearly solved the paradox of acting—that feeling should be left entirely outside the performance. The actor must be capable of presenting mirth, sorrow, rage, hope, love, despair, but if in his acting he indulges himself in the pleasure of his emotions he becomes ineffective to the audience. If he cries real tears, he is likely to choke his utterance. I can recall so many young players who have said: "I know I can act, because whenever I read the scenes I cry real tears." I knew but one person who could weep real tears and who could also cause the audience to weep real tears: that was Clara Morris. It was little matter whether or not she shed those real tears, but it amounted to much that she could cause her audience to shed them.

We find authority for the elimination of the actual emotion of the actor in the words of Molé, a noted French comedian, who once noted in his diary his disgust with his work when he allowed himself to go too fully into the emotion of his character. "I was real, as I would have been at home," he said. "I ought to have been real in another way in accord with the perspective of the theater." But when the mechanics are too pronounced, the effect is gone. We must be filled with spiritual exaltation, body and mind alert to meet any contingency. The only way that we can figure out this paradox is to say that we must present the feeling, but we must always have it under control. It must be method plus the spirit of the occasion; not emotion minus the method.

When all is done, the actor will have accomplished little of permanency. He has writ his name in water. Nothing of his achievement is left behind to tell what manner of man he was. And in the words of Garrick:

He who struts his hour upon the stage,
Can scarce protract his fame through half an age.

So, let us not begrudge him his hour, though it be filled with overlaudation. All too soon the clock strikes the ensuing hour wherein is heard the cry: The King is dead! Long live the King!

OTIS SKINNER

The Art of Acting

Ladies and gentlemen, I feel very much flattered indeed to see before me such an assembly, and more particularly as I have seen on the plan that it is mainly composed of my fellow members and colleagues of our own profession. I am glad that they have so great an interest in questions that we are about to-day to discuss. I am not going to give you a lecture in any sense, much less to keep you to hear me speak on every form of acting. Nobody could do that in an hour, or an hour and a quarter. All of you know that perfectly well. All I have to do to-day is to explain how acting can be taught, and I hope you will agree with me, before I end, that this is the way acting should be taught. There was, you are aware, a few weeks ago, a lively discussion with regard to the establishment of a permanent school. There was one project that was put forward by members of our own profession. I say of our own profession, because I know I am addressing actors and actresses, my colleagues, and my fellow students. That project was dropped, suspended, put aside, because certain good patrons of the drama had organised another project and pushed it forward with a great deal of energy. During this discussion certain influential members of the public press—graciously taking, as they have always done, great interest in the art dramatic—in their editorials pronounced their opinion that acting could not be taught; that it was not an art at all; that it was a gift; that it was the effusion of enthusiasm; that, in point of fact, actors, like poets, were born, not made. Now that appeared to me to place our art below that of a handicraft, for no art becomes respectable or respected until its principles, its tenets, and its precepts are recognised, methodised, and housed in a system. If it be said that we cannot teach a man to be a genius, that we cannot teach him to be talented, that is simply a fact; but I ask you in any art what great men, like, for example, Michelangelo, Landseer, Murillo, would have existed if some kind of art had not preceded them by which they learned the art of, say, mixing colours, the principles

145

of proportion, and the principles of perspective. Where would Shakespeare have been if he had accidentally and unfortunately been born in some remote region at the plow-tail, where there was not within his reach the drama school of Stratford-on-Avon? He would have perished at the plow-tail and have been buried in a furrow, and we should never have known it. You must absolutely have principles in all arts. You cannot produce your own thoughts, your own feelings, unless you have some principles as some guide, some ground. I am not an eloquent man. I am simply an actor, an author, one who is in the habit of giving speech to others and supplying speeches for others, rather than delivering speeches myself.

Now, you know in all good wine-growing countries the best of the produce is exported. That is the reason why you get such very bad wine when you are there. Well, this is, as I have said, a large subject. I cannot do more in an hour than just skim the surface. I can, as Newton said, but wander on the shore of the great ocean and pick up the shells. I can but give you enough to make you understand what our art is, its philosophic principles; that a good actor is not due to accident, that a man is not born to be an actor unless he is trained.

You know that in Paris acting is taught. You are aware also that actors and authors are in the habit on the stage of teaching the actors how the characters they have drawn should be played. I allude, for example, to the great Mr. T. W. Robertson, one of the greatest productions of our age, who has revolutionised the drama of his period. That man was in the habit of teaching and conveying his ideas to actors on the stage, and as to how the parts should be rendered. I may also refer to M. Sardou in Paris, who, it is notorious, does the same thing, as well as many of the stage-managers of the present day. Alexandre Dumas is known to be constantly doing the same thing. I may refer also to Mr. Gilbert, the author, who does the same thing, and so stamps the character that that character is entirely new, and one that you have never seen before. You know that all active managers, such as Mr. Irving, Mr. Wilson Barrett, Mr. Bancroft, Mr. Hare, Mr. Kendal, all teach the younger actors and actresses how to play their parts. They are obliged to do so in the present condition of affairs, because there is no school in the provinces to lick the novices into shape and to teach them the ground of their art, how to walk and how to talk—that is, to teach them acting.

Acting is not mere speech! It is not taking the dialogue of the author and giving it artistically, but sometimes not articulately. Acting is to perform, to be the part; to be it in your arms, your legs; to be what you are acting; to be it all over, that is acting. The subject of acting may be divided into the voice for the treatment of the production; the expression of feature or gesture. I call gesture that action of the body above the waist—the arms, the neck, the head, and the bust. The carriage is that action of the body which is below the waist.

Then there is the study of character. Now, there is no speechifying in that. It has nothing to do with dialogue, it has nothing to do with posture. It applies practically to that portion of the profession with which you have to do before you begin anything of the sort. Now, with regard to the voice, the secret of being heard is not a loud voice. I am not now speaking with a loud voice, yet I hope I am heard all over this place. ["*Yes.*"] Thank you. Now I will tell you why. Because I have practised speaking articulately. Every syllable of every word is pronounced, and, as far as I can, every consonant and every vowel is pronounced. That is the secret of speaking plainly, speaking easily, and being heard over a large assembly. Now it is the vowel which gives support, and value, and volume to the consonants. When you want to give strong expression it is the consonant you go at, and not the vowel; but when you want to be expressive, when you want to be agreeable, you go at your vowel.

The next thing a young actor has got to do is to measure his breath. Usually he gets anxious, he gasps, he takes breath in the wrong place, he expands his breath in the beginning of the phrase, or too much of it, and when he gets to the end of it he has got no more; the consequence is he is pumped out. All young actors fall off in the end of their phrases, and all go down in consequence. The first fault of a young public speaker is that he begins with a great rush, and then falls in the distance. The next thing for the young actor to study will be the letters *l, m, n,* and *r,* the four liquids in the alphabet—the four letters out of which you cannot possibly compose an unmusical word. You may tumble them about in any way you please, but you cannot use those four letters without giving sweetness to the remaining consonants as a consequence, if you give them their due value. What have you English people done? One thing that you have done is that you have abolished the letter *r.* There is no more splendid letter in the whole alphabet than the letter *r.* Some people pronounce it like *w.* That is a misfortune that they cannot help. But the majority of you, and I dare say a great number of you, who are now laughing at those who pronounce it like *w* do not pronounce it at all. Some of you pronounce it as if it was an *h*, and when you are speaking of the Egyptian war you say "the Egyptian wah!" and you say "that is rathah!" when you mean "rather," and "mothah," when you mean "mother"; whereas there are no such words in the English language. I am now speaking the straight and simple truth, and I hope nobody will be offended.

Then another fault of young actors and actresses is that they condense their words. Words having three syllables they put into two. For "syllable" they will say "syllble," and for "appetite" they say "apptite." They do not say "A Limited Liability Company," but "A Limted Libility Compny." That is the modern way of pronouncing the English language. People have a habit of clipping their words. This is bad for the stage. I do not know whether it is a contemporary fashion outside it. An old stager holds great stress on all the letters in order that he shall maintain the standard of purity and the proper pronunciation of the English language. There is another fault that young actors and actresses have, and that is that they pronounce vowels wrongly. They pronounce the letter *i* sometimes like *oi,* and sometimes *a-eh*. They talk of "Moi oie" or "Ma-eh a-eh"; yet neither of those is the pronunciation of *i* in the English language. In the better theatres and theatres of the first class, actors are kept in check in this respect, because the acting managers are educated men, and therefore prevent actors from doing so; but when I go to theatres of a second class I hear the English language pronounced in a way that—well, if the audience are of my opinion I should express myself very loudly. Now, there are young people who go upon the stage sometimes who are inclined to think they cannot get on because their voices are so weak, and so they are discouraged. I will give you an instance of what I mean. About twenty-two years ago I was producing a play at the Adelphi Theater. It was *The Colleen Bawn*. In the last act a young lady played a part where she had only about three lines to utter in one of the conversations. The young lady was sweet and interesting-looking, and I went up to her and said, "My dear young lady, do speak a little louder, you cannot be heard." I tried to persuade her, but it was hopeless. I said, "A little louder, please, try." At last she burst into tears as she said, "I am trying." I went to the leader of the orchestra and said, "Do you hear this lady speak?" They hesitated, but I pressed them, when they said, "No, we do not." She subsided, and went down. One of her relations came to me the next morning and said, "I am sorry you are troubled with my relation on the stage;

pray do not encourage her to go on, she will never succeed; she had much better do something else." Well, I thought so too, but three years afterwards I found that young lady playing a leading part in *The Colleen Bawn.* I also found her playing a leading juvenile part in a piece at the Olympic Theatre, and holding her own by the side of the best actors, and now she possesses one of the sweetest, most sympathetic, and best voices that I ever heard on the stage in any country. It was one of the most charming organs for perfection and sweetness that to my recollection I have ever heard. That was done by practice and self-tuition. Her name is Miss Lydia Foote.

I must now go to a subject of a rather delicate nature, and that is really the first part of my subject—the voice. You know there are certain voices on the stage—you are perfectly aware of this—that the actor does not use off the stage; that are exclusively confined to tragedy. It is not the actor's ordinary voice. The idea is that the tragedian never has to use his own voice. Why? What is the reason? Before this century the great French tragedians before Talma and the great English tragedians before Kean used their treble voice—the tea-pot style. They did it as if they played on the flute. Then came the period when the tragedian played his part on the double bass *so.* [*The speaker imitated a very deep bass amid much laughter.*] There was no reason for it. Now we perform that part in the present age in what is called the medium voice. The reason is this. It is the transcendental drama tragedy. When I call it transcendental I mean unreal, poetic, to distinguish it from the realistic or the drama of ordinary life. The transcendental drama assumes that the dialogues are uttered by beings larger than life, who express ideas that no human being could pour out. The actor has accustomed himself to feel that he is in a different region, and therefore he feels if he uses his ordinary voice it might jar on the transcendental effect. I have fought out this very question with the great tragedians in France; and it seemed as if the tragedians were afraid of destroying the delicate illusion of the audience, who are sent about four hundred years back, as if they were living with people whom they had never seen and had no knowledge of. The consequence is those characters are too big for any ordinary human being, and the actor tries to make his manner and his voice correspond.

I will now leave the question of voice, and go to the question of gesture. Now gesture on the stage must be distinct and deliberate. When you look at a person you do not turn your eye, but you turn your whole head. If you want to point, do *that* [*with the arm straight out from the shoulder*]—the action must go from the shoulder. Every novice does *that*—[*pointing with finger only*]—particularly little women. If you have to shake your head, it must be full. Now, there is one cardinal rule—no, I will not say that, because in the theatre there is no such thing as a cardinal rule. Great men and great women often make the greatest effects by inverting the well-known rule; but the rule is that all gesture should precede slightly the words that it is to impress or to illustrate. If I am making an address to heaven I raise my arms first *so* [*illustrating*]—"By heaven!" The gesture indicates slightly to the mind what is going to be given in words, and the words complete that idea and satisfy the mind of the audience. If I were to say "By heaven!" *so* [*raising the arms after words*], that is comic, is it not? If I were to say to you, "Now, look here," that is right [*the action of the hand preceding the words*]; but if I say, "Now, look here" [*the action following the words*], that would be wrong. Then, no one except in doubt and in very exceptional circumstances puts his hand to his head. It is a bad habit, or it is a bad gesture. It is only called in when the man is in trouble, or, as old Kean did it, in despair. It is very exceptional. Of course great men may do these sorts of things, just as a great painter puts characters in attitudes that are wrong, but which are right in him. Why in the attitude of appeal do you put your hands up *so?* Because you want them. You cannot appeal *that* way [*with the palms downwards*]. Why in deprecation do you put your hands downwards? You cannot do it *that* way [*the palms upwards*]. Common sense will tell you that many of these little matters are matters that depend upon philosophy. They are so simple, so clear, and distinct, that you laugh at them. But do you know they are not generally known? The actor picks up these things by degrees on the stage. Rules are scattered about the stage and transmitted, gipsy-like, in our vagrant life from one generation to another; but do you know that sometimes it is ages before they are learned, and that an actor has to go on picking up these things one by one? Do you know how many years an actor is in doing that? What was Irving doing antecedent to 1870? He had been several years on the stage. I first met Mr. Irving in 1866, in Manchester. He happened, very fortunately for me, to have been selected to play a part in a piece of mine which was first produced there. He played it, and I said at once, "Here is the man, here is somebody!" A short time afterwards I said to him, "Why are not you in London?" He said, "Because I cannot get there." I said, "Oh, that is very simple; I am going to produce this piece in London, and I shall make it an absolute condition that you play this part." Therefore he came in 1866. Now from 1866 to 1870 what were you about? Were you stone blind that you did not know him? No, it was not your fault. During all that time he had been gathering together, painfully and laboriously, all these arts of his profession, and while he was gathering them he could not, till he got them together, be sure of his art. He had not that internal power which should have enabled him to know the stage so as to take his stand upon the stage and possess you! When he felt that he could do it he did it, but not before.

But that is a digression from gesture. Now, I will say a word as to superfluous gesture, and I would say, Let the gesture be exactly such as pertains to what you say, so as to help the meaning, and no more. Do not use *gesticles*— little gestures—that is, fidgety. The audience are very much alive to gesture, and if they see you constantly on the stage, and find that your gestures mean nothing, they will pay you no further attention. Gesture is not a small thing. Ask the man in the House of Commons! Ask the man speaking after-dinner speeches! and they will tell you. That the knowledge of it is necessary is quite clear from the way he puts his hands into his pockets, or down on the table, or anything or any-where, simply because nothing interferes with a man so much as not having learned the appropriate gesture. Now, in gesture you will observe that when the face is delivered to the public in the ordinary way in which an actor acts you see two cheeks, two eyes, the whole of the mouth, and the whole of the nose, but the gesture is foreshortened; but in profile you see half a face, one eye, one half of the mouth, and one half of the nose, but then the gestic assistance becomes pow-erful. *So [full face]*, the gesture is weak; *so [profile]*, the gesture is strong.

Then, gesture must be subordinate to the spectator him-self. All things in this art must be subordinate to that. It is a sort of picture. Therefore, the arm farthest from the audience must, as a general rule, go up. These, you will say, are slight rules; but still they will jar on the audience occa-sionally if they are not followed. I beg to observe, as far as I have gone, these are not altogether rules that apply to the stage. They apply to oratory. They belong to the pulpit, they belong to the bar, and they belong to the House of Commons. If they did not, they would not be true. They do not belong to one more than another. Now, there is a very important thing about gesture which we will call byplay—that is, the gestures that are used while another person is speaking, so that the recipient, by receiving the speech from the stage, may transmit its effect to the audience. That is a very delicate process, and one that is very difficult for a novice to understand and perform; but he should know, if he is properly instructed, how to keep that gesture to listen to the principal actor, for if he does not do so he will not convey it to the audience, and he may conclude: "If his speech has no effect upon me it will not have any effect upon them."

Another thing is, do not let your gesture be too short. It seems that some cannot give the appropriate gesture. They say, "Go away!" [*with a quick gesture*]. They cannot rest long enough in a gesture. You do not know how long you can rest upon a good one. It tires you, but it will not tire the spectator. He does not like it, and does not understand that quick change. Then you should very rarely reach across your own body. Everything that is strictly natural is not always right. If I were in a room I should take my hat from this table with my right hand and turn, but here I should turn my back on the audience if I do so, therefore I take it *so* [*with the left hand, and passing it to the right*] when I am going out, although I have no right to take it in my left hand naturally. I could say a good deal more upon gesture, but I am afraid I am keeping you here too long. [*"No, no!" and cheers.*]

Now let us go to posture and to character. I now come to a most important fact. I am going to ask you what has become of the lost art of walking? Some waddle, some roll, and some toddle; but there is but one man in five hundred —nay, in one thousand—that really walks. Examine the Greek friezes, where the lines of persons are represented in the true attitude of a person walking. Nowadays on the stage, or in the street, you will find the action is totally different, and I will explain it. There are some southern Spaniards who still possess the lost art, and some Arabs do. I will tell you why presently. Let me explain the process. The English and French walk with their knees never brought straight. That is ungraceful, and not a proper method of walking. Walking means a stride with the foot from one position to another. That is the art of walking. If that stride is taken properly it is a walk. One reason for this is the modern walker is not accustomed to bend the foot, but unless those joints can play you cannot walk. The leg must be brought back into a perfectly straight position, because the walk is made by propulsion from one position to another. The leg is thrown forward, but should never be kicked out, but as the leg advances the propulsion is like that of the Greek friezes. The right leg is forward, or if the left is forward the right is always straight. The foot is brought perfectly level with the ground. The foot must not be dragged as some actors do it. There is no elasticity in it that way. I have not the slightest intention to be personal to anybody. The foot being brought forward slowly and level with the ground, the shoulders are kept back and the body is perfectly perpendicular.

Now, how is that to be obtained? I will tell you. If you place a pad on the head, and if you place on the pad a weight of say thirty or forty pounds—oh, you can bear sixty pounds without any trouble; you do not know what power there is in the backbone—that obliges you to carry your weight strictly over the backbone and to hold your head up; the head and neck immediately assume a uniform and erect attitude. The weight being where it is, the whole body assumes a perfect attitude and the arms drop in the right place. If you attempt to walk, the legs must be kept cleanly and clearly underneath, the body must be kept perfectly straight, and you can walk —a little stiffly, perhaps, because if you do not you will fall. When you get into the habit of carrying anything on the head you will walk with ease and grace under it. That is why the Arabs walk so well, because they are in the habit of carrying things on their heads. That is, perhaps, the reason the Greeks walk so well, because they were likely to carry something *in* their heads.

Now, in walking let us study some living thing. You know that some birds are noticeable for their grace; and you will find that with animals like those of the feline tribe there is at the middle of the walk a very slight pause. The walk is not continuous and continual, but there is a pause in the middle. You will also find that birds of a certain class walk in that way. That also adds grace to the movement; and you will find when you carry a weight of that kind upon your head you will feel when you get to the centre of the step that you make a slight pause, and this habit cultivates that peculiar touch of grace which is essential to an exceedingly graceful and full walk. Some ladies have it naturally, and it is always better if these things come not by art, but by nature. Then, again, the leg farthest from the audience should be always farther forward than the other. Starting for a walk, you should commence it with the off leg. If you kneel on the stage, kneel on the knee next the audience. These are ordinary facts that we should all know.

Now, when you walk backwards and forwards, do not turn upon the ball of your foot in turning round; but, when you come to the end of the walk, it is more dignified to take one step and bring your foot back, and then take the movement back again. A lady, if she attempts to do it, walks on the tail of her own dress. She is obliged, therefore, to be more graceful. Then measure your distance. Novices always fall short, or turn back; but good actors, by habit, render this impossible. A good actress gets to the table, if she wants to get to it, without difficulty. In the old style, actors used to have a number of tricks on the stage, which, fortunately, recent tragedians have abolished. One of these was what was called "taking the step." Your Richard and Macbeth could not act except in a circle; but then they made a point of taking the stage [*the speaker walked rapidly across the stage*], and that was the cue to the audience to applaud! When the performer had given a remarkable speech, and when he came to its point, he walked into one of the corners. It was impossible in the palaces of the kind and elsewhere for the performers to get into the corners, especially a lady, therefore he did not continue to cultivate a habit which was not only so unnatural, but so inartistic.

Another trick which comedians as well as tragedians used in taking an exit was to commence the speech in this way, "So, my Lord, I take my leave," and then go to the other side of the stage and finish it. This was equally conventional; the actor would reserve the last three or four words of his scene, and, walking to the side, would turn and speak those words "to take him off." So that twenty or thirty years ago an actor often said, "Would you give me a few words to take me off?" They could not get off the stage!

I think I have said enough on that branch of the subject, so that I may leave that in order to leave a little room for that part of the subject which relates to the study of character. Now, the great fault of young actors in the present day, novices particularly, before they go on the stage, is to imagine, when they have got the words into their heads, that all is done. That is not all. A child could do that, because it has a much better memory than a grown-up man—a much better memory. Young actors think when they know the part they know the work. But it is not the getting of the words into your head, it is the getting them out again. He goes to the stage, dresses nicely, parts his hair properly, and provides himself with patent-leather boots; but, if he does not study character, it is no use. You may look the thing very nicely; but the audience will discount that in a very few minutes. The question is whether you can do it. I am sorry to say that the young actors of the present day do not give so much attention to the inside of the subject as they ought to do. The first lesson an actor has to learn is, not to speak. It is to learn to walk on the stage, stand still, and walk off again. That appears very simple, but it is very difficult. When he walks on the stage he fixes his attention on what is said and what is done on the scene, never removing it to follow the speakers. But his part is to listen, and if he can perform that part well—that is, the part of a good listener—he will have achieved a progress in his art that many very favourite and prominent actors have never yet achieved. That one lesson alone, if it is perfectly learned, will actuate his whole career. He will never forget it, and it will be one reason of his success. Now, the finer part of the acting is to obtain an effect, not altogether by what is given you to speak, but by listening to what another person speaks, and by its effect upon you, by continuing your character while the other man is speaking. Your performance on the stage by that byplay may not be as great as his, but still it prepares the audience for the scene; the gesture helps the tone. The effect is exhibited on the actor who listens, and from him on the rest of the audience. If the beginner allows his mind to be employed in this manner it has this effect, his mind is no longer in attendance upon his arms; that terrible egotism, that vanity sickness that we call stage fright, he is relieved of nearly altogether. He cannot help feeling it because he rushes into it in consequence of the great pains he is at to obtain a judgment that is of value for its sweetness, and is acutely feared for its censure. If the man fixes his mind upon some other object, if the mind is over *there*, not *here* on himself, ease will naturally follow, because he is naturally there as a listener. That is his first lesson; when he has accomplished this he must come to the study of character.

To the young beginner I would say, when you go upon the stage do not be full of yourself, but be full of your part. That is mistaking vanity for genius, and is the fault of many more than perhaps you are aware of. If actors' and actresses' minds be employed upon themselves, and not on the character they wish and aspire to perform, they never really get out of themselves. Many think they are studying their character when they are only studying themselves. They get their costume, they put it on, see how it fits, they cut and contrive it, but all that is not studying their character, but their costume. Actors and actresses frequently come to me and say, "Have you any part that will fit me?" They never dream of saying, "Have you any part that I can fit? that I can expand myself or contract myself into; that I can put myself inside of; that I, as a Protean, can shape myself into, even alter my voice and everything that nature has given to me, and be what you have contrived? I do not want you to contrive like a tailor to fit me." That is what is constantly happening.

Now, I will give you an example of what happens when a new play is brought into the theatre. It is usually read in the green-room. I do not think that is a good plan. My experience, which extends to forty years, is that actors listen to the parts that others have to play, but never to their own, and are dissatisfied. "Oh, yes," says Smith, "I have a fine part, but look at Jones." Jones, grumbling, says, "Oh, yes; I suppose I shall do something with it; but see how it falls off in the last act. Miss Popkins has the best part." Miss Popkins is the leading woman. She comes and says, "Mr. Boucicault, I do object to be the mother of Miss Brown, whom I knew as a leading actress when I was a child." Then Miss Brown comes to me the following day full of anxiety, and, taking me aside, says, "What am I to wear?" I say, "Study your character." She still says, "What am I to wear?" and "Can I change between the second and third acts?" Then I am button-holed by Mr. Smith, who says, "Please, what is your idea about my wig?" This is not the study of character. It is jealousy of the other parts, and not their own.

It was not so forty years ago. They had their faults, many of them, but they did not constitute costume and make-up as the study of character, which it is not. I will tell you what did happen forty years ago. I was producing a comedy in which Mr. Farren, the father of the gentleman who so ably bears the same name (old Farren), played a leading part. He did not ask what he was going to wear, but he came to me, and said, "Who did you draw this party from; had you any type?" I said, "Yes, I had," and mentioned the names of two old fogies who, at that time, were well known in London society. One he knew, the other he did not. He went and studied Sir Harcourt Courtley, and he studied by the speediest method, for the study was absolutely and literally out of the mouth of the man himself. That will give you an idea how they studied character.

Once Mr. Mathews came to me and said, "Do you know Dazzle?" I said, "Yes." He said, "Do you know really a good type?" "Yes, I do." "Will you kindly let me see him?" I said, "I am in some difficulty, for if he thought I was going to put him on the stage he would shoot me, and I do not want that, but I can describe him." "Very well," he said, "what sort of a man is he?" I described him exactly. I said,

"The other day I was standing on the hearth rug, and a mutual friend, a young plunger, came in in a great state of excitement and announced to us that a distant relative had left him £10,000. Dazzle looked at the ceiling and said, 'If I had only £10,000! Bless me! I should be having £20,000 a year for six months.' " From that he understood immediately what the character was.

That is the way to study character, to get at the bottom of human nature, and I am happy to say that, amongst some young actors who have come out within the last ten or fifteen years, I have seen a natural instinct for the study of character and for the drawing of character most admirably, and much more faithfully than they drew it twenty or thirty years ago. There is a study of character that we may call good and true that has been accomplished within the last fifteen or sixteen years.

Now, I will say something by way of anecdote to show how utterly unnecessary it is for you to bother your minds so much about your dress. I was producing *The Shaughraun* in New York. I generally had enough to employ my time. I get the actors and actresses to study their characters, and generally leave myself to the last. But the last morning before the play was produced I saw my dresser hobbling about, but afraid to come to the stage. At last he said, "Have you thought of your costume?" I said I had not done any such thing. It was about three o'clock in the afternoon, and I had to play about seven o'clock in the evening. I went upstairs and said, "Have you got a red coat?" "Yes; we have got a uniform red hunting coat." "Oh, that is of no use!" "We have got one that was used in *She Stoops to Conquer*." That was brought, but it had broad lapels and looked to belong to about one hundred and fifty years ago. "Oh!" said the man, "there is an old coat that was worn by Mr. Beckett as Goldfinch." When he came to that it reached all down to my feet, and was too long in the sleeves. So I cut them off with a big pair of shears, and by the shears and the scissors I got some sort of a fit. Then I got an old hunting cap, a pair of breeches, and sent for some old boots that cost about 2s. 6d. and did not fit me, and that is how I came on the stage. The editor of one of the newspapers said, "Where on earth did you get that extraordinary costume from?"

Believe me, I mention these circumstances simply to show that the study of character should be from the inside; not from the outside! Great painters, I am told, used to draw a human figure in the nude form, and, when they were proposing to finish their pictures, to paint the costumes; then the costumes came right. That is exactly how an actor ought to study his art. He ought to paint his character in the nude form and put the costume on the last thing.

Now, let me give this particular advice to all persons going on the stage. Many of you are already on the stage, but others may be going on. Having arrived at that conclusion as to what your line is going to be, always try to select those kinds of characters and the line that is most suited and more nearly conforms to your own natural gifts. Nature knows best. If you happen to have a short, sharp face, a hard voice, an angular figure, you are suited for the intellectual characters of the drama, such as Hamlet and so forth. If you are of a soft, passionate nature—if you have a soft voice and that sort of sensuous disposition which seems to lubricate your entire form, your limbs, so that your movements are gentle and softer than others—then this character is fitted for a Romeo or an Othello. You will find, if you look back at the records of actors, there are few great actors that have shone in the two different lines, the intellectual and the sensual drama. Kemble could do Hamlet, but he could not do Othello. Kean could do Othello, but he could not do Hamlet. The one was passionate and sensual, the other was an intellectual, a noble, grand actor.

Now, after you have made this preliminary study you will recollect that in every great character there are three characters really. We are all free men, in one sense, speaking, of course, of our inner life; but we have three characters. First there is the man by himself—as he is to himself—as he is to his God. That is one man, the inner man, as he is when alone; the unclothed man. Then there is the native man, the domestic man, as he is to his family. Still there is a certain amount of disguise. He is not as he is to other men. Then there is the man as he stands before the world at large; as he is outside in society. Those are the three characters. They are all in the one man, and the dramatist does not know his business unless he puts them into one character. Look at Hamlet in his soliloquies: he is passionate, he is violent, he is intemperate in himself, he knows his faults and lashes his own weakness. But he has no sooner done that than Horatio comes on the stage with a few friends. Horatio is the mild, soft, gentle companion; with his arm round his neck, Hamlet forgets the other man; he gets a little on, but he is the same man to Horatio as he is to his mother, when he gets her in the closet. But when he encounters the world at large, he is the Prince! the condescending man! You have seen Hamlet played, and if you watched closely, you have seen those three phases of his character have been given on this stage! So it is in nearly all characters—comic or otherwise. You will find that the three characters always combine in the man.

This should be studied to be preserved. It is one of the charms of comedy, as all dramatists know very well how to employ. Take, for instance, where the woman is the affected woman of society. Something occurs to break her down, and she is bound to break down; the audience immediately recognise it, because they recognise the true woman. The truth comes out, and they do not like affectation; they prefer nature. When Pauline, in *The Lady of Lyons*, carries on the proud woman—that is, the woman of society—as she falls in love she struggles for what? To maintain the woman of society. During the struggle the audience watch with intensest interest whilst they gradually see her breaking down. Eventually, crash! and the true woman bursts out. There you see the preservation of those two characters. The observation of the three characters is one secret of the true and the highest form of the dramatic art, and the dramatist, if he would be true to nature and to his art, must carry them out. Now, it may be said that these things are not altogether high art. They may not be high art, but the high art rests on them. You cannot get on without them. They are the pedestals on which the statue rests. They are as necessary to the great picture as they are to the life they represent.

Now, ladies and gentlemen, I have kept you a long time. All I say now is that I have to give you most heartily and conscientiously, as an old man, an old dramatist, and an old actor, this advice. Whatever is done by an actor let it be done with circumspection, without anxiety or hurry, remembering that vehemence is not passion, that the public will feel and appreciate when the actor is not full of himself, but when he is full of his character, with that deliberation without slowness, that calmness of resolution without coldness, that self-possession without overweening confidence, which should combine in the actor so as to give grace to comic and importance to tragic presence. The audience are impressed with the unaffected character of one who moves forward with a fixed purpose, full of momentous designs. He expresses a passion with which they will sympathise, and radiates a command which they will obey.

Now, ladies and gentlemen, I have detained you here longer than I intended. I thank you very sincerely for the kindness with which you have attended to me. I do not know that I have given you anything very valuable, but I hope you will think that I have given you sufficient, and more than sufficient, to help you to study this, the art of acting, although it is simply a bit of a very great deal that can be taught to the young actor, who should be taught if he is to approach perfection in the period of probation which he has to go through. Let us give him the sound principles of his art. Do not let us leave the managers to be obliged to take the most ignorant people, and have to do here on the stage what should be done elsewhere. Let them be properly and fairly prepared and brought into such a position as to be able to do some of the minor parts of the drama which they profess to follow. If you believe anything I have said is good and worthy of your attention, and that I have not employed your hour foolishly and infructuously, then I will ask you to be kind enough to help me to thank Mr. Irving for his very great kindness in giving me this stage, and you the free use of this house, this afternoon, so that we may *collogue* together. I will ask you to be kind enough to say that you thank Mr. Irving, and to help me to thank Mr. Stoker and other gentlemen of this house, who have gone through an immense deal of trouble (more than I can explain) in putting me in a position so as to be able to address so brilliant and so kind an audience.

Actors and Acting

A Discussion by

Constant Coquelin, Sir Henry Irving, and Dion Boucicault

With an Introductory Note by Brander Matthews

Introduction

Constant Coquelin contributed to *Harper's Monthly* for May 1887 a paper entitled "Actors and Acting." This promptly evoked from Henry Irving a retort, "M. Coquelin on Actors and Acting," which appeared in the *Nineteenth Century* for June 1887, only one month later. Then, two months after Irving's article, Dion Boucicault printed in the *North American Review* for August 1887 an article which he called "Coquelin—Irving."

Finally, in *Harper's Weekly* for November 12, 1887, Coquelin replied first to Henry Irving and then to Dion Boucicault.

These five papers, taken together and in their proper sequence, contain a body of doctrine about the art of acting which has permanent value, in addition to the piquancy of the spectacle afforded by the triangular duel of three eminent practitioners of the histrionic art. And there is advantage, therefore, in bringing together these essays, partly that we may enjoy the skill of fence displayed by the three distinguished actors, but mainly that we may profit by what they have severally to tell us about their art. When accomplished craftsmen come forward to discuss the secrets of their calling, the rest of us will do well to listen attentively and to profit by what they have to tell us.

BRANDER MATTHEWS

Actors and Acting

I

Art I define as a whole wherein a large element of beauty clothes and makes acceptable a still larger element of truth.

Thus in the execution of a work of art the painter has his colors, his canvas, and his brushes; the sculptor has his clay, his chisel, and his modeling tools; the poet has his words, rhythm, harmony, and rhyme. Every art has its different instruments; but the instrument of the actor is himself.

The *matter* of his art, that which he has to work upon and mold for the creation of his idea, is his own face, his own body, his own life. Hence it follows that the actor must have a double personality. He has his first self, which is the player, and his second self, which is the instrument. The first self conceives the person to be created, or rather—for the conception belongs to the author—he sees him such as he was formed by the author, whether he be Tartuffe, Hamlet, Arnolphe, or Romeo, and the being that he sees is represented by his second self. This dual personality is the characteristic of the actor.

Not that the double nature is the exclusive property of actors alone; it undoubtedly exists among others. For example, my friend Alphonse Daudet takes delight in distinguishing this double element in the personality of the storyteller, and even the very expressions I am now using are borrowed from him. He confesses that he also has his first self and his second self—the one a man made like other men, who loves or hates, suffers or is happy; the other a being belonging to a higher sphere, whose balance nothing can disturb, and who in the midst of tumultuous emotions can observe, study, and take notes for the future creation of his characters.

But this double nature of the writer is neither so essential nor so conspicuous as that of the actor. The first self of the author watches the second self, but they never mingle. In the actor, on the contrary, the first self works upon the second till it is transfigured, and thence an ideal personage is evolved—in short, until from himself he has made his work of art.

When a painter is about to execute a portrait he first poses his model, and then, concentrating, as it were, in his brush all the striking features that his trained eye can seize, he transfers them to the canvas by the magic of his art, and when he has done this, his work is finished. The actor, however, has still something to do—he must himself enter into the picture. For *his* portrait must speak, act, walk in its frame, which is the stage, and it must convey the illusion of life to the spectator.

Therefore when the actor has a portrait to execute—that is, a part to create—he must first read the play carefully over many times, until he has grasped the intention of the author and the meaning of the character he is to represent, until he has a clear understanding of his personage, and *sees* him as he ought to be. When he attains to this, he has his model. Then, like the painter, he seizes each salient feature and transfers it, not to his canvas, but to himself. He adapts each element of this personality to his second self. He sees Tartuffe in a certain costume, he wears it; he feels he has a certain face, he assumes it. He forces, if one may say so, his own face and figure into this imaginary mold, he recasts his own individuality, till the critic which is his first self declares he is satisfied, and finds that the result is really Tartuffe.

But this is by no means all, otherwise the resemblance would be only external; it would merely convey the outward form of the personage, not the personage himself. Tartuffe must be made to speak with the voice that he hears Tartuffe using, and in order consistently to represent the part the actor must learn to move, talk, gesticulate, listen, and also think, with the mind which he divines in Tartuffe.

Now, and not till now, is the picture completed; it is ready to be framed—I mean put on the stage—and instead of exclaiming, "Look at Geoffroy!" "Here comes Bressant!" or whoever it may be, the audience will cry, "Ah, this is Tartuffe!" If otherwise, your labor is lost.

To sum up, the first thing necessary must be a deep and careful study of the *character;* then there must be the conception by the first self, and the reproduction by the second, of the person such as his character inevitably makes him. This is the work of the actor.

Like Molière, he takes his own wherever he may find it; that is, to complete the resemblance he may add to his portrait any striking traits which he himself has observed in nature; thus Harpagon was composed of a thousand misers melted and cast in the mold of a masterly unity.

II

The two natures which coexist in the actor are inseparable, but it is the first self, the one which *sees,* which should be the master. This is the soul, the other is the body. It is the reason—the same reason that our friends the Chinese call the *Supreme Ruler;* and the second self is to the first what rhyme is to reason—a slave whose only duty is obedience.

The more absolute the subjection to this mistress, the greater the artist.

The ideal would be that the second self, the body, should be a soft mass of sculptor's clay, capable of assuming at will any form, who would become a charming *jeune premier* for Romeo, a diabolical and intellectually fascinating humpback for Richard III, for Figaro a ferret-faced valet with an expression of audacious impertinence. Then the actor would be all-accomplished, and granted he also had equivalent talents, he could undertake every part. Alas! nature forbids this: he would be too fortunate. However supple may be the body, however mobile may be the face, neither one nor the other can be changed indefinitely at the will of the artist.

Sometimes it happens that a man's exterior will prevent him from acting certain parts which he is, notwithstanding, well able both to grasp and to expound. Sometimes nature relentlessly confines an actor to certain kinds of parts; but this touches the question of physique, of which I will speak later.

There are some in whom the *second self,* or the *ego,* rebels, on whom their own individuality exerts so much influence that they can never put it aside, and instead of their going to their role and clothing themselves in its semblance, they make the role come to them and clothe itself in theirs.

This becomes another way of conceiving art, and I do not hesitate to pronounce it inferior to the first, although I am well aware how much can be done in this direction by a highly gifted artist.

The first drawback is that a man becomes, in a measure, the man of a single part; it also leads to the neglect of the study and digestion of the character—to me the only important thing—for the quest of that of the exterior, and of picturesque detail.

Of course picturesque detail is not to be despised, but it

should never become the object of exclusive attention, and above all no picturesque trait, however natural, should ever be taken as the starting point of a role.

It is the *character* that is the starting point for everything.

If you have assimilated the essence of your personage, his exterior will follow quite naturally, and if there is any picturesqueness, it will come of itself. It is the mind which constructs the body.

If Mephistopheles is ugly, it is because his soul is hideous. I have seen him admirably played in Vienna by Levinski, who represents him lame and humpbacked, which is quite appropriate to the character.

But Irving, who also made a name for himself in this role —Irving, who is a kind of methodical Mounet, setting great store by the exterior of his parts—Irving cannot avoid seeking after the picturesque even in his slightest movement. If he wishes to touch his chin, he raises his arm and encircles it, his hand makes the tour of his head, striking the audience as it does so with a sense of its leanness, and never seizes the point of his beard till after it has described a complete circle.

Rouvière exaggerated to the utmost this view of a character, and suffered the lay figure which was in him to get the better of the actor.

The love of dramatic effect, and a very praiseworthy dislike of the hackneyed and commonplace, often induce very intelligent actors to err on this side. They choose first the aspects which they suppose to be characteristic of the person they can represent; then they allow themselves to be tempted by others which are purely picturesque, without considering, or perhaps without caring, if they belong really to the part; and the end is a caricature, not a portrait, a monster or a puppet, never a human being.

Even from the point of view of immediate success, this method of proceeding has one great drawback. The public tires of nothing so quickly as mere picturesqueness of effect. Your entrance once over, they pay no further heed to you; you have missed fire if you have not style, delivery, and the development of the character to fall back on. The style is the man, said M. de Buffon.

More than this: if by a misplaced anxiety to individualize your part you end by catching up a trick, oh, then beware! Instead of amusing your audience, you will prejudice them against you. The public, though it may laugh the first time, will soon become bored, and will not fail to convey its feelings to you by coldness and reserve, or by something more disagreeable still.

III

Do not misunderstand me. I forbid no one to borrow from observation of a model the peculiarities which betray the inner man. As I have said above, it is one of the necessary qualities of the actor to be able to seize and note at once anything that is capable of reproduction on the stage; but these traits must be adopted with discretion. For example, those must be avoided which are purely individual; the actor must take care not to adopt the characteristics of some special miser whom he may know but whom the public does not know, but instead he should give, as Harpagon, the concentrated essence of *all misers,* which his audience would recognize instantly.

There was one actor, Lesueur, who was pre-eminent in this art of true portraiture. No one has ever done more with his second self, or created out of his own personality characters more different in themselves, or with more intense expression. It was really astonishing. But then he studied with the fury of enthusiasm. In his house there was a sort of dark room, with closed windows and locked doors, where he used to shut himself in with his costumes, his wigs, and all his paraphernalia. There, alone before his mirror, he would sit trying experiments with his face by the light of the lamps. He would make up twenty, he would make up a hundred, times before he would succeed in producing the ideal which he felt to be the true one, and of which he could say, "Yes, that is he."

And when he had put the finishing touch to the likeness, he would work for hours at one wrinkle. The result was so extraordinary that judges of acting will never forget his absinthe drinker, his madmen, or his old gentleman playing piquet. He was one day Monsieur Poirier, that incarnation of the middle classes, and the next he would be Don Quixote, the type of starving knight-errantry. When he entered the stage in this last part, although he was really a small man, it seemed as if there was no end to his stature; he seemed to draw himself out, like a telescope, till he was as long as his lance. It was indeed the hero of Cervantes in all the melancholy of his interminable leanness.

But in spite of this wonderful talent, fortified by a close study of his parts, he lacked one element necessary to make the illusion complete—command of his voice. He never could manage to train his, and it remained to the last, in all his parts, the voice of Lesueur—very comic, but always comic in the same way, and with a terribly ponderous articulation. In the *Chapeau d'un Horloger* he has to say, *"Monsieur, madame me désire,"* and he pronounced it "madameu meu désieureu."

Now, articulation is to speech what drawing is to painting. A single sentence of Samson's, articulated as he knew how to articulate, was as good as a portrait by M. Ingres for enabling you to grasp the character of the person he was representing.

When this master in the art of speaking appeared in *Mademoiselle de La Seiglière*, if you had had your eyes shut you would have known from the way in which he put the question, *"Jasmin, Madame La Baronne de Vaubert n'est pas encore arrivée?"* what manner of man he was. It was the insolent *grand seigneur*, who looks on Jasmin as a being of different clay from himself, the empty-headed *émigré*, the egoist to whom it is nothing if Madame de Vaubert should have arrived or not, who makes the inquiry merely from politeness, mingled with a certain anxiety as to what effect her absence will have in delaying breakfast, after which he, the Marquis de La Seiglière, must be starting again, mighty hunter as he is before the Lord.

And when he referred to Bonaparte—to "Monsieur de Buonaparte"—he would catch himself up in order to exalt his enemy, so that the honor might redound on himself; for the sole object of M. de Buonaparte in winning so many victories had been to gain him, the Marquis de La Seiglière, over to his cause, and he, the Marquis, had turned a deaf ear to all his advances—to Marengo, Austerlitz, and Jena. The simple articulation of the syllables was enough to convey the naive self-sufficiency of the man and all his headstrong pride of race.

The power of a true inflection of the voice is incalculable, and all the picturesque exteriors in the world will not move an audience like one cry given with the right intonation. Articulation therefore should be the first study of the actor.

The public *must* understand every word he says, however quickly he may say it. A word must be able to draw tears or laughter from the mere manner of its articulation.

The voice should not be less finely trained than the exterior. It belongs to the second self, and should be specially supple, expressive, and rich in modifications of tone. According to the part, the voice should be caressing, smooth, insinuating, mocking, bold, eager, tender, despairing. You should be able to ring the changes from the clarinet to the bugle.

The lover's voice is not like the lawyer's voice. Iago has not the voice of Figaro, nor Figaro the voice of Tartuffe. Intonation, key, and note all differ with the role. As Madelon says, "It contains the chromatic scale." In a word, your character should be drawn and portrayed so that even the blind may see him by your articulation, your delivery, and your intonation.

All this should be added to the care that you bestow on your exterior; with the same minuteness as Lesueur, if you will, provided it be also with the same truth to nature. I mean always keeping in mind the character of which the exterior is only the illustration——the person who must be set before men's very eyes without the deformity which comes from exaggeration.

Physiognomy, gesture, and voice should all make one whole. It often happens that characters which are apparently quite insignificant need the greatest efforts of metamorphosis on the part of the actor. For instance, look at Thouvenin in *Denise*. One would think I could not have a more easy role than this extremely simple one. I am not speaking now of my success, but only of my struggles to attain it, of my long hours of study of the character. Thouvenin takes no part in the action; he talks and argues as any honest man would, as I might do myself any day. That is the very rock on which I might wreck myself. In virtue of the relationship between this personage and the man that is in me, the man such as I am in common life, I may be tempted to endow him with my gestures, to make him speak with my voice—to be, in fact, Monsieur Coquelin; and if I did this, I should have betrayed the author, who required that I should be Thouvenin. So it was necessary to watch more carefully than usual to restrain myself, to correct my ordinary ways, to modify my walk, to tone down the eagerness of my voice, to keep only the exact vibration that is required for the great speech at the end; to mold my physiognomy in such a manner as to give to Thouvenin his appropriate exterior as an ex-working-man who has educated himself and fills creditably his place in the world, but who brings to bear on the usages and conventions of society a liberty of judgment and an originality of language which reveal at once his origin and his character.

The special advantage of a serious study of the parts is to facilitate these transformations. Samson and Régnier hardly ever painted their faces; they contrived to change their expressions solely from within. In this art, as in so many others, Frédérick was the greatest master. The word *trans-*

figuration was applied for the first time, as far as I know, to an actor when he appeared in *Ruy Blas* with such splendid success. Transfiguration will hardly be thought too strong a word to describe the successive representations of Robert Macaire and Ruy Blas. His personifications of the scoundrel, with his shabby hideousness, and of the servant and lover of the Queen, with the tragic splendor of his face, were alike the work of a master; for he was beautiful in *Ruy Blas*. He contrived to throw a shadow of passionate melancholy over everything that was irregular, sharp, and severe in his countenance, till nothing was left but the light of genius, and he seemed to put on beauty like a mask. As no one ever had more accentuated features than he, he deserved all the more credit for his extraordinary transformations. This power is not given to all. Not even the hardest work will enable us always to grasp it; and this brings us back to the question of *physique,* so important on the stage.

IV

As I have said before, the exterior of an actor, certain details of his physical conformation, of his "architecture," may confine him exclusively to one special kind of part.

There are men whom nature has made *lovers* to the end of time, like Delaunay; there are *duennas* from the cradle, like Madame Jouassain. This indication of a special line often arises from some very slight peculiarity—from the angle made by the nose with the horizon, for example. But on the subject of the influence of the nose, everyone should read what Pascal says of Cleopatra: "The destinies of the world would have been different had Cleopatra's nose been shorter." One sort of face only suits tragedy, or, at most, serious comedy. Another face, bristling with queer irregularities, is out of place save in farce.

Happy indeed are these actors if their physique which forces them into a certain line allows them to add to it by the help of their talent an amount of universal truth and humanity sufficient to constitute a type. They will leave their image and an undying recollection behind them. This was the case with Henri Monnier in M. Prudhomme. He was never anything but M. Prudhomme; he could not be anything else; but he created in the person of M. Prudhomme a face which has become traditional, a type, a representation of an epoch and of a class. He and his creation will live forever.

But do not misunderstand me. The actor of one part,

however fine a study it may be, is inferior to the actor who has the command of many.

It is also an error to hold that the only really admirable creations are those in which the outward conformity of the actor with his role is absolute and entire.

Frédérick created a type which is, in its way, quite as immortal as M. Prudhomme. This was Robert Macaire, to which I have already alluded, and to which I shall have occasion again to refer. To Frédérick alone the creation is due, but this did not prevent him from also creating Ruy Blas.

Notwithstanding, he resembled in himself neither the one nor the other of these two persons, whom he may be said to have almost amalgamated in Don César, and he would be a bold man who would dare affirm that he was better as an artist in one than in the other. He was, in truth, wonderful in comedy, and sublime in tragedy. He had great powers, and his face was not of a kind to interfere with their outward expression.

The truth is that as long as an actor is free from any natural defects of structure, as long as his countenance is not more laughable or more unpleasing than the countenances of the generality of men, and the face is sufficiently mobile, even though it may lack beauty, to be able to assume at will a dramatic expression—given all these things, there is no reason why he should not distinguish himself both in comedy and tragedy.

It is all a question of degree, and of course a question of talent. It is hardly necessary to quote instances; they abound everywhere, and it is impossible it should be otherwise.

Tragedy and comedy are so closely blended in the contemporary stage that the capacity for the double impersonation is demanded of nearly all. Look at Régnier, my dear master. What admirable creations we owe to him! Was it laughter he provoked in *Gabrielle,* or in *Le Supplice d'une Femme?* And who will ever forget him as Balandard in *Une Chaîne,* or the shouts of irresistible merriment which he raised all through the theatre?

Physical beauty, or charm, is indispensable to *jeunes premiers.* In order to make and to receive gracefully declarations of love before an audience, it is necessary to possess no peculiarity which can excite a smile. The actor must either be handsome or be able to appear so.

For there is a difference. It is possible to appear handsome, and to have the power of attracting all hearts, without being in the least a model of beauty. I am sure I shall not wound the feelings of my friend Delaunay if I say that his nose is not exactly Grecian in its outline; and yet no one more fascinating ever appeared on the stage. He had so much charm, something so ineffably young and tender and airy, something which I do not hesitate to say has left the stage with him.

Charm, that is the one thing needful for the *jeunes premiers*. How is it that certain faces have so much of it that are entirely destitute of classical beauty? In what does their attraction lie? Why is it they can bewitch women? It is a problem I cannot undertake to solve. All I know is, let a man succeed in fascinating a single woman, and the rest will run after him. We are all like the sheep of Panurge, and women are the ewes.

As regards the *jeunes premières*, the case is the same. Beauty is not essential, but charm is. We all recollect what Victor Hugo said to Madame Dorval—"You are not beautiful; you are worse!" The charm which he felt, which he described exactly in this epigram, was the charm of genius; of the genius of the stage. So stage lovers must be handsome, like Laferrière, or look so, like Delaunay. The public, like their sweethearts, must fall in love with them at first sight; they must belong to the class who are worshiped from their cradles. Not that all love need be confined to them. On the contrary, one sees every day in our modern plays persons far less gifted outwardly than these *jeunes premiers* rob them in the long run of their myrtles and laurels. But only in the long run. Never at once. They win love by their genius, by their courage, by their devotion, and this love only grows with time, and the audience has gradually to get accustomed to the idea of it.

To take myself as an example, if I may be allowed to do such a thing, the audience would never for a moment suffer that on my entrance on the stage in the first act, I should receive a declaration of love from a beautiful woman.

I have, however, acted Jean Dacier, where I ended by being loved by a girl of noble birth. But I did not receive her confession till the last act, and then only because I was at the point of death. But it was love that gave the piece its success, and the public accepted it and watched its progress with interest, because, plow boy as I was in the first act, then soldier, and finally officer, I raised myself from one height of devotion to another, till I merited the supreme honor of being loved by my wife; for the lady was my wife.

I have been bitterly reproached by many critics for wishing

to play serious parts. On this point my artistic conscience is perfectly easy. I have never played parts which were beyond me. No one ever saw me act a lover. Jean Dacier is a character. Who could call Le Luthier de Crémone a lover? He is a humpback whom nobody loves. And Chamillac? He is an eccentric person, a sort of mustached apostle, who atones for a moment of madness, and who wins love indeed, but only in the end. It is a part full of reserve and capable of expression, but without the excitement of passion. And Gringoire, the unlucky poet condemned to the gallows, can *he* be called a lover? The very first *word* he hears from the girl when her eyes are directed to him is, *"Il n'est pas beau."* This is the position, and if I succeed in the end in winning love, it is with the help of poetry and of pity; it is that I am transformed by the aid of song, at any rate in the fancy of the maiden.

There is a race of actors who cannot get outside the limits of prose, others who are bound to be lyrical. I have done my best to belong to the latter class, and it is partly owing to my friends among the poets who have so often intrusted their verses to me. The most culpable of all is the most lyrical of all—Banville, the father of Gringoire, for whose divine Socrates and many other winged strophes it has been my happy lot to win applause—strophes instinct with the eternal dawn which glows in the heart of their author.

v

It is obvious that this essay rests on the theory with which I started, that in the actor the first self should be the master of the second; that the part of us which *sees* should rule as absolutely as possible the part of us which *executes*. Though this is always true, it is specially true of the moment of representation. In other words, the actor should remain master of himself. Even when the public, carried away by his action, conceives him to be abandoned to his passion, he should be able to *see* what he is doing, to judge of his effects, and to control himself—in short, he should never feel the shadow of the sentiments to which he is giving expression at the very instant that he is representing them with the utmost power and truth.

I will not return to what I have already said on this subject in "Art and the Actor," but I emphatically repeat it. Study your part, make yourself one with your character, but in doing this never set aside your own individuality. Keep the control of yourself. Whether your second self weeps or laughs, whether you become frenzied to madness or suffer the pains of death, it must always be under the watchful eye of your ever-impassive first self, and within certain fixed and pre-scribed bounds.

The best mode of representing a part once decided on, it should henceforth never vary. You must grasp your concep-tion in such a manner as to be able to recall the image you have created, identical down to the minutest particular, when and where you please.

The actor ought never to let his part "run away" with him. It is false and ridiculous to think that it is a proof of the highest art for the actor to forget that he is before the public. If you identify yourself with your part to the point of asking yourself, as you look at the audience, "What are all those people doing here?"—if you have no more con-sciousness where you are and what you are doing—you have ceased to be an actor: you are a madman. And a dangerous madman too. Conceive Harpagon climbing the balustrade and seizing the orchestra by the throats, loudly demanding the restoration of his casket!

Art is, I repeat, not identification, but representation.

The famous maxim, If you wish to make me cry, you must cry yourself, is therefore not applicable to the actor. If he has really to cry, he would, more likely than not, make his audience laugh; for tragedy often becomes comedy to the spectators, and sorrow frequently expresses itself in a grimace.

I can quite well understand how a young man on his first appearance should lose himself in his part and get *run away* with. Uneasy as to his reception by the public, the emotions which he has to represent become confounded with his personal feelings. This has occurred to me as well as to every-one else, and I can recall it without shame, for I was then only seventeen years old. I was acting in public for the first time, and my part was Pauvre Jacques. Pauvre Jacques is an unhappy musician who goes mad from being crossed in love (another proof that I was early corrupted by my prefer-ence for tragic parts). I was suffocated with emotion; still I managed somehow to act, and perhaps some of the audience were moved to tears, but when I went behind the scenes I know I felt quite ill. This is the way with all raw recruits. But if it were to happen to me today, I should consider myself dishonored. A practiced actor should be beyond the reach of such accidents.

I am aware that this theory has been questioned by many great artists. I remember an intelligent and appropriate remark made on the subject to Madame Ristori by a young English lady full of artistic instincts. Madame Ristori was arguing that the actor could only represent truly what he was really feeling. "But, madame," said Miss T——, "what happens when you have to die?" Plainly Madame Ristori had no intention of really dying. She acted as if she were dying, and acted extremely well, for she had previously studied, considered, and determined the manner of her death, and when the moment of representation came, she rendered her fixed impressions with all her wonderful intelligence, with the full force of her vigor and of her self-possession.

Occasionally an actor who is completely master of himself may indulge in experiments before the public, for he knows that he has himself in hand, and can always pull up. Those who have not their faculties perfectly under control run a great risk of losing their heads and not being able to regain their self-possession for the rest of the evening. And the worst of it is that it is invariably those actors who are always trying new tricks. As they never have a firm grip of their character, they are incessantly experimenting on it. They even go the length of glorying in the fact. I once overheard some-one say of Worms, "I don't care to see him act; I know exactly what he is going to do." At any rate, the speaker might have known that everything Worms did would be done well, and, after all, is not that the chief thing? It is more satisfactory than to watch an actor who, for all we know, will be perpetrating some folly the next minute. That reminds one of the Englishman who followed Batty, the lion tamer, from place to place in the hope of one day seeing him torn in pieces by his own lions. The interest of the theatre appears to me to be of quite another kind.

VI

There still remains the delicate question, how far great intelligence is necessary to the actor. There is much to be said on both sides. Examples are by no means rare of actors and actresses who have varied talents. Many are distinguished in literature, in painting, and in both, not to mention in ballooning.

But, after all, this intelligence is a superfluous luxury; the only intelligence indispensable to the actor is *that which belongs to his art.*

Someone, I forget who, once told me that the only French poetry Corot knew was *Polyeucte,* and he had never read all of that. But this did not prevent him from being a wonderful landscape painter and a poet down to the tip of his brush. In the same way an actor may be totally ignorant of painting, of music, of poetry even, and yet be a good actor, and a poetical actor. It is enough for him to be steeped in his own art, which is different from these others.

And though it is different, it is equally important, and it is unfair to scoff at the special intelligence of the actor. The faculties which can touch and move men are by no means to be despised. And it is not the case that it is the author alone who gives rise to these emotions. To those who hold this I would instance Talma, Frédérick, and multitudes of others who created their own parts out of what was originally absolutely insignificant. It was to their skill and genius alone that the public owed that profound, almost divine, trouble which seizes all of us when we contemplate beauty which rends for the moment the veil of our egotism, and which is the sensation that approaches most nearly to love.

It has been said of endless pieces, "What an absurd play, but wasn't Frédérick magnificent!" Take Robert Macaire, to which I have already alluded—was not the creation of this character a prodigy, showing to what heights an actor's special intelligence can rise? The very authors were the first to be struck dumb at this astonishing conception, which substituted for their solemn puppet an imperishable comic figure.

The dramatic art is, above all, the art of humanity, and this is what makes a play the highest of pleasures, the pleasure which moves the people most powerfully, while it offers to the refined the most exquisite enjoyments. In my opinion, therefore, it should always remain an *art;* that is, it should add the sweetness of poetry and the representation of the ideal to the expression of truth.

"Naturalism" on the stage is a mistake. In the first place the public won't have it. It always resents the exhibition of revolting hideousness, of pitiless and naked realities. People do not come to the theatre for that sort of thing. Even in parts that are vile and degraded they demand a gleam of ideality. Paulin-Ménier as Choppard appears at first revolting in his debased realism, but it is not so. There is a certain reckless touch about the character which does something to redeem it: *"Eh bien! quoi prenez ma tête—c'est pas un fameux cadeau que je vous fais là!"* How defiance was hurled at Death! his power was mocked at. It was the gleam of the ideal.

Just as I would not allow any departure from truth on the plea of picturesque effects, so I would not permit a representation of commonplace or horrible things on the pretext of reality. I am always on the side of nature, and against naturalism.

Nature in art! How much there is to say about it! It is a subject that is understood differently according to the country and the century. When Garrick came over to France he admired our actors greatly, but thought they were hardly natural enough. Perhaps some one will say the reason was that they were acting tragedies. But when Talma appeared he introduced into tragedy a natural manner of speaking and moving, and it was to this that he owed his influence and his success. Was his idea of what was natural the same as Garrick's? I do not know; for the genius of the two races is very different, and the love of originality it too deep-seated in our neighbors to allow them always to use a due measure of self-restraint; and anyway today it is we who find fault with Irving for not being sufficiently natural. The English idea of "nature" does not correspond with ours: that is the whole truth of the matter. We must also make reserves as to the German conception of nature, unnaturally tearful, resembling in its philosophic affectations the "nature" of Diderot and the susceptible school at the end of the eighteenth century.

It was they who, we must remind our readers, were really the innovators. The style which to our ears rings so false was introduced by them to the stage in the name of "nature." And it was likewise in the name of nature that the standard of the romanticists was raised—a standard which today is thrown aside and trampled in the dust by those who are weary of grandiloquence and of posing. They desired to substitute for conventional tragedy a drama which is really human, in which smiles and tears are mingled, and gave us *Antony, La Tour de Nesle, Lucrèce Borgia.* With the same object in view, Baron Taylor collaborated with the well-known and delightful Nodier and put on the stage *Melmoth, ou l'Homme errant, Les Vampires, Honte et Remords, Amour et Étourderie,* etc. These were obviously "natural" in quite another sense from that of Voltaire; and the actors, making common cause with the authors, declared Talma to be unnatural. They took it into their heads to speak as people "really speak," in such a way that no one could hear them, and to sit with their backs to the audience. They recited the poetry of *Athalie* precisely as they would have said, "Good morning, how are you?" "Good heavens, yes," said Abner, "I have come to worship the Almighty in His temple. I have come just as I am, cane in hand, to celebrate with my friends the famous occasion on Mount Sinai, where, if I am not vastly mistaken, the law was given to us. *Sapristi!* how times have changed!" They flattered themselves that in this manner they were introducing "nature" into Racine. On the other hand, when they were on their own ground—that is, in the melodramas—the emphasis of the meter once more reasserted itself. It was not indeed the sepulchral and monotonous singsong of yore; it was a halting kind of sublimity—wild bursts of verse, and a sudden alacrity in sinking. They no longer said, "How are you?" but "Let me grasp that manly hand." There were hidden meanings everywhere. They wore an air of doom from head to foot. It was an era of hat and feather. But is there no feather on the hat of M. Zola? Were he to have his way we should be threatened with a new madness of extremes, but this time it would be the extreme of the trivial and commonplace. What I mean by art that is natural in the modern sense is equally remote from both these extremes. It is classic rather than romantic, for everywhere it regards limit, everywhere it shuns violent antitheses.

The actor with this ideal does not give an exaggerated importance to different aspects of his part. He does not try to play three or four different characters at once; he aims, on the other hand, at unity and a broad general representation of humanity. He sees things as they are, but he conforms to the general rules of theatrical conventions and to the particular necessities of the part he is interpreting. The "nature" of the tragedy differs from that of the melodrama, and that again from the comedy, and it is impossible to render it in the same way. Hence Frédérick ought never to be reproached for not acting always naturally. The kind of parts he undertook demanded certain exaggerations. He would, after the manner of his school, speak ten lines in a conventional fashion, in order to be able to give to the eleventh a truer and more natural ring. He was forced to say the verses as they were written, and when he at last made his point with the true intonation, it left behind it a deeper impression of naturalness than the foregoing lines had done of unreality.

And here I must close, for this is not a formal treatise on acting, still less an apology. Every artist in speaking of his art seems in some degree a special pleader. Of course he only wishes to preach what he believes to be true, and that which he believes to be true is what he tries to do himself. I have said what the comedian should be, but I am far from flattering myself that I realize my ideal, and if I have alluded to myself, it is only for the sake of illustrating more clearly my arguments. I should have preferred to erase any personal note from these pages, as I have always tried to do from my parts, where my wish is to be, to enter into, nothing but the characters I play. For, after all, that is the essential point, and it is with that I must end. Is not the greatest poet he who has managed to efface himself the most entirely, in whose pages you find every kind of man, but never himself?

It was thus with the father of poetry, Homer; it was thus with Shakespeare and with Molière: all are absent from their works, where humanity in its thousand varied aspects lives eternally.

Herein standeth our honor, the honor of all us players: namely, in this, that these two men, its chief creators after God, were players like ourselves. Therefore should we study their works religiously and without ceasing, nor ever turn from them, save it be to peruse that eternal Comedy of Human Nature.

CONSTANT COQUELIN

II

M. COQUELIN ON ACTORS AND ACTING

It is some years since I had the privilege of recording in this review a few casual observations connected with the Drama. They related chiefly to characters in Shakespeare, and had no personal drift. My renewal of them now is suggested by the article which M. Coquelin has contributed to the May number of *Harper's Magazine,* and by certain personal considerations which are an inevitable result when one player has undertaken to criticise his fellows. As a rule, this kind of review is much to be deprecated, for it is easy to conceive that, if every artist were to rush into print with his opinions of his compeers, there would be a disagreeable rise in the social temperature. Criticism is generally sufficient in the hands of the professors of the art; but when an actor takes up its functions for the enlightenment of other actors, and, with the freedom of M. Coquelin, invites comparisons and suggests parallels, he runs no little risk of a grave misapprehension of his purpose. I take it for granted, however, that in this instance the object of the writer is to lay down certain immutable principles of the actor's art.

I do not propose to follow M. Coquelin through the details of his thesis, which contains a comforting proportion of truisms. Nor is it necessary to devote much space to the initial difficulty—which, by the way, he only discovers at the end of his discourse—namely, the difference between English and French ideas of natural acting. This difference may be considerable enough, but it need not be made greater by hasty generalisation. Even my insular training does not, I hope, disqualify me from an intelligent admiration of M. Coquelin's genuine accomplishments; nor does it, I venture to think, blunt my perception of the misdirected zeal with which he associates the elements necessary to make up the art of what he calls true portraiture. In a word, I believe that he completely misses the vital essence of tragedy, and that his criticism is of the earth, earthy.

It is hardly within the scope of this note that I should discuss with M. Coquelin as to how far the resources of a comedian may be suitable for tragic parts. There seems to be a deep-rooted conviction in his mind that the qualities which enable an actor to observe certain types of character, and to embody their salient features in a consistent whole, will invariably enable him to scale the heights of the poetic drama. But the most odd feature of this assumption is his labour to prove that an actor must give to each character a separate physiological maintenance, so that every fresh impersonation may begin the world with a new voice and a new body. That an artist, with an individuality so marked as M. Coquelin's, should imagine that his identity can be entirely lost seems singular. It must be granted that this art of transformation, even in part, is of great importance in that large range of the drama where M. Coquelin is quite at home, and where the purely mimetic faculty has its chief significance. When, however, we are asked to believe that the representation of a great tragic part depends on the simulation of a physical apparatus which the actor has not previously exhibited, we must seek refuge in a respectful incredulity. It would almost seem as if M. Coquelin, in the midst of his dissertation on the significance of a wrinkle, had lost sight of the fact that in tragedy and the poetic drama it is rather the *soul* of the artist than his form which is moulded by the theme. Edmund Kean sometimes passed from one part to another with little more external variation than was suggested by a corked mustache; but the poetry, the intensity, the fiery passion of the man made his acting the most real and vivid impersonation that his contemporaries had seen. M. Coquelin perhaps takes it for granted that the actress is exempt from the burden of change—the perpetual metamorphosis—to which he dooms the actor. If there be no such exemption, then the task of the artist who must vary her face and figure for Rosalind, Juliet, and Imogen is likely to become unpopular. What did Rachel owe to any transformation of physique? She, as M. Coquelin must be well aware, was the most trained actress of her time. She knew all that Samson could teach; she spared no elaboration of art; but all this experience and labour would have counted for little without the divine fire which made her so great. This electric quality is the rarest and the highest gift the actor can possess. It is a quality which, in varying degrees, distinguishes those who tread the highest walks in the drama, and which has given fame to-day to Salvini, Barnay, Booth, and Mounet-Sully.

When M. Coquelin maintains that an actor should never exhibit real emotion, he is treading old and disputed grounds. It matters little whether the player shed tears or not, so long as he can make his audience shed them; but if tears can be summoned at his will and subject to his control, it is true art to utilise such a power, and happy is the actor whose sensibility has at once so great a delicacy and discipline. In this respect the actor is like the orator. Eloquence is all the more moving when it is animated and directed by a fine and subtle sympathy which affects the speaker though it does not master him. It is futile to deny absolutely to the actor such impulses as touch the heart by the sudden appeal of passion or pathos. Kean was not a player who left anything to hazard, and yet he had inspired moments, which anyone holding M. Coquelin's views might ascribe to insanity. Diderot and Talma pointed out, and M. Coquelin repeats the lesson, that an actor has a dual consciousness—the inspiring and directing self, and the executive self. Yet it was also Talma who remarked that an actor will often leave the stage at the end of a scene trying to remember what he has done, instead of thinking what he has still to do. This, at all events, is idealism in art, and my complaint of M. Coquelin is that he seems to allow to idealism only a very small place in his philosophy. Not the least striking illustration of this defect is his proposition that a hideous soul should have a hideous body, and that Mephistopheles should therefore be represented as an image of deformity. History and fiction alike rebel against such a dictum; for, if this critic be right, then the Borgias, Iago, Macbeth, Tito, Ulric should embody moral disease in their physical tissue. It is true that Mephistopheles need not be a handsome demon, but why should a hump be a symbol of cynicism? Some of the most exquisite spirits that ever reflected the radiance of divine love upon earth have been shrouded in ugliness! The greatest infamy in Italian history smiles down upon us in old picture galleries from the perfection of manly dignity and the most delicate loveliness of woman. M. Coquelin's conception is as primitive as the orthodoxy which used to insist that the devil wore horns and a tail. The demand that the incarnation of evil shall be pre-eminently distinguished by physical distortion is, to say the least of it, scarcely in harmony with the enlightenment of our age. *Faust* is a mixture of legend and philosophy—a great human drama, with the intense reality of life over-shadowed by the supernatural. Mephistopheles is both man and spirit, and should not the actor suggest to the imagina-tion of the spectators an almost exaggerated idea of the commanding, all-embracing influence of the evil principle, while presenting the personality of the "squire of high degree"? It is imposible to represent such a creation in any adequate fashion without summoning picturesque aids to heighten the spiritual effect of the play. To what extent the picturesque may be legitimately carried in dramatic art will always be a moot point. "Picturesque" is a word often used vaguely, but if it mean beauty—the selection of what is pleasing and harmonious in illustration—then by all means let us be picturesque. To discard this element in action, colour, and expression would surely be a serious error. I fear that if I understand M. Coquelin aright, his philosophy is much more material than would be expected from an actor who tells us that he is nothing if not "lyrical."

There is, of course, much in M. Coquelin's article that is true and that is admirably put—notwithstanding that he fre-quently upsets in one paragraph the proposition of another. Nobody would deny that the study of character is the founda-tion of our art, or that the detail which is foreign to a char-acter ought not to be presented for the sake of theatrical effect. But the essay is not a primer for beginners, it is ad-dressed to the writer's colleagues and contemporaries. It deals out praise in this quarter and blame in that, and it has a strong flavour of autobiography. This distinguished comedian scarcely does justice to his intelligence when he forgets that no two actors of any originality will play the same part alike. An actor must either think for himself or imitate someone else. Such imitation produces a reverence for certain stage traditions that is sometimes mischievous, because an actor is tempted to school himself too closely to traditional interpreta-tion, instead of giving fair play to his own insight. Probably it is of our departure from this rule that M. Coquelin is thinking when he sighs over "the deep-seated love of orig-inality" in the English race. But that originality, after all, is only the very natural assertion of the principle that the representation of character can never be cast in one unchanging mould. The individual force of the actor must find its special channel. Salvini's Othello is a great impersonation, but judging from all we know of Edmund Kean's performance of the Moor, it differed widely from the Italian's. There seem to be no difficult problems in Othello's character, and yet it would be idle to expect a succession of great actors to play the part in precisely the same way. M. Coquelin divides actors into two classes—those who identify themselves with their characters, and those who identify their characters with themselves. Excellent as this definition is, it is somewhat misleading. M. Coquelin tells us that when he played Thouvenin it was his greatest difficulty to repress his own idiosyncrasies. His study was to efface Coquelin entirely—voice, walk, gesture—and to present only the man he conceived Thouvenin to be. This is very good as far as it goes; but why should Edwin Booth, when he acts the part of Hamlet, try to forget that, physically speaking, he was ever Edwin Booth? His mind is absorbed in the character—he looks and speaks the melancholy, the passion, the poetry, and the satire of this supreme creation; yet is he to be told that, if in some detail of aspect, gesture, or movement, he remind the audience that he is still Edwin Booth, he is making the character a part of himself, instead of losing his own nature for the time in the world of imagination? The actor who portrays with the grandest power the Titanic force and energy of Lear, or the malignity and hypocrisy of Shylock, will be truer to the poet than another who interests us chiefly in the characteristics of age or a type of the Jewish race. M. Coquelin would, I fear, in tragedy teach us to be too prosaic; for however important realistic portraiture may be in the comic drama—and there are noteworthy examples of its success on the English as well as the French stage—in tragedy it has a comparatively minor place.

HENRY IRVING

III

COQUELIN—IRVING

M. Coquelin is an accomplished comedian whose great natural gifts were cultivated in the College of the Histrionic Art, the Comédie-Française, where he graduated as a star.

Mr. Irving is a comedian who has had no collegiate training for the stage, as there is no school of art in England.

The Frenchman, therefore, acquired his principles before he acquired his experience. The Englishman acquired his practice, from which he deduced his principles. These two artists discuss the pathology of tragedy. They describe the artistic process by which the tragic actor embodies the passions delineated by the tragic poet.

We cannot regard Mr. Irving as a tragedian. He is a versatile character actor, who, like Frédérick Lemaître, plays everything, but shines chiefly in character parts. Frédérick was equally great in *Ruy Blas* and *Robert Macaire*; Irving is equally great in *Louis the Eleventh* and *Jeremy Diddler*. But Frédérick was not a Talma, and Irving is not an Edmund Kean.

It is questionable, therefore, whether these two eminent artists are equipped with experience of the kind required to pass judgment on this matter. Let us see!

Comedy aspires to portray by imitation the *weaknesses* to which human beings are subject; and, it may be, to correct such frailties by their exposure to our ridicule. Character, in our dramatic sense, is the distinction between individuals, and it is exhibited by *the manner* in which each bears and expresses his or her trouble, or deals with his neighbours.

Tragedy aspires to portray the *passions* to which strong natures are subject, and a resistance to their influence. But strong natures exhibit no distinctive character. Heroes are monotonous. Othello, Richard, Macbeth, Lear, Hamlet are great sufferers from various causes, but they suffer alike; they all cry in the same histrionic key. Edwin Booth, Forrest, Macready, Kean, Salvini always presented the same man in a different costume. Rachel was always Rachel. Bernhardt is always Bernhardt. But Irving in *Louis the Eleventh* is not Irving in *Mephistopheles*. Coquelin in *Le Luthier de Crémone* is not Coquelin in the *Duc de Septmonts*.

We may surmise, therefore, that as the object of the comedian differs so diametrically from the object of the tragedian, the principles and the practice of one of these branches of the same art may not be applicable to the other.

M. Coquelin denies poetic afflatus and impulsive effusion to the tragedian. He claims that every feature in the actor's face, every note in his voice must be under his complete control, as the musical instrument is to the performer. In this opinion he is backed by Shakespeare, who counsels the tragedian "in the torrent and tempest of his passions to beget a temperance that will give it smoothness." But it may be said this is, meaningly, an advice to repress rant.

May I, without intrusion, exemplify from personal experience the action of the mind under the two different affections while engaged in tragic and comic composition? While writing comedy the mind of the dramatist is circumspect and calculating, careful in the selection of thoughts, a fastidious spectator of the details of his work, thoroughly self-conscious and deliberate. Such is not the condition of his mind when writing tragic scenes, or scenes of deep pathos. The mind of the poet becomes abstract, his thoughts shape themselves into language—the passion wields his pen. The utterance is impulsive —he is an actor, not a spectator in the scene, and when he awakes from this transport of the mind he looks round to recover consciousness of where he is! Surely every author must have experienced this illusion, and under these circumstances. I have never known, in all my experience, that scenes so composed have failed, when fairly acted, to convey a like emotion to the audience.

M. Coquelin says the voice of the heart is inartistic; it must be controlled and moulded by the brain! Yes! in comedy —into which the emotions alluded to never enter, or, if so, in a very modified degree. I am not a tragedian; therefore can only speak with much reserve; but if the poet, under the great impulse of tragic composition, can lose his perfect self-control, and in that state his thoughts shape themselves into exquisite language, if grammar and spelling become instinctive work, as the pen follows the mind without circumspection or aforethought; if this can be with the poet, may it not be likewise with the tragedian? May not the rules and principles of his art be so much a part of his nature that he can give rein to his passional spasm while retaining his seat and control of Pegasus? If he fail to do so, he becomes, I admit, ridiculous; but if he succeed, he mounts to the verge and edge of the sublime. Such a feat can only be safely attempted by the perfectly trained artist. When novices give way to their effusion they inevitably become grotesque.

M. Coquelin describes his method of building up a character. It affords an admirable lesson to comedians, and should be preserved by an imperishable record in the archives of our art. But as comedy is largely a physiological study, tragedy is largely pathologic. Doubtless there are many great tragic figures in the drama that should be treated from the outside, as are the great comic figures; but this part of them is comedy; such for example is the grim comedy of *Louis the Eleventh*. And, in so far and so much, the play is less purely tragic. The process, therefore, so valuably detailed by the French comedian is applicable to comedy only, inasmuch as it is applicable only to the moulding of character, and character belongs to comedy.

Salvini goes so far as to declare that domestic passions, such as love, are beneath the grandeur and dignity of the tragic muse. I suggested that *Othello* and *Lear* and even *Romeo and Juliet* were able to stand beside any works of Sophocles. He could not admit they were so. He regarded them as being on a lower plane.

I concede to M. Coquelin that the tragedian of the day follows the principles he has laid down, but with all the admiration justly due to great merit, I doubt the application of Zolaism to our art. For example: The last scene in *Adrienne Lecouvreur*, as performed by Sarah Bernhardt, exhibits a powerful scene of physical agony. The girl, under the excruciating torture of the poison she has inhaled, dies in convulsions, writhing between her two lovers, moaning over her loss of life, so young, so happy. The spectators watch the throes of death as if they were present at a terrible operation. It is very fine.

Many years ago I witnessed the performance of Rachel in the same play. I remember the gaze of wonder with which she recognized the first symptoms of the poison, then her light struggles against the pain that she would not acknowledge. And when the conviction came that she was dying, her whole soul went out to her young lover—her eyes never left his, her arms clung to *him,* not to life, or only to life because life meant him. There was no vulgar display of physical suffering excepting in her repression of it. And she died with her eyes in his, as though she sent her soul into him.

I have known her pause hysterically in a scene when she heard the barking of a little dog confined in one of the dressing-rooms. If she had herself completely in control, as M. Coquelin describes, so small a matter need not have discomposed her.

Those who have travelled in Italy have seen artists making copies of the celebrated pictures in the galleries at Florence and Rome. I saw before the Beatrice Cenci, in the Barberini Palace, one of the most perfect duplicates imaginable; the minutest examination could not detect a touch in the original that was not reproduced. What was wanting? There was something. Out of the original there came that tender, reproachful, beseeching look that haunted the spectator. It was not in the copy. It marked the difference between talent and genius. There is in all great works an almost imperceptible something so fine that it evades description, sensible rather than palpable, and of that faint, heavenly light the aureole is made.

Surely this exquisite touch of the soul cannot be the effect of cerebro-mechanism such as M. Coquelin describes. May not such a process, applied to great minds, tend to crib, cabin, and confine their effulgence? Is it not just possible that with a little less of this mechanical practice in the Comédie-Française and a little less of admiration for Zola, Sarah would have been a head and shoulders (including her heart) higher than she is?

The dependence of the artist on mechanism, so eloquently and truthfully laid down by M. Coquelin, may be accepted as applicable to comedy and to such parts of tragic plays as may contain an infusion of comedy; but—with great respect to him—no further.

The independence of the artist from mechanism, claimed *per contra* by Mr. Irving, is admirable so far as pure tragedy is concerned, and only in scenes where such effusion is indicated by the eruptive language of the poet, which, if given with mechanical deliberation, might appear beneath the level of the volcanic passion.

DION BOUCICAULT

IV

A REPLY TO MR. HENRY IRVING

I

In the English review *The Nineteenth Century* Mr. Henry Irving has published a reply to the study on "Actors and Acting" which appeared in *Harper's Magazine* last May. The opinion of so distinguished an artist as Mr. Irving could not be a matter of indifference to me; I have therefore read his article with the greatest attention, and I beg leave, as we do not agree, to reply to his reply.

I cannot believe that Mr. Irving was offended by my estimation of his talent. In attempting to define his talent I am not aware that I depreciated it. And this is all the answer I shall make to Mr. Irving's reproach that I have sat in judgment upon my colleagues and contemporaries. I neither judged nor condemned any one. My purpose was to explain various theories. I cited examples, and I made those examples contemporary, because thus their verification was easy. It is only natural that my theory should seem to me to be the best, and in that respect Mr. Irving is not constituted otherwise than I am; but I do not think that I have allowed myself to be carried away so far as to deny the talent of those who profess a different faith from my own. It is likewise, I hasten to say, the doctrine and not the man which Mr. Irving attacks. And he attacks stoutly, and in a tone which at times reaches indignation, as if I had been wanting in respect to that holy of holies which he calls the "poetic drama"; but this vivacity needs no justification; on the contrary, it is most creditable to Mr. Irving, because it shows to what a degree he is passionately devoted to his art.

As for the question whether Mr. Irving really answers my thesis, that is another matter. Did I express myself badly? It is to be feared I did, for in more than one case Mr. Irving seems to have represented me as saying either what I did not say or the contrary of what I said. The only points on which he consents not to combat me are the "truisms," of which, he observes, my essay "contains a comforting proportion." He ought then to admit as a truism what I said on the difference between the English and French ideas of "natural acting." Here I do not pretend to have made any discovery; many more competent writers have advanced these views before me, and Mr. Irving's article, and his talent too, are a new confirmation of their truth.

Yes, the English are above everything "original," and they carry their taste for originality so far as to love even eccentricity. We in France are generalizers; the English, on the other hand, concern themselves chiefly with the individual; I will even say with exceptional individuals. Let us consider their most powerful types. Macbeth is not the universal ambitious man: he is Macbeth, the somnambulist of ambition, a fatal, strange, unique figure. Othello is not the type of the jealous man, the same as Venice or at Cyprus as in all other latitudes: he is a particular jealous man—jealous as a man can be who partakes of the nature of a hero and of a child, and who, like this noble Moor, combines the candor of a primitive soul with the sudden and formidable impetuosity of African blood. And so with the others. The characters of Shakespeare are individuals, profoundly human, without doubt, but nevertheless exceptional. And perhaps that is excellent in drama, for as drama sets man struggling with destiny, the more powerfully organized are the beings whom it depicts smitten down by fate, the more soul-stirring and striking is the lesson.

Comedy, on the contrary, knows no other fatality than the

logic of the characters; it depicts the usual course of things—common life, and men as they really are; it lives on generalities. And it is in this point that Molière triumphs. While the great English comic writer Ben Jonson delights to paint odd people—individuals and not types, *humors* and not characters—Molière puts on the stage general personages who are universally true and who live our own daily life; it is our humanity, ourselves as we are. There is nothing excessive in them, and nothing eccentric. The same is the case with our tragic personages. The characters of Racine, and even the characters of Corneille, in spite of the poet's austere personal accent, are more general than those of Shakespeare. There are none of those spurts of individuality which give such exorbitant relief to the grand figures of the English poet. As in antique art, our characters keep in the ranks; they remain in the tone of the whole, which is harmony and measure. Drama, I repeat, perhaps demands more. But this is a fact, and a fact which, to my mind, reveals the difference in the genius of the two races. Let Mr. Irving play Nero in Racine's tragedy of *Britannicus*: I am sure he will feel how impossible it is to give to this terrible jealous emperor the transports of an Othello. Even in their fury our heroes do not know wild excess.

It is natural that this difference in the manner of conception should recur in the manner of rendering a character. English comedians, as it seems to me, are like English writers: their chief care is originality. Mr. Irving will not contradict me, for his whole article is, after all, nothing more than a claim in favor of this precious quality. He fears that my theories may smother originality by casting representation of character "in one unchanging mould," and so he pleads vigorously for personal inspiration against tradition. This in reality is the true reason of our disagreement. Mr. Irving represents genius as independent and solitary, deriving everything from itself, or receiving from above certain sudden enlightenment, thanks to a special quality which he calls "electric," and which "distinguishes superior artists," or, in other words, idealists. I represent, or endeavor to represent, prosaically perhaps, but passionately also, that *ensemble* of traditions which constitutes the Comédie-Française, that mass of accumulated observations, that inheritance of those who have gone before, by which the newcomers profit—the results of two centuries of study placed at the service of those who are beginning. Mr. Irving maintains that respect for this glorious past leads to imitation, is an obstacle to free personal inspiration, and, in a word, kills all individuality. This may be true for actors of second or third rank (though at any rate the system has the result of rendering them endurable, which is something); but for actors of talent, no. Great actors have not been wanting at the Comédie-Française: have there been two alike? Did Talma resemble Lekain? Did Samson stifle the genius of Rachel? Genius always makes its way. Far from obstructing true originality, study develops it and sets it off to advantage; it removes that rust of oddness, of exaggeration, and of convention which so often clings to originality, and which would end by spoiling it; study polishes the blade and renders it more brilliant. Mr. Irving, speaking of Rachel—it is he who cites this example—says that she knew all of her art that could be taught, and that she elaborated her roles with the utmost care; but that all this "experience and labor would have counted for little without the divine fire which made her so great." If it counted for little, why should she have imposed upon herself this overwhelming labor? To say that the "divine fire" is everything is to say too much or too little. Without the "divine fire" a man cannot be an artist, but the "divine fire" is not equivalent to innate omniscience. It does not give an actor diction, nor does it teach him how to compose a role. And what is an artist without diction and composition? With the "divine fire" alone, and no study, an artist is necessarily incomplete, odd, capable here and there of fine bursts, but oftener of false cries and mistaken movements. Work alone makes an accomplished artist.

In reality, this, I am convinced, is Mr. Irving's own opinion. He is probably also of my opinion on the question whether an actor ought actually to feel the emotions which he represents. He does not pronounce clearly, it is true; he even quotes an anecdote which seems to refute the theory of absolute self-possession. But the reason is that if he frankly adopted this theory, Mr. Irving would be afraid of seeming to condemn those sudden inspirations, those flashes of enlightenment, which he holds to be the mark of genius, and which happen spontaneously on the stage. He cites Kean, who was certainly not a "player who left anything to hazard," and who yet had "inspired moments." Kean was not the only one. Frédéric Lemaître also had "inspired moments." But let Mr. Irving read my essay over again, and he will see that I by no means deny inspiration. I said precisely that when one is sure of a role, when, like Kean, one leaves nothing to hazard, then indeed one can without inconvenience try some of those traits which are suggested by the heat of the representation. What I protest against is the idea that one can be inspired in a role which one has not studied, and the belief that one is inspired when one is merely extravagant. The "electric quality" was possessed by Talma in the divinest degree, but it was always by the simplest means that he made this quality produce the most powerful effects. When he exclaimed as Oreste (Racine's *Andromaque*), "Dieux! quels ruisseaux de sang coulent autour de moi!" (Heavens! what streams of blood flow around me!) he did not begin to stride about the stage toward the four cardinal points; he brought his legs together tightly, one against the other, his elbows clung closely to his body, his ribs shrank in, his shoulders rose in a movement of inexpressible horror, and almost without moving he became terrible. There is nothing supernatural in our art, and inspiration, far from being infallible, may often be mistaken. Frédérick had admirable inspirations, but he also had inspirations sometimes so wild that he had to ask pardon of the public.

On the other hand, a second-rate actor, carried along by his part or excited by some particular circumstance, may have one of those movements of inspiration which produce the illusion of genius; in vain afterward he will try to recall the flame; he will remain Gros Jean just as he was before. It is not therefore very reasonable, in my opinion, to represent inspiration as the essential mark which distinguishes superior artists. The question, for that matter, is of small importance to the public. By what token shall the spectator know whether such and such a thrilling cry has just been hit upon by the actor there on the spot, or whether it has been tried, thought over, learnt, and repeated a hundred times beforehand?

Does Mr. Irving mean to maintain that the cry found on the stage by inspiration will be for that very reason infallibly truer and finer than the other? The whole history of dramatic art would rise in protestation against such an assertion. But behold! because I deny the divinity of inspiration I am once more arraigned and convicted of materialism. Yes: Mr. Irving has discovered that I am a materialist in art, and his chief ground for this conclusion is the importance, as he thinks excessive, which I attribute to physical exterior. He represents me as maintaining that every tragic impersonation imperatively demands a new body and a new voice, absolutely different from the voice and body which the artist has previously employed. Alas! I said on the contrary that this was the unattainable ideal, and I dwelt at length on the obstacles which the physical construction of an actor opposes to his playing certain parts which otherwise his intelligence would render him capable of undertaking. What I said, and what

I repeat once more, is that an actor must modify his gait, his general bearing, and, if he can, his voice according to the character of the role. I cannot admit that Charles I be made to walk and to talk like Mathias in *The Bells*, like Hamlet, and like Iago. Mr. Irving, I observe, is somewhat negligent in this matter; but still he sometimes conforms: he changes his voice for Louis XI, for instance: this being so, I fail to comprehend why he plays Mephistopheles with the voice of Romeo. Do those differences prevent being as poetic and sublime as is desirable? In no way. For the matter of that, they are obtained by profoundly studying the role, which I recommend the actor to do before everything else; for, far from having forgotten the soul of the role for the exterior, I said, and I repeat, that the actor must first become penetrated with the essence of his personage, that he must in a way swallow and digest it, and when once he has assimilated it, the exterior will follow of itself quite naturally. *It is the mind which constructs the body*, I said. I do not see that this axiom is so materialistic. Mr. Irving cites Kean, "who sometimes passed from one character to another with little more external variation than was suggested by a corked mustache," but whose impersonations were nevertheless most real and vivid. This does not astonish me at all; I consider it to be the perfection of art. I will, however, answer two things: the first is that on the stage Kean, in order to pass from Romeo to Richard III, did not limit himself to so summary an exterior modification; and the second is that even in drawing rooms he did not remain the same man in the two roles. I guarantee that his voice changed, that, ardent and passionate in Romeo, it became sarcastic and crafty to express Richard; that in the same way his breast, instead of being broad, manly, and throbbing, shrank up; that his shoulder grew humpy; that his attitude became cringing; and that when he drew himself up it was with the movements of a serpent. And this I imagine did not impair the poetry of Shakespeare.

"But," says Mr. Irving, "you affirm that a hideous soul should have a hideous body, and that Mephistopheles should therefore be represented as an image of deformity; a conception," he adds, "scarcely in harmony with the enlightenment of our age, and as primitive as the orthodoxy which used to insist that the devil wore horns and a tail." And Mr. Irving takes the trouble to remind me of a number of historical personages whose portraits fill the old picture galleries, and who were consummate scoundrels while being at the same time very handsome men. This is the brilliant passage of his article. But what is the drift of it all? What have we to do here with "the enlightenment of our age"? Was Mephistopheles a personage of our times? Is it my fault if the Middle Ages, which created the character, made him deformed, obeying therein an old human tendency of which there still remains something, whatever Mr. Irving may say to the contrary? Is it my fault if Goethe conformed with the legend? For in plain words Mephisto's cloven foot is mentioned twenty times in *Faust*, and his walk must evidently be affected by this peculiarity. Does not Marguerite conceive a horror of him on account of his ugliness? I did not find it contrary to the spirit of the role when I saw Levinski represent Mephistopheles with a slight hump on his back; not because, as Mr. Irving thinks, a hump is to my mind "a symbol of cynicism," but because, according to popular prejudices, it always implies wit and often malice, two characteristics which cannot be denied to Mephisto, and to which Levinsky gives extraordinary relief. In other respects, the attention of this remarkable artist has been especially directed to the negative side of the role. Mephisto is the one who says "No." His role is to disgust Faust with action by showing him its nothingness. Irony and sarcasm are his arms, and Levinsky manages these arms superlatively. The more vivid the expression given to the universal influence of the evil innate in Mephisto, and the more formidable and terrible he is rendered —and in this Mr. Irving succeeds marvelously—the better; but I think it is a mistake to make him handsome, inasmuch as both the author and the legend represent him otherwise.

I will not insist upon another error made by Mr. Irving in his adaptation of Goethe's masterpiece. This error is not absolutely imputable to the actor; it is imposed upon the actor by the theatrical manager. The error I allude to is the almost complete annihilation of the role of Faust. If it is difficult, as the saying is, to conceive *Hamlet* without the Prince of Denmark, it seems no less difficult to play *Faust* without Faust. But this is almost what Mr. Irving is doing. And the explanation is obvious. The manager having at hand for Mephistopheles an exceptional actor, and having no such actor for Faust, solved the difficulty by sacrificing the latter role. The result is that the piece does what Mephisto does not: it limps. Mr. Irving does not seem to have noticed this fact, and the authority of his general observations on the work is detracted from all the more as manager and actor are in this case one and the same person, namely, Mr. Irving himself.

The special point of view of the manager is revealed in

Mr. Irving's article in other remarks, also at the expense, I think, of the point of view of the actor. For instance, after having accused me of materialism on account of the attention I pay to the exterior of the actor, he takes up against me the defense of those "picturesque aids" which, he says, heighten the effect of the action and contribute to its beauty. But is it not precisely these picturesque aids which contribute to complete that physical exterior about which, in his opinion, I take too much trouble? It seems to me—with all due respect be it said—that Mr. Irving is here contradicting himself for the mere pleasure of contradicting me.

Evidently, whether he employ picturesque aids, or whether he confine himself to the resources of his admirable talent, Mr. Irving seeks in the highest degree to mark all his roles with his personal stamp and seal. He means to remain Mr. Irving in all his creations, and he cannot understand why I advise him in certain roles to efface as much as possible his own personality in order to bring forward conspicuously the personality of the character he is playing. "What!" he says: "here is Edwin Booth, who plays Hamlet. He looks and speaks the melancholy, the passion, the poetry, and the satire of this supreme creation; yet is he to be told that if in some detail of aspect, gesture, or movement he remind the audience that he is still Edwin Booth, he is making the character a part of himself, instead of losing his own nature for the time in the world of imagination?"

By no means. We should have to say that only if he disfigured the role in order to get possession of it, and if he substituted his own personality for that of his personage. The mind of the spectator undergoes a kind of reduplication similar to that of the actor. Just as the actor is at once his personage and the person who plays it, so the man who listens to him is at once the spectator, I might almost say the dupe, who allows himself to be transported into the passions of this personage, who feels them, shudders at them, or weeps at them, and at the same time he is the critic who knows that he has before his eyes an artist, and who, as the case may be, applauds or hisses that artist. And a still more curious thing is that the more the spectator sees the personage, and the more complete the illusion, the more the critic applauds the actor. Edwin Booth is never so loudly applauded as when he is exclusively Hamlet; and for that matter I am told that this is always the case. If he reminded the spectator too frequently that he is Booth and not the Prince of Denmark, the illusion would be broken, and pleasure would consequently become impossible for the listener-spectator, who would soon communicate his coldness to the listener-critic, and the actor would suffer for his fault.

Mr. Irving ends his article with the Parthian arrow that *realistic portraiture,* so important in the comic drama, occupies a comparatively minor place in tragedy. The consequence, which he does not object to indicate, is that those who are most skillful in this realistic portraiture—which, by the way, is nothing less than the exact and living representation of characters—may be perfectly incapable of rising to the heights of poetic drama. And such, alas! would be my case.

This sentence must have been passed in a moment of that divine inspiration which Mr. Irving makes out to be the privilege of superior artists, for he dispenses with mentioning human reasons in support of his verdict. It becomes me, therefore, to bow my head. I might mention artists, and not the least eminent, who are excellent in both kinds; I might ask if this inaccessible poetic drama, written by men, after all, and which puts men on the stage, really requires something more than men to play it. But this is simple trifling. Tragedy or comedy, which is the superior form? The question is as old as art itself, always disputed and never solved. For my part I am satisfied with what Molière says in the *Critique de l'École des Femmes.* And now to conclude, turning against Mr. Irving himself his accusation of prosaism, I will reproach him with attaching too much importance to those picturesque aids which he thinks are poetry, and which are simply conventionality; I ask him if he does not fear lest by dint of seeking beauty in the rare, the unexpected, and the extraordinary he may forget to take it where it really is, in nature. I'm afraid, I confess, that Mr. Irving sacrifices a good deal to scenery; that in making the personages too grand he will finally cause them to lose that humanity which is the true principle of their sublimity; and I do not regret that I have preached above everything the study of truth, of that truth which reveals to us the human heart, of that truth which is, after all, the eternal basis of art, inasmuch as beauty is nothing but the splendor of it.

Constant Coquelin

V

A Reply to Mr. Dion Boucicault

I did not read the article by Mr. Dion Boucicault in the *North American Review* of August until after having written the above reply to Mr. Irving. It happens, however, that in answering Mr. Irving I have also answered Mr. Boucicault, at least on many points. But the article is substantial, interesting, and clear; it is most kind toward me; I am therefore bound in politeness to add a few lines addressed directly to its eminent author.

In order to give the casting vote in the question, Mr. Dion Boucicault takes his stand at his special point of view as a dramatic author who excels in both departments. He describes his method of comic composition as entirely a matter of calculation and deliberation, and compares it with his method of tragic composition, which is entirely a matter of impulse and of passion. Supposing that something analogous to this difference must also exist between the process of the comic actor and the process of the tragedian, he therefore concludes that Mr. Irving is right as regards tragedy; but so far as concerns comedy, and even characteristic drama, I am not perhaps in the wrong; and thus he nonsuits us both in the most charming manner possible.

What Mr. Dion Boucicault says about his two ways of working, according as he puts on Shakespeare's cap or Molière's, is very interesting, and gave me great pleasure; but it seems to me that the conclusions he draws are too hasty. The differences between the author and the actor are greater than he imagines. All is over for the author the moment he leaves his desk; for the actor, on the contrary, one may say that it is then that all begins. The work that he brings to the theatre is a mere sketch, which becomes definitive only by means of the rehearsal; the actor is only a part of a whole, he cannot work alone; finally, he has to face the public, which places him, with regard to the author, on the same footing as the soldier marching in person to the assault of batteries stands with regard to the strategist who from his chamber directs the operation by telegraph. This fact justifies many differences of method.

Every writer who composes has his hours of inspiration, or of poetic "eruption," to use Mr. Boucicault's word, when he seems to write under the dictation of some spirit. Since Mr. Boucicault says that it is so, I must believe that these moments are peculiar to the tragic author, although I do not clearly see the reason, and although what is called the *vis comica* seems to me, on the contrary, to be altogether of a nature to procure for those who cultivate it a sort of intoxication and frenzy of which it would not be difficult to find traces in Aristophanes, Molière, Regnard, and their successors. But when the tragic author has fallen again to the earth, and seeks to find his whereabouts, what does he do? He criticises his inspiration. He revises, he judges, cuts out here, amplifies there; and his work is not finished until after this second operation. Now is not this second operation even more necessary to the actor? and how can he go through this operation if he abandons himself to inspiration in presence of the public itself? This is why I recommend him to be absolutely master of himself on the night of the first performance, and Mr. Dion Boucicault implicitly agrees with me when he says that these "passional spasms" are only to be safely attempted by perfectly trained artists, and that "when novices give way to their effusion they inevitably become grotesque." I have not made any assertion stronger than that.

To sum up: Inspiration is imagination; that the actor does not shut his door against it, all well and good; but the *folle du logis,* the madcap imagination, must not become the mistress of the house.

I find Mr. Dion Boucicault somewhat severe toward tragedy. He denies it the quality of variety. Why? That tragedy is concerned with beauty more than comedy seems to me incontestable; and beauty, is it not sublimated truth? And are not the manifestations of truth innumerable? The characters of tragedy can therefore be as varied as those of comedy. I cannot admit that all heroes are alike. In the tragic authors, just as much as in Homer, they are dissimilar. Œdipus is not Lear; Orestes is not Hamlet. Their tears are *chemically* the same; *humanly* there is nothing more unlike. I can scarcely understand any better why the painting of passions should be held to lower tragedy, and why in consequence, as Salvini thinks, Shakespeare should be ranked below Sophocles, who, according to the great Italian tragedian, confined himself, we must suppose, to dramatizing the great strokes of destiny (as if the domestic affections did not play the leading part in that adorable *Antigone,* the most winning conception of Greek genius). No; man cannot abstract himself from his creation; there is no masterpiece in which he is not. Man is the end and aim of tragedy, as of comedy; and the tragedian, like the comedian, having to render man, I do not see why their methods should differ so radically.

The tragedian must be master of himself quite as much as the comedian. Perhaps this is more difficult for the tragedian; that is all. Mr. Dion Boucicault relates the anecdote of Rachel being disconcerted on the stage by the barking of a little dog confined in one of the dressing rooms. Will he allow me to tell him that this proves nothing either against Rachel or against me? Admirably mistress of her role, sure of saying only what she had previously tried and proved, holding herself, in a word, thoroughly in control *so far as the actress was concerned,* Rachel, *so far as the woman was concerned,* might very well not have the same power over her nerves, and not be able to command so despotically impressions received from *outside.* I think that I myself am fairly cool and self-possessed on the stage, but I would not guarantee myself to be proof against similar accidents. The case here is very different. I claim that the actor should see and hear himself play, but no *exterior* circumstances must prevent him doing so. I should have protested vehemently if a broad aisle had been cut down the middle of the orchestra stalls at the Comédie-Française, as there was talk of doing not long ago. Why? Because I know how terribly the actor on the stage in the middle of a tirade would be irritated by one single gentleman walking carelessly down this passage and distributing discreet nods and greetings right and left. Certainly it is better not to be susceptible; but when you are absorbed completely in a certain task, and when you are just realizing that difficult problem of being two persons in one, it is most annoying to feel obliged to reckon with accidents in the auditorium, however puerile they may be; and as for a little dog barking in a dressing room, it is enough to exasperate all the actors on the stage, and all the spectators in the house as well.

But, I repeat, this is a different thing; and when a tragedian, undisturbed by any exterior accident, loses control of himself on the boards, if he is badly inspired he must not imitate his heroes and say, "It is destiny," but rather he must say, "I do not know my part," and set to work to study again.

Certainly no mechanical practice can give genius. I never made any such monstrous assertion. A man is born with greater or less natural gifts, and the reason why remains a mystery. But he must cultivate his gifts and he must work out his genius. Mr. Boucicault speaks of that indescribable something which makes an original picture superior to the most perfect copy imaginable. Well, I know in what that indescribable something consists. It consists, on the one hand, in the author's manner of feeling, which, in its turn, depends upon his personality—that is to say, on something of unknown and, if you like, of divine origin—and on the other hand, it consists in his manner of rendering what he feels; that is to say, his artistic process. Now while he has little or no power over his personality, the artist has every power over his process; and so it came about that Raphael thrice changed his manner.

One thing which quite astounds and puzzles me is that I am accused of preaching Zolisme, or Zolaism, whichever may be the preferable orthography. I must, indeed, have expressed myself very obscurely. However, when my article appears in book form with full development, it will be seen clearly that I am a partisan of *naturalness* as opposed to *naturalism*. I shall never admit that ugliness can be in art a principle equal to beauty, and that it can claim the right to be worshiped. Ugliness is an accident, a source of contrast, and the moment it no longer serves to bring beauty into relief it is superfluous. This doctrine is also, I am sure, that of Sarah Bernhardt. Mr. Dion Boucicault doubts it. He compares her manner of playing the fifth act of *Adrienne Lecouvreur* with Rachel's performance in the same play, which he once witnessed, and he gives us to understand that while Sarah is superior in physical realism, her predecessor was superior poetically. But, after all, is it so sure that the classic Rachel did not have flashes of romantic or naturalist boldness? Here is a little-known anecdote related by M. James Darmesteter in his excellent edition of *Macbeth*. Rachel was once on the point of playing Lady Macbeth in England. The memory of Mrs. Siddons haunted her, and as she was told that the English actress had exhausted every resource, especially in the sleepwalking scene—"Oh, but I have an idea of my own," replied Rachel. "I should lick my hand."

If I am not mistaken, this extraordinary inspiration approaches very near to Zolaism. *Que voulez-vous?* Art is great, and genius can pass strange things into the sanctuary. Rachel might have been sublime when she licked her hand; Sarah may be sublime in the realistic agony of Adrienne. In any case, I am sure that over her most terrible convulsions the angel of grace still hovers. For Sarah is a woman of high intelligence, very sensitive withal, and instinctively, like the criticism of our day, open to the charm of the poetry of all epochs; she adores all that is exquisite, being herself exquisite. But she admires and appreciates simple grandeur, and the brutalities of an abrupt genius may be not displeasing to her. Thus she may admit in Zola undeniable power; but if at certain lofty elevations she happens to be of the same mind with Zola, I will guarantee she is not the woman to descend with him to *La Terre*.

The reproach of monstrosity brought against Sarah also seems to me to be exaggerated. The misfortune is that authors will write roles expressly for her; they cut them to the pattern of her nature, so that in consequence she has only to be herself in order to be excellent.

At the Comédie-Française this would not have been the case. The ancient and the modern repertory would have forced her to diversify herself more. But she did not stay there long enough. How can Mr. Dion Boucicault accuse this "college of the histrionic art" of having inoculated her with that "mechanical practice," so dangerous, he says, for the independence of the artist? There is no "mechanical practice" taught at the Comédie-Française. Tradition reigns at the Comédie, but it does not govern; and those who wish may emancipate themselves from that tradition. At the present day do we not see there at the same time Worms, who is the personification of correctness, and Mounet-Sully, the incarnation of all that is unexpected and impulsive? Let us then say no more about uniformity of teaching.

To conclude, I am not throughout in agreement with Mr. Dion Boucicault, but, as he will see, we are of the same mind on more points than he imagined. I feel very much flattered by the attention which has been paid to my little essay by the eminent dramatist, and it is a great satisfaction for me to have been appreciated in so impartial, and on the whole so favorable, a manner by a theatrical man so completely equipped as Mr. Dion Boucicault.

CONSTANT COQUELIN

On the Stage

by

FRANCES ANNE KEMBLE

With an Introduction by George Arliss

Introduction

I am grateful to the editor of this series for having drawn my attention to this paper written by an actress whose name and fame are so familiar to all students of the drama. Considering its brevity, it is perhaps the most careful analysis of the actor in juxtaposition with his art that one is likely to find in dramatic literature. And it has the inestimable value of having been written by an actress of considerable experience and acknowledged ability. Whether one entirely agrees with her is another matter. It is written with such conviction and such skill that it is worthy of careful study and consideration. I imagine that the lay reader would accept her conclusions without question; and it is perhaps hardly fair that an actor should permit himself to be too critical of her decisions. Towards the end of her paper Mrs. Kemble says: "This same dramatic art has neither fixed rules, specific principles, indispensable rudiments, nor fundamental laws." In my opinion, there can be no question as to the truth of this assertion. And it is because of this absolute freedom of mental and physical action that no two actors in the discussion of acting are likely to agree whole-heartedly on how it should be done—how results should be arrived at. I remember my utter surprise when I first discovered that Coquelin considered it bad art for the actor to feel the emotion that he was portraying and attempting to convey to an audience; that Coquelin himself felt nothing, and that he considered the actor who did feel was lacking in one of the fundamental demands of the stage. But, although it is to me inexplicable that a part could be developed on such premises, how can one argue the point, since Coquelin became Coquelin, and what more could any actor ask?

It is interesting to consider how far the observations of Mrs. Kemble, which we may reasonably accept as true of her day, are also applicable to our own time. She says: "Greater intellectual cultivation and a purer and more elevated taste are unfavourable to the existence of the true theatrical spirit." This I think is equally true to-day. The majority of our best actors are drawn from the lower and middle classes. I have no adequate explanation for this: it is possible that the higher cultivation results in a disadvantageous restraint of emotion, of a consciousness of the desirability of decorous behaviour in the presence of others; and this might rob a cultivated actor irretrievably of that natural abandon which is likely to be at once a charm and an asset on the stage.

On the other hand, her distinction between "theatrical" and "dramatic" (to the discussion of which she devotes a large part of her article) does not seem to me to apply to the theatre of to-day. She says: "They are so dissimilar that they are nearly opposite." To illustrate her meaning she instances children, whom she describes as always dramatic, but when they find themselves "objects of admiring attention" they become theatrical. I understand what she means by this. They immediately begin to over-act. Mrs. Kemble seems to use the term "theatrical" as we use it in common parlance when we say, "Don't be theatrical!" But is that a proper use of the word when discussing the stage? The only explanation I can give of her emphatic insistence on the distinction between the terms is that so large a proportion of the plays of that period were hopelessly artificial and had to be played in that exaggerated manner which we call theatrical. She mentions *The Duke's Motto,* which I know from personal experience to be an entirely unnatural play, requiring entirely unnatural acting—although I remember it gave great delight to a three-penny gallery and a sixpenny pit on the Surrey side of London. It is easy to realise that one might be theatrical without being dramatic; or have a strong dramatic instinct without being effective on the stage. But I find it difficult to agree with her that "things dramatic and things theatrical are so dissimilar that they are nearly opposite."

The article is undoubtedly one that should be preserved. It is valuable too for its side-lights on Mrs. Siddons and on Edmund Kean. As a whole, I get the impression that Mrs. Kemble had a tremendous admiration for the drama. But she confesses that the stage was repugnant to her; nearly all her relatives were connected with the theatre; she had grown up with actors and actresses; she was familiar with them and their habits; after reading her article, I cannot help feeling that perhaps she had a certain latent contempt for the actor as an artist, which it is quite possible she never admitted, even to herself.

GEORGE ARLISS

On the Stage

Things dramatic and things theatrical are often confounded together in the minds of English people, who, being for the most part neither the one nor the other, speak and write of them as if they were identical, instead of, as they are, so dissimilar that they are nearly opposite.

That which is dramatic in human nature is the passionate, emotional, humorous element, the simplest portion of our composition, after our mere instincts, to which it is closely allied; and this has no relation whatever, beyond its momentary excitement and gratification, to that which imitates it, and is its theatrical reproduction; the dramatic is the *real*, of which the theatrical is the *false*.

Both nations and individuals in whom the dramatic temperament strongly preponderates are rather remarkable for a certain simplicity of nature, which produces sincerity and vehemence of emotion and expression, but is entirely without *consciousness*, which is never absent from the theatrical element.

Children are always dramatic, but only theatrical when they become aware that they are objects of admiring attention; in which case the assuming and dissembling capacity of *acting* develops itself comically and sadly enough in them.

The Italians, nationally and individually, are dramatic; the French, on the contrary, theatrical; we English of the present day are neither the one no the other, though our possession of the noblest dramatic literature in the world proves how deeply at one time our national character was imbued with elements which are now so latent as almost to be of doubtful existence; while, on the other hand, our American progeny are, as a nation, devoid of the dramatic element, and have a considerable infusion of that which is theatrical, delighting, like the Athenians of old, in processions, shows, speeches, oratory, demonstrations, celebrations and declarations, and such displays of public and private sentiment as would be repugnant to English taste and feeling; to which theatrical tendency and the morbid love of excitement which is akin to it, I attribute the fact that Americans, both nationally and individually, are capable of a certain sympathy with the French character, in which we are wanting.

The combination of the power of representing passion and emotion with that of imagining or conceiving it—that is, of the theatrical talent with the dramatic temperament—is essential to make a good actor; their combination in the highest possible degree alone makes a great one.

There is a specific comprehension of effect and the means of producing it, which, in some persons, is a distinct capacity, and this forms what actors call the study of their profession; and in this, which is the alloy necessary to make theatrical that which is only dramatic, lies the heart of their mystery and the snare of their craft in more ways than one; and this, the actor's *business*, goes sometimes absolutely against the dramatic temperament, which is nevertheless essential to it.

Every day lessens the frequency of this specific combination among ourselves, for the dramatic temperament, always exceptional in England, is becoming daily more so under the various adverse influences of a state of civilisation and society which fosters a genuine dislike to exhibitions of emotion, and a cynical disbelief in the reality of it, both necessarily repressing, first, its expression, and next, its existence. On the other hand, greater intellectual cultivation and a purer and more elevated taste are unfavourable to the existence of the true theatrical spirit; and English actors of the present day are of the public, by being "nothing if not critical," and are not of their craft, having literally ceased to know "what belongs to a frippery." They have lost for the most part alike the dramatic emotional temperament and the scenic science of mere effect; and our stage is and must be supplied, if supplied at all, by persons less sophisticated and less civilised. The plays brought out and revived at our theatres of late years bear doleful witness to this. We have in them archaeology, ethnology, history, geography, botany (even to the curiosity of ascertaining the Danish wild-flowers that Ophelia might twist with her mad straws), and upholstery; everything, in short, but acting, which it seems we cannot have.

When Mrs. Siddons, in her spectacles and mob-cap, read *Macbeth* or *King John*, it was one of the grandest dramatic achievements that could be imagined, with the least possible admixture of the theatrical element; the representation of *The Duke's Motto*, with all its resources of scenic effect, is a striking and interesting theatrical entertainment, with hardly an admixture of that which is truly dramatic.

Garrick was, I suppose, the most perfect actor that our

stage has ever produced, equalling in tragedy and comedy the greatest performers of both; but while his dramatic organisation enabled him to represent with exquisite power and pathos the principal characters of Shakespeare's noblest plays, his theatrical taste induced him to garble, desecrate, and disfigure the masterpieces of which he was so fine an interpreter, in order to produce or enhance those peculiar effects which constitute the chief merit and principal attraction of all theatrical exhibitions.

Mrs. Siddons could lay no claim to versatility—it was not in her nature; she was without mobility of mind, countenance, or manner; and her dramatic organization was in that respect inferior to Garrick's; but out of a family of twenty-eight persons, all of whom made the stage their vocation, she alone pre-eminently combined the qualities requisite to make a great theatrical performer in the highest degree.

Another member of that family—a foreigner by birth, and endowed with the most powerful and vivid dramatic organization—possessed in so small a degree the faculty of the stage that the parts which she represented successfully were few in number, and though among them were some dramatic *creations* of extraordinary originality and beauty, she never rose to the highest rank in her profession, nor could claim in any sense the title of a great theatrical artist. This was my mother. And I suppose no member of that large histrionic family was endowed to the same degree with the natural dramatic temperament. The truth of her intonation, accent, and emphasis made her common speech as good as a play to hear (oh, how much better than some we *do* hear!), and whereas I have seen the Shakespeare of my father, and the Shakespeare and Milton of Mrs. Siddons, with every emphatic word underlined and accentuated, lest they should omit the right inflection in delivering the lines, my mother could no more have needed such notes whereby to speak *true* than she would a candle to have walked by at noonday. She was an incomparable critic; and though the intrepid sincerity of her nature made her strictures sometimes more accurate than acceptable, they were inestimable for the fine tact for truth, which made her instinctively reject in nature and art whatever sinned against it.

I do not know whether I shall be considered competent to pass a judgment on myself in this matter, but I think I am. Inheriting from my father a theatrical descent of two generations and my mother's vivid and versatile organisation, the stage itself, though it became from the force of circumstances my career, was, partly from my nature, and partly from my education, so repugnant to me that I failed to accomplish any result at all worthy of my many advantages. I imagine I disappointed alike those who did and those who did not think me endowed with the talent of my family, and incurred, towards the very close of my theatrical career, the severe verdict from one of the masters of the stage of the present day, that I was "ignorant of the first rudiments of my profession."

In my father and mother I have had frequent opportunities of observing in most marked contrast the rapid intuitive perception of the dramatic instinct in an organisation where it preponderated, and the laborious process of logical argument by which the same result, on a given question, was reached by a mind of different constitution (my father's), and reached with much doubt and hesitation, caused by the very application of analytical reasoning. The slow mental process *might* with time have achieved a right result in all such cases; but the dramatic instinct, aided by a fine organisation, was unerring; and this leads me to observe, that there is no reason whatever to expect that fine actors shall be necessarily profound commentators on the parts that they sustain most successfully, but rather the contrary.

I trust I shall not be found wanting in due respect for the greatness that is gone from us, if I say that Mrs. Siddons' analysis of the part of Lady Macbeth is to be found alone in her representation of it; of the magnificence of which the "essay" she has left upon the character gives not the faintest idea.

If that great actress had possessed the order of mind capable of conceiving and producing a philosophical analysis of any of the wonderful poetical creations which she so wonderfully embodied, she would surely never have been able to embody them as she did. For to whom are all things given? and to whom were ever given, in such abundant measure, consenting and harmonious endowments of mind and body for the peculiar labour of her life?

The dramatic faculty, as I have said, lies in a power of apprehension quicker than the disintegrating process of critical analysis, and when it is powerful, and the organisation fine, as with Mrs. Siddons, perception rather than reflection reaches the aim proposed; and the persons endowed with this specific gift will hardly unite with it the mental qualifications of philosophers and metaphysicians; no better proof of which can be adduced than Mrs. Siddons herself, whose performances were, in the strict sense of the word, excellent, while the two treatises she has left upon the characters of

Queen Constance and Lady Macbeth—two of her finer parts —are feeble and superficial. Kean, who possessed, beyond all actors whom I have seen, tragic inspiration, could very hardly, I should think, have given a satisfactory reason for any one of the great effects which he produced. Of Mlle. Rachel, whose impersonations fulfilled to me the idea of perfect works of art of their kind, I have heard, from one who knew her well, that her intellectual processes were limited to the consideration of the most purely mechanical part of her vocation; and Pasta, the great lyric tragedian, who, Mrs. Siddons said, was capable of giving her lessons, replied to the observation, *"Vous avez dû beaucoup étudier l'antique," "Je l'ai beaucoup senti."* The reflective and analytical quality has little to do with the complex process of acting, and is alike remote from what is dramatic and what is theatrical.

There is something anomalous in that which we call the dramatic art that has often arrested my attention and exercised my thoughts; the special gift and sole industry of so many of my kindred, and the only labour of my own life, it has been a subject of constant and curious speculation with me, combining as it does elements at once so congenial and so antagonistic to my nature.

Its most original process, that is, the conception of the character to be represented, is a mere reception of the creation of another mind; and its mechanical part, that is, the representation of the character thus apprehended, has no reference to the intrinsic, poetical, or dramatic merit of the original creation, but merely to the accuracy and power of the actor's perception of it; thus the character of Lady Macbeth is as majestic, awful, and poetical whether it be worthily filled by its pre-eminent representative, Mrs. Siddons, or unworthily by the most incompetent of ignorant provincial tragedy queens.

This same dramatic art has neither fixed rules, specific principles, indispensable rudiments, nor fundamental laws; it has no basis in positive science, as music, painting, sculpture, and architecture have; and differs from them all in that the mere appearance of spontaneity, which is an acknowledged assumption, is its chief merit. And yet—

> This younger of the sister arts,
> Where all their charms combine

requires in its professors the imagination of the poet, the ear of the musician, the eye of the painter and sculptor, and over and above these a faculty peculiar to itself, inasmuch as the actor personally fulfills and embodies his conception; his own voice is his cunningly modulated instrument; his own face the canvas whereon he portrays the various expressions of his passion; his own frame the mould in which he casts the images of beauty and majesty that fill his brain; and whereas the painter and sculptor may select, of all possible attitudes, occupations, and expressions, the most favourable to the beautiful effect they desire to produce and fix, and bid it so remain fixed for ever, the actor must live and move through a temporary existence of poetry and passion, and preserve throughout its duration that ideal grace and dignity of which the canvas and the marble give but a silent and motionless image. And yet it is an art that requires no study worthy of the name; it creates nothing; it perpetuates nothing; to its professors, whose personal qualifications form half their merit, is justly given the meed of personal admiration; and the reward of contemporaneous popularity is well bestowed on those whose labour consists in exciting momentary emotion. Their most persevering and successful efforts can only benefit, by a passionate pleasure of at most a few years' duration, the play-going public of their own immediate day, and they are fitly recompensed with money and applause, to whom may not justly belong the rapture of creation, the glory of patient and protracted toil, and the love and honour of grateful posterity.

A Company of Actors:
The Comédie-Française

by

FRANCISQUE SARCEY

Translated by M. Barbier

With an Introduction by Brander Matthews

Introduction

In 1871, during the dark days of the commune in Paris, a number of the members of the Comédie-Française headed by Got went over to London for a brief season, earning money which helped to support the company of the House of Molière; and in the spring and early summer of 1879 the entire company paid a visit to London while the Théâtre Français was being repaired and redecorated. The season lasted for six weeks and at every performance the Gaiety Theatre had to turn away many playgoers who wanted to profit by the opportunity to study the foremost company in Europe, then at the moment of its most brilliant prosperity.

The French organization was accompanied to England by Francisque Sarcey, the most important French dramatic critic of his time. He was as expert in expounding the principles and the practices of the art of acting as he was in declaring those of the art of playmaking; and he was as familiar with the annals of the French theatre as he was with the history of the French drama. He had earlier published *Comédiens et Comédiennes,* a series of biographical and critical studies of the leading members of the Comédie-Française; and no one else was as well equipped as he to explain the organization of the Comédie-Française, to describe its traditions, and to expound the unwritten laws which assure its stability. This he did in a lecture delivered one afternoon at the Gaiety Theatre, on the stage of which the Comédie-Française was appearing every evening. At the request of James Knowles, the editor of the *Nineteenth Century,* he wrote out his lecture, which was translated into English by M. Barbier and published in that monthly review in the number for July 1879.

Henry James, an assiduous attendant at the Théâtre Français whenever he was in Paris, had taken Sarcey's *Comédiens et Comédiennes* as the text for an essay on the Théâtre Français, originally published in the *Galaxy* and later reprinted in his volume on *French Poets and Novelists* (1878). He dwelt with reminiscent delight on the satisfaction

212

he had always had in taking his seat in that noble theatre and he emphasized the main point that Sarcey brought out clearly:

> The traditions of the Comédie-Française—that is the sovereign word, and that is the charm of the place—the charm that one never ceases to feel, however often one may sit beneath the classic, dusky dome. One feels this charm with peculiar intensity as a newly arrived foreigner. The Théâtre Français has had the good fortune to be able to allow its traditions to accumulate. They have been preserved, transmitted, respected, cherished, until at last they form the very atmosphere, the vital air, of the establishment. A stranger feels their superior influence the first time he sees the great curtain go up; he feels that he is in a theatre that is not as other theatres are. It is not only better, it is different. It has a peculiar perfection—something consecrated, historical, academic. This impression is delicious, and he watches the performance in a sort of tranquil ecstasy.

It may be noted here that Henry James was not so careful as he might be to observe the distinction Sarcey scrupulously makes between the Comédie-Française, which is the organization itself, the company of comedians and tragedians, and the Théâtre Français, which is the name of the building that happens now to be the home of the organization—the august company in its two centuries and a half of existence having migrated half a dozen times from one worthy edifice to another.

After the Comédie-Française had brought to an end its triumphant season in England, Matthew Arnold wrote a pungent paper on "The French Play in London" (reprinted in his *Irish Essays,* 1882). He was an old playgoer, missing no opportunity to see the best that could be afforded by the playhouses of England, France, and Germany. In the course of his essay he recorded his intense admiration for Rachel, whose exquisite art he had commemorated in three sonnets; he contrasted the dramatic poetry of the French with that of the English, to the advantage of the latter; and he expressed his dissatisfaction with the later social drama popular in his time in Paris, the plays of Augier and the younger Dumas. But he was cordial in his praise of the French players and of the organization which gave them occasion to display their histrionic gifts to the best advantage. And he seized the chance to point a moral for the benefit of his fellow countrymen:

What then, finally, *are* we to learn from the marvellous success and attractiveness of the performances at the Gaiety Theatre? What *is* the consequence which is right and rational for us to draw? Surely it is this: "The theatre is irresistible; *organise the theatre.*" Surely, if we wish to stand less in our own way, and to have clever notions of the consequences of things, it is to this conclusion we must come.

The performances of the French company show plainly, I think, what is gained—the theatre being admitted to be an irresistible need for civilised communities—by organising the theatre. Some of the drama played by this company is, as we have seen, questionable. But, in the absence of an organisation such as this, it would be played even yet more; it would, with a still lower drama to accompany it, almost if not altogether reign; it would have far less correction and relief by better things. An older and better drama containing many things of high merit, some things of surpassing merit, is kept before the public by means of this company, is given to perfection. Pieces of truth and beauty, which emerge here and there among the questionable pieces of the modern drama, get the benefit of this company's skill, and are given to perfection. The questionable pieces themselves lose something of their unprofitableness and vice in their hands; the acting carries us into the world of correct and pleasing art, if the piece does not. And the type of perfection fixed by these fine actors influences for good every actor in France.

Moreover, the French company shows us not only what is gained by organising the theatre, but what is meant by organising it. The organisation in the example before us is simple and rational.

To *Munsey's Magazine* for September 1908 I contributed an account of the vicissitudes of the Comédie-Française in which I asserted that any attempt to duplicate the French institution in Great Britain or the United States would be difficult, not to say impossible:

To suggest an English equivalent for this French institution we should have to imagine that the performers of the York or the Coventry plays had established themselves in London, and that their rude playhouse had been taken over by Shakespeare and his comrades. We should have to imagine further that this company, having acted the chief plays of the Elizabethan dramatists, survived the Commonwealth and was transferred under the Restoration to Drury

Lane, where it performed the comedies of Congreve and Wycherly, Vanbrugh, and Farquhar. We must imagine, also, that this company, to which Burbage and Betterton had belonged, welcomed in time Garrick and Cooke, the Kembles and the Keans, Macready and Irving; and that after producing the comedies of Sheridan and Goldsmith, it had been hospitable in time to the later plays of Gilbert and Pinero, Henry Arthur Jones and James M. Barrie, preserving unbroken the splendid traditions bequeathed to it by the past.

And yet, even if a rival to the Comédie-Française cannot now be achieved in London or in New York, it might at least be attempted. Even if there is not now in any theatre of the English-speaking world the historic continuity which has given stability and longevity to the Comédie-Française, we have the material for the organization for which Matthew Arnold pleaded; we have in Great Britain and the United States actors and actresses unsurpassed in France, and we have dramatists no longer inferior. Even if traditions cannot be improvised, we might begin to create men now for the benefit of those who are coming after us, in the hope that one or another may take root to burgeon abundantly in the future.

Here in New York we have a model; we have here an organization for the opera, which has endured now for more than a generation and which shows few signs of lessening vitality. We may very well ask ourselves if the devotion and the generosity which have done so much for the prosperity of the music drama might not be enlisted for the support of the drama. To create an institution which may in the years to come withstand comparison with the Comédie-Française will take time and wisdom and money; it will demand not a little of each of these elements of permanence, but the result would be worth while.

BRANDER MATTHEWS

A Company of Actors:

The Comédie-Française

I

Ladies and Gentlemen: In addressing a public before whom I have the honour to appear for the first time, I ought to speak of the emotion I feel, and, at the same time, solicit your indulgence. Such is the usual exordium of lecturers when making their début. But the truth is, I am not moved in any way, and do not feel the shadow of a fear. It is your fault if I express this unwonted confidence, and you have only yourselves to thank for it. The fact is that, ever since I landed on the hospitable shores of England, I have met with so much courtesy, kindness, and attention—a cordiality so frank and so obliging—that, in speaking to you, I feel as if I were addressing my friends at home rather than my hosts abroad. Hence I do not think it necessary to solicit an indulgence which I feel sure you have already granted to me.

I am about to speak to you of the Comédie-Française and its organisation, and particularly the latter point, for it is the organisation of that institution which constitutes its power and greatness. It is, in fact, owing to that organisation that it is able to-day to lay before your eyes the imposing and marvellous sight it offers to the world.

The Comédie-Française took possession of the Gaiety Theatre a few weeks ago, and during this lapse of time a fresh bill has been issued every day, and every night a series of new plays submitted to your judgment. This ever-changing variety will continue to the end of its stay in London. The Comédie-Française intends to remain here for forty-five days, and its programme comprises forty-three plays. These forty-three pieces constitute only a small portion of its repertory. Thus, although four or five of the dramatic master-pieces of Corneille are constantly played in Paris, only one, the *Menteur*, a comedy, has been selected for representation here; Racine also is represented by only one tragedy; from Molière three or four comedies have been chosen, while

Regnard and Beaumarchais supply but one work each—the *Joueur* and the *Barbier de Séville*. The names of Lesage and Marivaux are altogether absent. Coming lower down, Scribe, who contributed so much to the Comédie-Française, is likewise absent; and as to contemporary dramatic authors, we shall see with regret what an amount of dramatic treasure the Comédie-Française has been obliged to leave aside.

The *répertoire courant*—that is to say, the pieces which the company can play at any moment, all the parts being known beforehand, without any other preparation than one of those summary rehearsals known in the language of the French green-room as *raccords*—its *répertoire courant* includes about one hundred plays, out of which the manager can choose as he likes. A single order to the storekeeper, a notice posted up in the green-room, is all that is required: the same night the scenery is ready, all appurtenances in order, and the actors at their posts.

Need I tell you that all the plays are acted with remarkable *ensemble?* You have been able during the past fortnight to ascertain this fact by your own experience; and I find by your papers that it is precisely the perfection of that *ensemble* which has most deeply struck the theatrical critics of the English press. At the Comédie-Française the most insignificant parts are filled up, if not by first-class actors, at least by persons who have already studied long and know their business. In plays like *Hernani* and *Mademoiselle de Belle-Isle,* for instance, in which, as you may have seen, there are a certain number of very secondary personages, some of whom have but a few words to utter, while others say nothing at all, these obscure parts, instead of being given up to common supernumeraries engaged for the night, are filled either by young actors who have their trial to go through, or by old actors who have no other talent but their perfect knowledge of the boards—in short, by actors who form part of the company, and who are thoroughly acquainted with the traditions and manners of the house.

Such a numerous and homogenous company in possession of such a vast repertory is a most singular phenomenon, and one well worthy of arousing your astonishment. There are, no doubt, in all the great towns of Europe, and especially in London, theatrical companies in which some great actor may be found, like your Henry Irving, some striking individuality perhaps superior to the most eminent actors of the Comédie-Française. But this is an exception, a kind of accidental occurrence. Supposing you brought together for a season two or three great actors, they would no doubt offer very attractive entertainments, but they could not be compared with the Comédie-Française, which possesses a repertory, and which, to use the consecrated expression, *joue d'ensemble*.

So very true is this fact, ladies and gentlemen, that eminent Englishmen have often proposed to copy the organisation of the Comédie-Française, and to establish a similar institution in London, formed on the same model and worked according to the same rules. This idea is no doubt an enticing one: unfortunately it is next to impossible to realise it. If you wish to transplant an old tree, you must, in order to keep it alive, transport along with it the mass of earth in which the roots are embedded: both must be transplanted together and at the same time. In the same way, when it is sought to transport into one country some old institution which has been born and grown, and become great and strong, in some other country, it is necessary to transport along with it the manners and customs from which it derives its life, and all the traditions which create, as it were, a special atmosphere around it, and in the midst of which it can alone be grown. This process is an impracticable one. There is, besides, one element over which we have no command, and that is time.

Certain nations have tried to borrow from you, and to acclimatise in their own country the parliamentary form of government which it was your glory to be the first to establish in Europe. Nothing was easier than to copy your constitution, to regulate, according to the model furnished by yourselves, the respective rights and duties of the different powers of the State towards one another. But it was not possible to import at the same time the long experience and practice you have had of that constitution, the manners and traditions which form around it a rich soil in which its roots are so firmly and deeply planted—the inviolable respect of the Crown for the rights of Parliament, and the feelings of deference and love for the Crown, the loyalty in a word, which distinguish the English people. Certain other nations may have assumed all the apparatus, all the outward forms of parliamentary government, but they have lacked the guiding spirit which should animate it, the traditions which support it.

Tradition alone constitutes the power of the Comédie-Française. In order, therefore, thoroughly to understand this ancient institution, it is necessary not so much to study the rules by which it is at present governed as the whole of the customs and traditions from which it has gradually risen. The cause of its glory can be fully understood only by searching its past history and studying it from its very beginnings.

II

A child, on his birth, brings into the world a certain number of natural dispositions which, on being developed later by education, will contribute to give the man a character of his own and tend to form his individuality. Just in the same way there stand, at the origin of all old institutions, one or two initiative facts which gave them a distinctive character, and which regulated their ulterior development. It is necessary to find out and bear these facts in mind, for they are the key to the whole history of an institution.

Two such facts stand at the origin of the Comédie-Française. Both contributed to give it a certain shape and to lead it in a certain direction; the influence of both has acted through centuries, and is still felt to-day.

What are these primordial facts?

Any of you who visited the Paris Exhibition last year may have seen, in the room devoted to the history of the stage, an extremely curious old engraving. It represents a dozen or so actors, wearing their costumes, standing round a table lit up by a candle. He who appears to be the chief is counting out money and dividing it into parts. The engraving is entitled "After the Performance."

Such was, in fact, what used to take place. Every night, after the performance, all who belonged to the company, from the manager down to the lowest supernumerary, met together to reckon up the receipts. The total sum was then divided into parts—twelve parts was the number, if I remember right. One actor would receive the whole of a part; another was entitled to half a one; another would get only one-fourth; each according to his importance, merit, and labour, until the whole of the twelve parts were distributed. Thus Molière, the head of the company, received one part in his capacity as manager, and a second one in his capacity as author and actor. It was a kind of co-operative society which appointed its own manager, and in which every member could be a manager in his turn. This mode of sharing the profits, which certain economists of the present day are trying to adapt to trade and commerce, was put in practice in the first instance by humble actors. It has, with one exception, disappeared from all theatres, where now the director is a kind of foreman or master, and the actors so many paid workmen. It has, however, happily been preserved at the Comédie-Française, which has always been, and is still, a society in which all the share-holders are equal, though possessing different rights.

This is the first of the two primordial facts I alluded to a few minutes ago. The other will not be so easily understood by you, because it is singularly repugnant to English minds. And yet I must ask you to listen to it and to admit it.

In France, under the old régime, nothing could be published without a special authorisation of the king. It was a privilege: *cum privilegio regis* are the words which stand on all our old editions. If it were not possible to publish a book without the permission of the king, how much more difficult must it have been to open a theatre and act plays without the said permission! The king granted, according to his good pleasure, the privilege to act a certain play in a certain place.

Now privilege means favour, and he who graciously grants the favour is perfectly entitled to exact in return the conditions he pleases. The king who permitted a company to give performances naturally reserved to himself the right to demand that the performances should suit his taste. He would watch over and direct them and limit them to a certain ideal which he thought to be the best. He was entitled to do this by virtue of the privilege he had granted, and also by virtue of the favours which he was wont to shower on faithful and obedient companies. He sent for them to court, and, on their leaving, loaded them with rich presents. Sometimes he put them down on his private pension list and paid them a pension every quarter. To-day this would be called a subvention.

Thought, however, even in France, is now emancipated, and the theatre is free like the printing-press. But the sovereign—or, if you like it better, the Government—still subventions certain theatrical undertakings, and, like everybody who invests money in a concern, has always the right to examine what use is made of the sum granted. Government, therefore, keeps a right to interfere in these undertakings; and it is thus that the Comédie-Française, which, at its origin, owed its existence to the king, since it received from him first a privilege and then a pension, is still, owing to the subvention it gets from the State, under the hand of the Government.

Here, then, we have two principles before us: the republican principle, since a co-operative society is, according to the formula laid down by one of our most eminent public writers, the government of all by all; and the monarchical principle, since the king had in former times and the Government to-day has the right to interfere in the affairs of the society, and to impose a sovereign will on it. One might reasonably imagine that two principles so opposite would either exclude or destroy each other. Well, such is not the case; on the contrary, it is by the action and counter-action of these two principles, always struggling against each other and yet always united, that this great institution, the Comédie-Française, has been formed. We find them at its origin; we can follow their influence as the institution developed itself; to-day they are still contending to get possession of it, and it is that very contest which keeps it alive, for life can be found only where contrary forces struggle and harmonise with each other.

We can discover these same two principles at the origin of all theatres established under the Monarchy. And yet how is it that only one of them, the Comédie-Française, has survived?

It is because that theatre had the good fortune to have Molière for its founder and first master. When Molière came to Paris in 1658, a humble author of unknown farces and an obscure comedian, after having completed one of those provincial tours so amusingly described by Scarron in his *Roman Comique*, there were already two theatres in Paris in a flourishing condition: the Hôtel de Bourgogne, which was the king's theatre, and the Théâtre du Marais, where pantomimes were acted. Who would have imagined that the newcomer would so very soon outdo its rivals? The fact is, Molière was not only, next to your Shakespeare, or rather by the side of Shakespeare, the greatest dramatic writer that ever existed; he was also a clever administrator, an unequalled stage-manager, and an honest man, of large mind and warm heart, adored and respected by his little company, which closely gathered round him like a living organism of which he was the soul.

When he died in 1673, the little company which he had kept united together was on the point of breaking up, and the future Comédie-Française appeared doomed. One of the best actors of Molière, La Thorillière, went over to the enemy's camp—that is to say, joined the Hôtel de Bourgogne. Other defections less important followed. So great an ingratitude towards such a glorious name cannot fail to astonish us. The truth is, Molière was not looked upon by his contemporaries as he is by the present generation. He was not yet transformed into a kind of demi-god. Nobody is a great man during his lifetime, or immediately after his death: time alone completes great men, just as time transforms certain works into masterpieces.

Yes, it is undeniable that time has a great deal to do with

the formation of masterpieces. Every generation that passes before a work of genius looks at it from a different point of view, and finds in it new beauties which henceforth remain indelibly attached to it. Time enriches these works with the progress it has made, with the fresh ideas, feelings, and knowledge it has acquired; and it is thus, after the lapse of two long centuries and a half, that we now find concentrated in *Tartuffe* every kind of social, moral, and religious hypocrisy, as we find every species of jealousy in *Othello*; it is thus that these characters, enriched daily with the new forms of feeling unceasingly experienced by humanity, assume colossal proportions, and that the poets who created them are raised in the eyes of the world to heights of prodigious greatness. Homer perhaps is the greatest poet of all only because he is the oldest, and because three thousand years have laboured in his behalf, and made his statue a gigantic one.

We may feel indignant at the thought that the woman to whom Molière bequeathed his name could have changed that glorious name for that of an obscure actor. But we must remember that Molière, in the eyes of his contemporaries, was only a writer of comedies; they did not see in him the great man that centuries have made him for us. His memory was not sufficiently imposing to restrain his old companions from deserting it. There was only one exception, and his humble name deserves to be recorded in history, for it was unquestionably he who saved the Comédie-Française, and, next to Molière, was the real founder of that institution. His name was Lagrange. He was not an actor of great talent, neither had he much intelligence, but he had loved Molière seriously and deeply. If his mind was not large enough to understand the greatness of his genius, he at least felt it in his heart, and he repeated unceasingly to his comrades the words of the humble and the lowly: "Let us love each other in him and through him." The Comédie-Française recently gave this honest man a magnificent proof of its gratitude: it published in a rich form the diary in which Lagrange daily entered the most minute events of the life of Molière's company.

Thanks to him, the company remained united before the public, while the Hôtel de Bourgogne struggled to regain the lead in the theatrical world. The two rival companies fought a hard and, it must be added, an unsuccessful campaign. The king resolved to blend them into one. Had he joined Molière's company to that of the Hôtel de Bourgogne, it is probable that the destiny of the Comédie-Française would have taken a different direction. It would have been deprived of that fixed and luminous star, of that lighthouse which has always guided its way through the rocks and shoals of revolution—the name of Molière. But it pleased Louis the Fourteenth, who had always protected Molière and made great use of him, to cast the remnants of the company of the Hôtel de Bourgogne into Molière's company. This fusion took place in 1680. Henceforth there was but one company—the company of the king. The Comédie-Française was definitely established. We, in France, love to call it La Maison de Molière, and that glorious name it fully deserves.

Thanks to the fusion, the repertoires of Corneille and Racine were added to that of Molière. It is true that Molière, out of respect for the great Corneille, had played some of his tragedies which the actors of the Hôtel de Bourgogne had rejected. But these tragedies, the works of his old age, were not his best. The great and immortal masterpieces of the poet were the property of the Hôtel de Bourgogne, as was also the repertory of Racine, who, after having been guilty of a petty meanness towards Molière, had quarrelled with him and given his tragedies to the rival actors.

It was a singular fortune, and this happened only once during the lapse of centuries, that three men of genius, very different in character, although nearly equal in talent, should have lived almost at the same time. These three men had written a number of great works, which constituted for the stage a repertory the like of which for richness and beauty has never been excelled. This repertory was an inestimable treasure and an exhaustless resource to the company of the king, for it furnished it with first-rate material to depend upon in times of scarcity; and even now, when we have bad literary seasons to go through, we have recourse to this repertory to satisfy the public curiosity when it is tired and weary of novelties.

III

Such is the starting-point of the organisation of the Comédie-Française.

The Comédie is a society, or, should you prefer another expression, a republic, which governs itself. Rome elected two consuls every year; the Comédie-Française elects two chiefs every week, who are styled *semainiers*. Each member is a *semainier* in his turn. The *semainiers* on duty draw up the bills of performance, preside over the rehearsals, and distribute the profits: in short, they are the captains of the vessel. The engagement of actors and the reception of pieces take place at a general meeting of the society.

The king appointed two or four commissioners to preside or to watch over the company; these commissioners, called *les gentilshommes de la chambre,* had for their duty to enforce the views or taste of the king, and to defend his interests. And what were their rights? Exactly the same as those which the company now exercises, either by itself as a body or by the medium of its *semainiers.* They could make engagements, accept pieces, impose their programmes, and interfere with everything concerning the theatre. Such were their rights, and they constantly used them.

But where did the respective limits of these two rival powers end? As regards limits, there were none very precise. On one side as on the other, there was no law to go by. If there were written rules, nobody knew them, or at least paid any attention to them. Conflicts arose constantly and filled up the whole of the history of the French stage during the eighteenth century. However, the rival parties generally managed to come to an agreement. How, I can hardly explain, except by comparing the process with the English way of settling difficulties—that is to say, by relying more on common sense and custom than on the technicalities of the law, and by making mutual concessions in accordance with public opinion. For do you imagine that public opinion has had nothing to do with the affairs of the Comédie-Française? No, you cannot think so. The public has been a third power which joined the other two and became the regulator of them. It has played a great part in the history of the Comédie-Française, and it has been one of the most active elements in its final organization. It deserves, therefore, a few words of notice.

Under this name of public or audience, we must not imagine the international crowds which, at the present day, congregate within the theatres of Paris and London. The public to-day is unquestionably a public—there is no other term to describe it—but it is a public devoid of homogeneousness, a compound of individuals who do not know one another, who have no ideas in common, who cannot respond to the same feeling. The public of former days was a real public. On one side were the noblemen who met again at the theatre in the evening after having seen one another at court all day long; on the other side were the well-to-do burghers of old Paris, who, having closed their shops and done with their business for the day—and at that time, when people did not lead the kind of feverish life we lead nowadays, shops were closed early, and business did not strain the mind—repaired to the play to enjoy their favourite pastime.

The stage in France is a national and especially a Parisian pleasure. Molière, Regnard, Beaumarchais, Voltaire, Scribe, and many other less celebrated dramatic authors were born within sight of the walls of Paris. Everybody in Paris is fond of the play and is a good judge of it. Even at the present moment, when this passion is not so strong as it used to be, many a young man will go without his dinner in order to treat himself to the play. How many will stand for three or four hours together at the doors of a theatre, in the midst of rain or snow, to see the piece in vogue! Everything that relates to dramatic literature is warmly discussed, and there is not a woman, however imperfectly educated she may otherwise be, who is not capable of giving expression to her opinions on theatrical matters, with a knowledge of the subject sometimes astonishing. Every soil has its own peculiar virtues; in the same way every nation has its own peculiar aptitude:

> Excudent alii spirantia mollius æra . . .
> Tu regere imperio populos, Romane, memento.

The passion of the French is the stage. The Parisian middle class was enraptured with it. Yet, at most, thirty or forty thousand persons went usually to the theatre, and out of this number only five or six thousand were regular frequenters. Hence a new piece, after about thirty performances, had exhausted the public interest, and fifteen to twenty performances were considered a fair success. I will not venture to say that all these fanatics of the theatre were acquainted one with the other; but they had received the same education, they knew the repertory so well that they could have prompted an actor in distress; they were imbued with the same feelings, and formed those compact and homogeneous audiences, the members of which understood each other perfectly, and by so doing laid down the law of the stage; for, after all, he who pays has a full right to be the master.

The quarrels which divided the actors among themselves, and the actors from the *gentilshommes de la chambre,* were known to these audiences, not by the papers, for there were none, but by the conversations in the *cafés,* and by those numerous imperceptible voices which escape from behind the scenes. They knew that *Messieurs les Gentilshommes* had, in spite of the unwillingness of the committee, engaged such or such an actress, who pleased one of them. The audience, in consequence, revolted unanimously, unless, by chance, the favourite of the court people turned out to be a true artist, and in this case they took part against the committee and forced it to give way. However intelligent and discerning it was, the public had none the less its moments of error and passion; in such a case the actors and the *gentilshommes* united to resist, and, if they held out long enough, they gained the day precisely because reason was on their side.

If you glance over the annals of the Comédie-Française, you will find that the whole of its history is a long series of quarrels and conflicts between the republic of the actors, the personal government of the *gentilshommes de la chambre*, and that third power, the public, who had no other weapons to fight their battles with than their whistles and hisses.

This public was a jealous and vigilant guardian of tradition. It no doubt accepted the innovations of writers and actors, but it was fond of rules and reminded the actors of them when they showed signs of departing from them. It was, in fact, the public that made the education of the actors; it placed under their eyes the models of past times, insisting that they be followed; so that in the composition and interpretation of pieces there was no sudden rupture of continuity.

It was thus that the Comédie-Française passed through the brilliant eighteenth century, adding to the repertory of its immortal founders an immense number of works, some of which are veritable masterpieces, while others, less important, form what is called, in theatrical parlance, *le répertoire de second ordre*. Before leaving this subject, let us stop for a moment and consider a circumstance which it is essential to point out, because it has contributed in a great measure to the formation of this repertory, whether of the first or second order.

You have perhaps noticed that, among the great pieces laid before you by the Comédie-Française, several small pieces have slipped in; some are simply vaudevilles and others mere farces. Perhaps you have not well understood how the House of Molière could stoop to such small works. It is because, as I have already pointed out to you, and cannot repeat too often, everything at the Comédie-Française is linked with tradition.

As there was formerly but one theatre in Paris which, by virtue of the privilege granted it, alone had the right to give dramatic performances, it was bound to open its doors to pieces of all kinds. In consequence, you will find in the repertory of Molière, by the side of great five-act pieces, *bouffonneries* which in our days would be acted at the

Variétés and the Palais-Royal—for instance, the *Médecin malgré lui* and the *Mariage forcé,* not to mention any others. But as the Comédie-Française assumed more importance in the world of letters, it was obliged to put on a graver tone; it appeared offensive to hear the language of Tabarin on the same stage where, on the previous night, the dignified Alexandrines of Corneille had been heard. An incident of Parisian life in the eighteenth century rendered the contrast still more striking.

Every year in Paris two fairs used to be held on public places, which were deserts then, but which are now covered with houses. The more celebrated of the two was the St. Laurent fair, and the older the St. Germain fair. Mountebanks repaired thither in great numbers, and among them were a few stage-managers. These impresarios of the booth came into contact with two privileges: if they desired to make their actors sing, they had the Opéra down on them, for the Opéra alone had the right to charm the ears of the Parisians; if they contented themselves with mere dialogues, they came across the Comédie-Française, which prohibited them, in virtue of its prerogatives, the right of exhibiting speaking characters.

But in France, the classic land of privileges, it must be said that privilege has never been favourably regarded by the public. The people have always taken the side of free competition. Is this feeling one of justice, or is it merely a love of finding fault? I will not attempt to decide. In any case the humble managers of the booth theatres found in the public a benevolent ally as witty as it was noisy. The censorship forbade these strolling companies to indulge in dialogues; so they resorted to mere gestures, while a voice behind the scenes recited the piece as it went on, and the audience applauded enthusiastically. When the moment came for singing a couplet, a great placard was suddenly hoisted in front of the public, on which were written the words and music of the song, and the audience sang the forbidden air, while the actors mimicked the words. The authorities added prohibition to prohibition, but it was all in vain; a thousand ingenious ways of evasion were always found; so they had to retreat, and to allow new theatres to be established with privileges which permitted them to play pieces of an inferior class.

From that moment the Comédie-Française closely confined itself to what are called the serious class of pieces. But, as long as lasted this little war, which amused the eighteenth century so much, and the history of which would take up a whole volume, the Comédie had followed in the track of Molière; it had mixed up farces, comic ballets, and even rhyming burlesques with great works. The tradition was founded; it has been preserved. In addition to certain *bouffonneries* of the classic repertory, the Restoration and the times that followed it up to the present day have taken advantage of this liberty to produce at the House of Molière light pieces like the *Petit Hôtel* of Meilhac and Halévy, which was played before you the other day, and gay little comedies, bordering on farce, like the *Voyage à Dieppe,* in which I have seen Provost and Got many a time.

Another tradition was created by this quarrel between the Comédie-Française and the secondary theatres. It was weak and timid at the beginning, but it has extended considerably of late years, and has become almost a dogma. The time came —I do not give the precise dates, neither do I enter into details, as it is less a history of the Comédie-Française than an explanation of the customs and prejudices on which it is founded, that I attempt to give here—the time came when the pieces of a secondary class, which flourished in the booths of the fair, were received officially on the stage of the Italiens, which had just been dispossessed of its Italian *bouffes,* France having gradually forgotten their language, and fashion having deserted them. A number of ingenious, elegant, and witty authors wrote for this new theatre several charming works which were very successful; among these authors I may especially mention Marivaux and Favart.

The Comédie-Française borrowed from this new repertory some of its prettiest works. For instance, *Le jeu de l'Amour et du Hasard,* which had been created at the Italiens by the beautiful and celebrated Sylvia, was transplanted to the House of Molière to please an actress who was famous at the time, and who thought she would shine in the principal character. The piece, having achieved a success, was placed in the repertory, and is often played at the present time. It, however, betrays in some ways its origin. The character of Pasquin requires a deal of burlesque acting which would appear little worthy of the Comédie-Française, if we did not know that it first saw the light on the boards where the harlequin of the Italians gave himself up to the coarsest pantaloonery. They have been kept on the austere stage of the Comédie-Française, because tradition is everything there.

During the past fifteen years the Comédie-Française has practised more extensively than ever this tradition which Molière has described in the celebrated phrase: "Je reprends mon bien partout où je le trouve." It is thus that the *Gendre de M. Poirier,* the *Fils Naturel*, the *Demi-Monde, Philiberte,* the *Marquis de Villemer,* and many more have been added to the repertory. The Comédie-Française has become of late a kind of museum, where good pieces, brought out at no matter what theatre, finally receive their consecration, in the same way as the paintings, after having been exhibited during the life of the painter at the Luxembourg Museum, pass after his death into the Louvre to take rank among the masterpieces if it be thought they deserve that honour.

While the Comédie-Française was forming for itself an admirable repertory of plays, it was also gathering a marvellous collection of objects of art, statues, busts, and paintings, which might be called its *trésor*, in the same way as we say the *trésor de Notre-Dame*. Who does not know the *foyer* of the Comédie-Française and the gallery which joins it? Who has not admired that superb marble where Molière—an ideal Molière, but no matter—seems to live again, and the pensive face of the aged Corneille, and that masterpiece of masterpieces, the inestimable jewel of the collection, the bust of Rotrou? Shall I speak of the statue of Voltaire sitting, which is known to the whole world by the copies that have been made of it; and of the bust of the same Voltaire which figures by the side of the statue? This Comédie-Française, being a lasting institution, has been able, day by day, and seizing good opportunities, to enrich itself with these marvels of art, of which our Louvre might be jealous. The history of each of these works of art is known, as well as the way the Comédie-Française got them. For this one the artist received a free admittance for life; that one was bequeathed to the house by a lover of the theatre; while others were offered by a member of the company, or given by the Government. Every half-century increases the splendour of this collection and enlarges the library and the archives. The House of Molière is at one and the same time a theatre, a palace, and a museum.

IV

All this—repertory, company, collection of art, archives, and glorious mementoes—narrowly escaped destruction or dispersion in the great Revolution of 1789. Politics invaded the house and divided the members into two hostile camps. The one clung to the old régime and Royalty; the other boldly espoused the new ideas. A schism was inevitable; it broke out. The Royalists remained faithful to the building in which the Comédie-Française was then installed, and which is now the Odéon; the others came and established themselves in the Rue Richelieu, at the same spot where the Théâtre

Français is now to be found. The dissidents were the more numerous, and, be it said, the most celebrated. At their head was the illustrious Talma, he who was to become the glory of tragedy under the First Empire. The public did not hesitate; they recognized in them the real heirs of Molière. Moreover, by one of those dictatorial measures in vogue at the time, the theatre on the left bank of the Seine was closed, and the actors who had not rallied to the Republic thrown into prison.

On the 9th of Thermidor there was a moment of inexpressible confusion. All the actors that formed the old company, each going his own way, were dispersed over various theatres. But this crisis was a short one; and in May 1799 they found themselves united together again in the *salle* of the Rue Richelieu. All the institutions of the past had fallen around them; they alone were left standing uninjured. It was still a republic governed by consuls elected for a week, and by their side was the sovereign represented by a commissioner of the Government. He loved the theatre, did the sovereign, who was no other than the First Consul. When he became Emperor, Napoleon the First interested himself in the house most deeply and took a proud pleasure in providing a royal audience for his actors in ordinary. He felt the necessity of codifying the customs in virtue of which the Comédie-Française was administered, and he issued the decree which is so celebrated in France under the name of Decree of Moscow. It was indeed from Moscow (1812) that the decree was dated. Napoleon, who had something theatrical and *charlatanesque* about him, did not dislike these contrasts and surprises, with which he thought to dazzle the imagination of posterity. It is useless to enter into the details of this new code; it merely consecrated old usages. The Comédie-Française is still regulated by this code, although it has been modified by an *ordonnance* delivered in 1830 and by decrees issued in 1850 and 1857. But neither *ordonnances* nor decrees have changed the great features of the company, the only features that interest us in this sketch, and those great features were fixed by Napoleon in accordance with tradition. He added only one point which had its importance as regards the maintenance of the perpetuity of the Comédie-Française through the ages. It had long been the custom that the actors, on retiring after long service, should receive a pension from their colleagues, levied on the profits. But it was necessary to provide for the possibility of the company making no profits. Napoleon, besides the annual subvention he allowed to the Comédie-Française, assigned a sum of 200,000 francs as a reserve fund to meet the deficit of bad years and to assure the regular service of the pensions. That measure was not useless, for the House of Molière had hard seasons to pass through.

Of the three elements which have co-operated in the formation and development of the Comédie-Française, we have already seen two at work. And the third? The public— that public of great lords and well-to-do burghers which I described a few minutes ago—that intelligent public, fond of theatrical affairs and jealous of artistic tradition.

The era of *gentilshommes* had passed, and they were no more spoken of. There were still some after the Revolution, but they no longer formed a separate body; they were mixed up with the great public, and, to use the expression of Charles the Tenth, they had, like everybody else, only their places in the pit. But the middle-class public was found again, almost the same as we saw it a few minutes ago: they formed round the orchestra of the Théâtre Français a kind of aristocracy in the matter of taste. They were called the *habitués* because they went to the theatre every night; and when the actor, entering on the stage, perceived those long rows of bald and shining heads on which the chandelier shed its rays, he was seized with a slight trembling. I saw the last remnants of this circle in my youth: to-day they have entered into the category of fossils. It was in talking with them that I learned all that I know about the contemporary theatre, for they were nearly all educated persons, men of taste, who went to the play not to be seen, but to see.

But this public of the Restoration and the Monarchy of July committed a grave mistake. It did not, like its predecessors, hold the balance equal between the respect for tradition and the taste for novelty. It leaned too much towards the side of tradition, and nearly caused the ruin of the Comédie-Française. It was natural that the great shock of the Revolution, followed by the magnificent Imperial epic, should have its influence on literature and the stage—that authors and actors should display to generations renewed by those prodigious events new modes of thought and sentiment.

But there is nothing so tenacious as a literary taste. The public of *habitués* had in its childhood admired classic tragedies and comedies in verse, of which the *Misanthrope* and the *Femmes Savantes* are the most perfect models. It would not admit of anything outside these two consecrated forms being tried. It might be tired and weary of them, but it would not confess the fact, and gaped and yawned in secret. It rejected with horror every innovation as a scandal;

and while in the field of literature that clamorous army known as the Romantic school arose, the Comédie-Française remained obstinately closed to the new art, or, if the latter succeeded in breaking open the door, it was immediately hissed out again, and the *habitués* returned to sleep over the tragedies of the imitators of Campistron, who like himself had imitated Racine.

What was the consequence of all this? The public—I speak of the great public, of that which was composed, as we say in these days, of the *nouvelles couches sociales*—no longer went to the House of Molière. It conceived such a deep hatred of the latest copyists of Corneille, Racine, and Molière that at length it got disgusted with the masters themselves. The Comédie-Française had hard times to go through then. Receipts of from three hundred to a thousand francs were not rare at that period: the company rubbed its hands with joy when it had (to use the consecrated term) 'passed the four figures,' that is to say, when the receipts amounted to more than a thousand francs. I have in my youth often seen classic works played by a company of eminent actors whose equals we do not possess to-day; altogether there were not more than a dozen of us in the pit, where the price of the places was not more than forty-four sous; the empty boxes looked like so many black holes in the wall; the stalls alone were filled; it was there where the *habitués,* most of whom paid nothing, gathered together.

If the Comédie-Française had not been subventioned, if it had not been under the hand of the Government, it would have broken up at that epoch; for it did not cover its expenses, and each member of the company would have gained more money by playing in another theatre. But the members were kept together by the honour of belonging to a national institution, to the *House of Molière,* and by the certainty of a pension regularly paid at the end of their career.

Rachel alone could draw receipts in those times. It was the great Rachel. But Rachel cost the theatre more than she ever drew, and she did more harm to art than she rendered it service. She would not become a *sociétaire* or Member, because, once a member, she would have been obliged to share her profits with her fellow-members; she remained a *pensionnaire* (the salaried actors are those who make their first appearance at the Comédie, and are in receipt of salaries until they become Members), because she could demand what salary she liked. The nights on which she played the receipts amounted to ten thousand francs, the whole of which went into her pocket. The next night the theatre was empty.

Rachel, moreover, must be blamed for having imparted a factitious life to tragedy and for encouraging her admirers to struggle against the advent of a new art. She obstinately confined herself to a dozen parts, in which she displayed incomparable power, and left imperishable memories. She did not lend the assistance of her genius to any of the contemporary poets, or, if she did so, it was with regret, and without decisive success.

v

It was after the Revolution of 1848 that more prosperous, if not more glorious, days began to shine on the Comédie-Française. The commissioners delegated by the Government to this republic of actors had already for some time been replaced by a general administrator. The names had been changed, but in reality the thing was the same. It was still the hand of the sovereign in the affairs of the Company. The rules which limit the action of the two powers are no more defined in the present day than they were two centuries ago. The amount of authority which falls to the general administrator depends on the prestige he enjoys. It is something entirely personal. He is the real master if he is capable and willing. I have known M. Arsène Houssaye in that post; he was master, but in such a clever and exquisite manner that nobody perceived it. M. Empis, on the contrary, acted the master in such a disagreeable way that he was removed. M. Thierry, who came next, exercised with all kinds of reticence, circumlocution, and delays, at the same time appearing to give way, an influence which was for a long time preponderant. Finally, M. Perrin, of to-day, has charmed and overcome all resistance by the clearness of his views, the brilliancy of his conceptions, and, above all, by the renown of a successful and fortunate manager, which he had acquired in all his undertakings, either at the Opéra or at the Opéra-Comique. And his good luck has followed him to the Théâtre Français, for never since its foundation has the house made such large receipts. They vary from 6,000 to 7,000 francs. Hence the dividends shared every year by the *sociétaires* have become enormous. The Members, besides the salaries they pay to themselves, last year had parts or shares which amounted to more than 40,000 francs. Add to this the supplementary expenses they allow themselves every time they play, or, as *semainers*, supervise the getting up of a piece, and you will see that a Member entitled to the whole of one part gets from 60,000 to 70,000 francs per annum. Add again the fact

that a portion of the profits has been deducted beforehand
and turned into two parts, one part to increase the general
fund, and the other to form for every Member a little heap
of money which he receives on the day of his retirement. It
was thus that Bressant, when he took leave of the Comédie-
Française, received 80,000 francs in a lump; his retiring
pension is, I think, 8,000 to 10,000 francs a year.

It is easy to understand that so many advantages, apart
from the honour of being able to put on your card the words,
Member of the Comédie-Française, which gives a position in
society, and which assures a certain consideration of which
actors are all the more jealous that it was long refused to
their calling—it is easy to understand that so many advantages possess an irresistible fascination for all young actors.
There is not one who does not dream of entering the House
of Molière one day, who does not make it the height of his
ambition and struggle with all his might and main to attain
it. The high study of elocution would long since have been
abandoned for the easier triumphs of the *vaudeville* and the
opérette, if the House of Molière did not appear in the distance offering its golden apples to candidates. No, you will
never know how many unfledged Delaunays and Sarah Bern-
hardts there always are on the streets of Paris, who work ten
hours a day at the old repertory, and who dine at restaurants
at sixpence a head waiting for glory. They try to raise themselves to the height which the Comédie-Française alone maintains in these days of decadence.

The decadence which affects all the theatres in Paris has
not yet made itself felt at the Comédie-Française, and yet of
the three elements which have contributed to its success
during centuries, one has already almost disappeared. There
is no longer any public. The Parisian is swamped amid the
multitudes which the railways daily turn out on the Boule-
vards, and which invade the theatre of the Rue Richelieu
every night. They prolong beyond measure the success of
pieces, and force the actors to play them a hundred times
running, thereby spoiling talents which cannot be renewed,
and which have not opportunities enough to seek fresh
strength in the great school of the classic repertory. Their
taste is neither delicate nor attentive. They neither instruct
nor support the actor. This state of things, unfortunately,
will only go on increasing, and I myself can see no remedy
for it. It has not yet done much harm to the Comédie-Française, which still presents a majestic aspect and relies on the
two principles which presided over its formation, and which
have constituted its power. On the one side, that *ensemble*

of actors governing themselves and guarding the traditions. Do you know that between Got and Molière there are only seven or eight names of great actors? We have, so to speak, only to stretch out our hand to be able, across several generations, to find the first Mascarille. Got played a long time with Monrose, who had seen Dazincourt. Dazincourt appeared young by the side of Préville, already old. Préville had known Poisson, who is the last link of the chain up to Molière. In this way the tradition has been preserved alive from one great actor to another. One feels how such or such a part was played in the days of Molière, and when by chance the interpretation is changed by the caprice of an actor, as happened in the case of Arnolphe, whose character was modified by Provost, that change forms a date, and the new tradition is established, unless the successors of Provost reject it. Here we see the distinctive mark of the Comédie-Française, which unites to tradition a wise spirit of innovation, that corrects and harmonises it to the tastes of the day, but at the same time, out of respect for tradition, always puts the bridle on this taste for novelty. The history of the Comédie-Française is only a perpetual compromise between these two contrary forces.

The administrator represents more especially the spirit of innovation. As he is always a man of influence and education, he brings with him into office personal opinions on art, and seeks to apply them. He therefore gives a stroke to the rudder which turns the ship in a new direction. He is disinterested, as the question of money does not affect him; or rather he has no other interest than glory. He does not, therefore, feel any desire to sacrifice art to big receipts. He is also above those petty rivalries, those mean jealousies, which often divide actors, and from which those of the Comédie-Française are not more exempt than others. He puts an end to their quarrels sometimes by imposing his own will, sometimes by compounding dexterously with their passions. *C'est la lutte: donc c'est la vie.*

Such is it still, this majestic body of traditions which is called the Comédie-Française. Everything is there, as in great family houses, rich and solemn. The employees of it stay there till old age, and are proud of it. You will find ushers there so ceremonious that they appear as if they dated from the Great Monarch and had formerly opened the doors to him. The box-openers know all the *habitués,* and salute them with a friendly smile. Costumers and assistants transmit their charges from father to son. The very forms which are used to reply to all who have anything to do with the Comédie smack of old times, and in everything the Comédie says or does there is a politeness and generosity which is like a permanent homage to the memory of Molière.

I think you will forgive a Frenchman for this panegyric. You have enough of other superiorities to admit with a good grace the glory of an institution which is lacking in your country. The people which is to-day at the head of the movement of contemporary philosophy, which has revolutionised the world of thought and science with the writings of such men as Darwin, Herbert Spencer, Sir John Lubbock, and Evans, has nothing to envy in anybody. It is great enough to render justice to the merits of its rivals, and I thank you for having done so with so much courtesy and warmth of heart.

Edmund Kean and Junius Brutus Booth

by

EDWIN BOOTH

With an Introduction by Lawrence Barrett

Note by Brander Matthews

Introduction

Edwin Thomas Booth was born on his father's farm in Hartford County, Maryland, November 13, 1833. Although he was not dedicated by his parents to the stage, his apprenticeship began in early youth. The care of a growing family keeping his mother at home, young Edwin was sent forth while almost a child himself to act as guide, companion, and friend to the most erratic genius that ever illumined the theatre in any age. As mentor, dresser, companion, the boy lived almost a servant's life in hotels, dressing rooms, among the wings, in constant and affectionate attendance upon him to whom the early drama of America owes so much of its glory. The applause received by the father rang in the lad's ears as a sweet prelude to that which was ere long destined to be his own. Indeed, he seemed already to participate in the glory of his father by the close and anomalous relation.

Curious and characteristic anecdotes are given of this strange union. Incidents were continually happening which were preparing the character of the boy for his own eventful career. Seeing much of the vicissitudes of the actor's life in that day of the drama's hardest probation in America, he learned lessons that were later to be useful to himself. Pathos and humor were strangely brought together in these tours of the elder Booth, accompanied by his bright-eyed, watchful assistant. The irregularities and vagaries of Junius Brutus Booth are made familiar to the reader of dramatic history by the annalist and biographer; but few knew the serious side of that strange nature, its love of home, its parental tenderness, its sweet indulgence, the royally stored mind, rich with the learning of foreign literature and graced with a wealth of expression that made his learning a wellspring from which all could drink. Thus the theatre was Edwin Booth's schoolroom, the greatest living master of passion his tutor, and the actors his fellow pupils, divided from him only by the disparity of years. Constantly ignoring any question of Edwin's ever becoming an actor, his father acquiesced willingly in the boy's amateurish acquirement of the violin and of a Negro's mastery of the banjo. These tuneful accomplishments, aided by the voice of the young musician in some of the then familiar plantation melodies, amused the leisure and gratified the paternal pride of a fond and sometimes over-indulgent father.

In many ways these simple graces served to assist the young guardian in keeping his father within doors when his restless spirit urged him forth upon some of those erratic wanderings that seem now almost like moody insanity; when, straying far into the morning through the sleeping city, striding for hours up and down an open deserted market place, morose, silent, he was followed by the pleading, faithful lad, who feared that some ill would result from such rashness. Lear in the storm, with no daughter's ingratitude as an urging cause, seems an apt parallel here. When the summer vacation came, or when the father drifted into idleness as he drifted into labor, Edwin was sent to school, but to be as suddenly dragged thence whenever one of the fitful engagements began. One can easily fancy how much more potent were the lessons of the theatre than those so irregularly learned in regular school; and it is demonstrated truly in his case that an actor's life is in itself a liberal education.

No wonder the boy grew up observant, grave, thoughtful, and melancholy beyond his years. As no thought had been given to his career, so at last it was determined by accident, and by no suggestion of his father's. On September 10, 1849 Edwin Booth appeared as Tressel to his father's Richard III on the stage of the Boston Museum. No trumpet of herald announced this important event; its necessity arose from the somewhat insignificant fact that the duties of prompter made it necessary that someone should lighten the shoulders of that official of a double burden, and the obscure actor was replaced by one who that night entered upon a career the consequences of which will affect the American stage more profoundly than any other event connected with it. The success of this maiden effort did not seem to win the father to the lad's side. Without openly condemning the step, the elder Booth tacitly showed that he did not approve of it. The report of Edwin's hit induced managers of other cities to request that father and son should appear together on occasions. This was stubbornly resisted. On one occasion an old friend, then managing a Western theatre, asked Mr. Booth to allow him to bill Edwin with his father. He was met by the usual curt refusal; but after a moment's pause, and without any sense of the humor of the suggestion, Booth said that Edwin was a good banjo player, and he could be announced for a solo between the acts.

His first appearance as Richard III was the result of an accident, and it was quite as unexpected as his original effort. His father, billed at the National Theatre, New York, for Richard, suddenly resolved just before the play began that he would not go to the theatre; entreaties were in vain. "Go act it yourself," said the impracticable father to his confused and half distracted son. On his carrying this message to the disappointed manager, that official, in his distress, accepted the alternative. The audience was satisfied, and the play went on to the end with no demonstration of disapproval. A brief experience in the stock company at Baltimore, uneventful and comparatively unsuccessful, preluded the departure for California from which so many results important to Edwin Booth's subsequent career were to flow. The Booths sailed in 1852, crossed the Isthmus, and appeared at San Francisco soon after their arrival.

The time for this visit was ill chosen. Financial depression had succeeded the early marvelous prosperity of the Golden State, and the drama, despite a fine company of actors, was languishing with the other industries of the Pacific coast. A few performances in San Francisco, some appearances in Sacramento, given to poor audiences and unremunerative both to actor and manager, make up the result of the only visit of the elder Booth to the far West. Returning home alone and believing fully in the future prosperity of California, he left his two sons, Junius Brutus and Edwin, behind him. The usual vicissitudes of the actor in those pioneer days were experienced by Edwin Booth: unpaid services in the cities, sad and trying wanderings in the mountains, where the surroundings were of the rudest, the audience the most indulgent, sickness, want, cold, hunger—these were the early discipline of the sensitive and gifted child of genius. During this time the news of his father's death reached him, bringing home to his heart the first great sorrow it had ever known. Now filling a subordinate place in a stock company at a mere pittance, now pushed prematurely forward into the parts his father had made famous, he journeyed hither and thither, reaching even as far as Australia, where his welcome was most cordial; then to the Sandwich Islands, with a king for his patron; and so back once more to the land of gold, where, in a happy hour, he yielded a ready ear to that voice which had been for years calling him to the scenes of his father's glory, and where his crown was in waiting for him.

His first appearance after his return was made in Baltimore as Richard III. Later, while playing in Richmond under the management of Joseph Jefferson, he met with the lady who became afterwards his wife, the lovely and accomplished Mary Devlin, then a member of Mr. Jefferson's personal and dramatic family; and at length, early in the spring of 1857, he made his bow as a star in Boston, the city where he had made his first essay as an actor, and where his father's memory was still cherished. Opening as Sir Giles Overreach, he was completely successful. He followed this auspicious beginning with a round of characters in which he sustained the reputation he had already gained. On May 4, 1857 he made his bow before a New York audience as Richard III at the Metropolitan Theatre. The writer may be pardoned if he here connects himself with the subject of this memoir by recalling the importance of the scene, of which he was a witness and a participant in a humble way, playing Tressel in a powerful cast of the tragedy.

Although Booth had but recently returned to the East, rumor had brought the story of his fame and success; and the stock company of the theatre awaited eagerly his appearance at rehearsal. The scene will long live in the memory of those who were present. A slight, pale youth, with black flowing hair, soft brown eyes full of tenderness and gentle timidity, a manner mixed with shyness and quiet repose, he took his place with no air of conquest or self-assertion and gave his directions with a grace and courtesy which have never left him. He had been heralded by his managers in the papers and on the fences as the "Hope of the Living Drama," greatly to his dismay, but his instantaneous success almost justified such extravagant eulogy; and while curiosity had brought many to see the son of him who had been their whilom idol, they remained to pay tribute to an effort which was original and spontaneous.

He arrived at an opportune moment. Forrest was beginning to lose his grasp upon the scepter which he had held so long; age and infirmity were showing their effect upon his once perfect frame, and his style was derided by a new generation of theatre-goers. The elder Wallack was playing his farewell engagement, Davenport was wasting his fine talents in undignified versatility; and a place was already made for a man who had original and creative power. Pursuing for the next few years the career of a wandering player, with frequent returns to New York and new additions to his repertory, Edwin Booth was acquiring new experience and valuable confidence in his powers. He was married in 1860 to Miss Devlin; and in 1861 he visited London, having made an ill-considered and hasty agreement with a manager there which forced him to come out at a comedy theatre, the Haymarket, in a part unsuited for a first appearance, although one of his best performances, Shylock. He paid too little heed to the importance of his London engagement, and it was only as it neared its close, when he had satisfied the people by his magnetic performance of Richelieu, that he woke to the magnitude of the event. He was obliged to quit the scene of his success at the moment of its arrival. Returning to his own country, he found the land agonized in the throes of civil war. During this first visit to England his only child Edwina was born. His home on his return was made at Dorchester, Massachusetts. Here he left his young wife, whom he never saw again, to go to his New York engagement in February 1863. His wife's death was bitter affliction which drove him to increased labor in his art as some poor solace for an irreparable loss.

He now took a lease of the Winter Garden Theatre, New York, having already purchased with Mr. J. S. Clarke the Walnut Street Theatre, in Philadelphia. His partners in the New York scheme were Messrs. Clarke and William Stuart. In November 1864 occurred the notable production of *Hamlet,* which ran one hundred consecutive nights. Adequately mounted, excellently cast, it fixed the fame of Mr. Booth as the Hamlet par excellence of the American stage. No such revival of a Shakespearean play had taken place since the days of Charles Kean, at the old Park.

While Booth was acting at the Boston Theatre in April 1865 the news was brought to him of the great calamity which had befallen the country and inflicted an incurable sorrow upon himself and his family. He at once resolved to abandon his profession forever; but after nearly a year of retirement, at the urgent solicitation of friends throughout the whole country, he appeared as Hamlet at the Winter Garden Theatre on January 3, 1866. The reception and performance were remarkable.

William Winter says of this event: "Nine cheers hailed the melancholy Dane upon his first entrance. The spectators rose and waved their hats and handkerchiefs. Bouquets fell in a shower upon the stage, and there was a tempest of applause, wherever he appeared. After this momentous return to the stage, he found a free-hearted greeting and respectful sympathy; and so, little by little, he got back into the old way of work, and his professional career resumed its flow in the old channel." This was a notable event in America's dramatic history. A series of revivals worthy of the refinement of any age succeeded each other at the Winter Garden Theatre. *Richelieu* was given as never before in the history of the stage. Shakespeare's *Merchant of Venice* as a whole, with a fidelity unsurpassed in scenic and historic annals, ran for several weeks to large and delighted audiences. At the summit of the success of these efforts to revive the glory of the earlier days of the drama, a fire broke out in the Winter Garden Theatre, which destroyed not only much valuable material, but also delayed for a time the purposes of the ambitious actor, who had no less a desire than the highest achievement for his beloved art. Setting out on his provincial tours once more, he formed the plan to create out of the ashes of his ruined theatre an edifice more costly and enduring. Selecting a site for his new house, he placed the earnings of his richly productive career in the lap of his new enterprise. Over a million of dollars were spent in the construction of the noblest temple yet erected to the drama in America. With the same liberality which had stopped at no sacrifice in the erection of the building, the actor now lavished large sums on the stage and its settings. The theatre was opened February 3, 1869 with a gorgeous production of *Romeo and Juliet* from the original text. Booth was himself the Romeo, his future wife, Mary McVicker, the Juliet, the gifted Edwin Adams the Mercutio, with a supporting cast of unusual excellence. The success of the theatre was instant and enduring. For the years during which Mr. Booth retained control the receipts were very large, although the lavish outlay left no margin of profit. *A Winter's Tale, Hamlet, Julius Cæsar, The Merchant of Venice, Much Ado about Nothing,* and others of the great Shakspearean plays were presented in an unprecedented style of magnificence, admirably cast. The original texts in all instances were restored, many years ahead of all English efforts in that direction. Disaster, owing to unskillful business management, and the impossibility of one man's remaining always at the helm, wrecked this noble venture. But although bankruptcy resulted to the enthusiastic founder, the glory of having given such a temple and such a series of revivals to the American stage will be linked inseparably with the renown of Edwin Booth.

His subsequent appearances in San Francisco after twenty years' absence, and in London, where he presented a round of his favorite parts with great eclat, and his crowning glory in presenting himself before the critics of exacting Germany, lead up so near the present hour of writing that these exploits must await another annalist.

The noble subject of these records is still in the zenith of his strength. He lives to lead the American stage of today with the same power as of old, and with the same love on the part of his followers to sustain him. Eulogy and praise stand mute in the presence of such merits. *Nil nisi mortuis bonum* is the admonition when the chroniclers gather up the records of a great man's life after the race is run. The biographer who shall truly write the story of Edwin Booth's career will have little need to observe this caution. Of him it may be said, aside from his great place and merit as the greatest exponent of our art today, that

> His life was gentle; and the elements
> So mixed in him that nature might stand up,
> And say to all the world "This was a man."

LAWRENCE BARRETT

Note

The foregoing was written in 1886. The next year the writer of this glowing tribute undertook to manage the tour of a Shakspearean company of which the two friends should be the chiefs. In 1890 Barrett withdrew for a year from the company while remaining the manager; and Madame Modjeska took a place by the side of Edwin Booth. The next season Booth and Barrett again joined forces, the younger actor relieving the elder from all the burdens of conducting the enterprise. In March 1891 Barrett died suddenly. Booth made his own last appearance on the stage in Brooklyn on April 4, two months before his death.

Three years earlier Edwin Booth, desiring to do something for the benefit of the profession that he and his father between them had adorned for more than threescore years and ten, had bought a spacious house, No. 16 Gramercy Park, had caused it to be altered, decorated, and furnished under the supervision of Stanford White, and had presented it to a specially organized club for which his old friend Thomas Bailey Aldrich had suggested an appropriate name, The Players. This clubhouse was opened on the last night of 1888; its founder read the deed of gift; and on the stroke of midnight he raised to his lips a silver loving cup that had belonged to his father, passing it then to the member who stood next him. And on every New Year's Eve since then The Players have gathered to greet the new year and to drink to the memory of the Founder. It was in the room that he had reserved for himself in the clubhouse that Edwin Booth died, June 7, 1891. The Players have kept this room sacred to his memory, exactly as he left it, even with the book he had been reading lying on the table where he laid it.

BRANDER MATTHEWS

Edmund Kean and Junius Brutus Booth

In my study, or my smokery rather, for little else but smoking is done in the small room to which only a chosen few are admitted, I have often sat until dawn alternately reading memoirs of great actors of the past and contemplating their portraits and death masks which hang upon the walls; and somehow I seem to derive a more satisfactory idea of their capabilities from their counterfeit presentments than from the written records of their lives.

What a void in the gallery of old masters of Dramatic Art is made by the absence of any portraits of Thespis, Roscius, or Burbage. We might perhaps get a taste of their quality, could we see some semblance of their features.

My impressions may have no worth. They are offered simply as the mere fancies of one who, while placidly puffing his midnight pipe, holds communion with the departed; not by means of spiritism, but, as I have said, through the medium of their biographies, their pictures, and the plaster casts of their dead faces.

To begin with our earliest tragic actor of whom we have any authentic portrait, I can read no line of tragedy in the face of Thomas Betterton, although Cibber's opinion must be respected; and I doubt if Quin's features, of which I have no likeness worth considering, would convince me of his excellence in the higher range of tragedy. Certainly those of Barton Booth and Spranger Barry do not; yet all of them manifest much dignity. The beautiful features of Garrick evince wonderful mobility, but they suggest more of the comic than of the tragic quality. All his best known portraits depict him as the incomparable comedian; even in Hogarth's Richard the expression of horror seems weak; and as his friend and admirer, the great Johnson, declared that his death eclipsed the gaiety of nations, I am inclined to believe that Davy was more favored by Thalia than by Melpomene. Old Macklin and George Frederick Cooke gaze at me with hard immobile features, denoting great force in a limited tragic range, such as hate, revenge, and cunning. Nothing poetic or sublime can be found in either countenance, nor anything approaching the humorous, unless it be a leer in the latter's eye which indicates cajolery, or the sardonic mirth of Shylock, Richard, or Iago. I cannot imagine either of these famed actors as being satisfactory in Lear, Macbeth, Hamlet, or Othello. From them I turn to the noble front of Kemble, whose calm majestic features seem to say, "See what a grace was seated on this brow!" whereon indeed is clearly set the impress of the tragic crown; and then to his sister, Siddons, the unexpressive she whose lips and eyes, made forever eloquent by Reynolds, tell us that her jealous mother, Melpomene, cabin'd, cribb'd, confin'd, and bound her in the limitations of the awful circle, although lavish Nature gave her the utmost range of human emotions, whether of joy or of grief, anger, remorse, or the very levity of mirth. Neither Kemble nor Siddons was able to doff the buskin for the sock successfully. Their spheres were high, but circumscribed.

The sweet, sad face of the great German, Ludwig Devrient, and that of his nephew, Emil—by many considered the better actor—and the feline loveliness of Rachel, which clearly shows the scope of her ability, must be passed by as foreign to the subject; my object being simply to compare the portraits of some of the most renowned English tragedians, as they affect me, with that of our great Protagonist—Edmund Kean.

There is no art to find the mind's construction in the face, the living face; but Death frequently reveals some long-hidden secret, a gleam of goodliness, a touch of tenderness, even a glimpse of humor, which life conceals from us. In the uncanny cast of the head of the dead Kean, which hangs above his portrait opposite my desk, I discover the comic as well as the tragic element, and in his ghastly, yet to me fascinating features, only, do I perceive any trace of the two qualities combined. All this there is to be seen, by my eyes at least, in the distorted face, even in its last agony, wasted by disease and suffering; and more than this, I perceive a smile for the weary-hearted wife who sobbed forgiveness at his deathbed, loving to the last.

Lewes, who certainly knew more of this subject than I do, and who was apparently a careful critic, says that Kean had his limitation in tragedy, and that he was devoid of mirth. Lewes, as a lad, had seen Kean in life. I have seen only his dead, weird beauty; and contemplating this as I have often done, and recalling the worlds of one who acted with and against him, I can hardly agree with Lewes. Once and only once my father gave me a glimpse of his reminiscences; on that occasion he, who seldom spoke of actors or the theatre, told me that in his opinion no mortal man could equal Kean in the rendering of Othello's despair and rage, and that, above all, his not very melodious voice in many passages, notably that ending with "Farewell, Othello's occupation gone," sounded like the moan of ocean or the soughing of wind through cedars. His peculiar lingering on the letter "l" often marred his delivery; but here, in the "Farewell," the tones of cathedral chimes were not more mournful. Now, I believe that he who could, as Kean did, perfectly express Othello's exquisite tenderness, as well as his somber and fiercer passions, must have been capable of portraying the sublimest, subtlest, and profoundest emotions. The fact that Kean disliked to act Hamlet and failed to satisfy his critics in that character is no proof that his personation was false. If it was consistent with his conception and that conception was intelligible, as it must have been, it was true. What right have I, whose temperament and mode of thinking are dissimilar to yours, to denounce your exposition of such a puzzle as Hamlet? He is the epitome of mankind, not an individual; a sort of magic mirror in which all men and women see the reflex of themselves, and therefore has his story always been, is still, and will ever be the most popular of stage tragedies. As for the absence of mirth in Kean, the same has been said of all actors with features severely molded. Kean played piano accompaniments to the songs he sang; he told quaint stories, and performed mad pranks in the very ecstasy of merriment. Besides, he made a giant stride from Harlequin to Hamlet, a godlike step from the lowest to the highest plane. Still, after treading the boards on the stilts of Tragedy, his descent to the lower walk may not have been graceful. Most players of what is called the old school, which simply means the only school of acting, now closed I fear forever, had similar training; but how many have ascended the frail ladder of Fame so successfully as Kean? In not retaining the lighter parts of his repertory he showed a worthy ambition to be regarded as a tragedian, a denizen only of the highest realm of Art. If he failed to satisfy in the lesser serious roles wherein he was but one of a group, it was because, like a riderless racer, he felt the need of weight. Accustomed to carry alone the burthen of a tragedy, he naturally felt ill at ease when others shared responsibility with him.

That the son of the only man who shook this monarch on his throne should be so bold in his defense may be considered strange, and indeed it is somewhat out of the way of human dealings; but I know that their rivalry was but the result of managerial trickery, which for a time estranged them. That their personal feelings for each other were of peace, the following anecdote related to me by my mother will attest.

She, with her husband, attended one of Kean's last performances in America, I forget when and where; the play was *Richard III*. At the close of it my father rose, saying he wished to bid Kean good-by, and left my mother alone in the private box to witness the farce or afterpiece which in those days always supplemented tragedy. After some time had elapsed, my father returned with moistened eyes and sadly said, "Let us go home," before the conclusion of the farce, for which my mother wished to wait. On the way to their lodgings she could get nothing from him but sighs and monosyllabic responses to her many queries respecting his interview with Kean.

Days passed before she succeeded in coaxing from him an account of what had happened. He told her, at last, that when he announced himself at the door of Kean's dressing room, the latter dismissed his valet and embraced his enemy. I can see this human trait even in this hideous dead face— my favorite portrait of the man. Hot toddies were sent for, and the two professional foes discussed their varied experiences since their last meeting. Declining Kean's invitation to supper, because he had to escort his wife home, and seeing that his comrade was much fatigued, my father assisted the little giant to disrobe, with many jokes between them. He told this story laughingly, but my mother said to me, "I am positive from your father's eyes and long silence on the subject, that there was more of pain than of pleasure in their parting."

They were so much alike in feature, in manner, and in stature—although my father boasted an inch above Kean in the latter particular, and in that only—that in the scenes where Booth's brown hair and blue-gray eyes were disguised by the traditional black wig of tragedy and by other stage accouterments, he appeared to be the very counterpart of his black-eyed, swarthy rival. Their voices were unlike—the latter's harsh and usually unpleasing to the ear, the former's musical and resonant. Their reading of the text was not the same. Kean was careless, and gave flashes of light after intervals of gloom. Booth was always even, a careful expounder of the text, a scholar, a student, and—but enough of comparisons; they were made, *ad nauseam,* long years ago, and belong to the written history of the London stage; they need have no admittance here. Suffice it that the mere similitude stamped the second comer as an imitator, although he had never seen his predecessor. Kean said, and I believe him, that he had never seen Cooke act; nevertheless many critics declared him to have been a copyist of the great George Frederick.

The word "imitation" seems to be used as a slur upon the actor alone. The painter and the sculptor go to Italy to study the old masters, and are praised for their good copies after this or that one. They are not censured for imitation; and why may not the actor also have his preceptor, his model? Why should he be denounced for following the footsteps of *his* old master? Why should he alone be required to depart from tradition? True, other artists see the works of their predecessors and can retain or reject beauties or blemishes at will; but the actor relies solely on uncertain records of his master's art, and thereby is frequently misled into the imitation of faults, rather than into the emulation of virtues.

In the main, tradition to the actor is as true as that which the sculptor perceives in Angelo, the painter in Raphael, and the musician in Beethoven; all of these artists having sight and sound to guide them. I, as an actor, know that could I sit in front of the stage and see myself at work I would condemn much that has been lauded, and could correct many faults which I feel are mine, and which escape the critic's notice. But I cannot see or hear my mistakes as can the sculptor, the painter, the writer, and the musician. Tradition, if it be traced through pure channels and to the fountainhead, leads one as near to Nature as she can be followed by her servant, Art. Whatever Betterton, Quin, Barton Booth, Garrick, and Cooke gave to stagecraft or, as we now term it, business, they received from their predecessors; from Burbage and, perhaps, from Shakespeare himself, who, though not distinguished as an actor, well knew what acting should be; what they inherited in this way they bequeathed in turn to their art, and we should not despise it. Kean knew without seeing Cooke, who in turn knew from Macklin, and so back to Betterton, just what to do and how to do it. Their great mother Nature, who reiterates her teachings and preserves her monotone in motion, form, and sound, taught them. There must be some similitude in all things that are True.

No reference to Kean can be made, it seems, without allusion to his frailties. That is well enough. It is the biographer's duty to be candid and not to hide his hero's faults; but those allusions have been mainly brutal. Why not deliver all with charity? By permission of my friend, Dr. A. O. Kellogg, whose lifework has been the study and treatment of mental diseases, I quote from his yet unpublished essay on my father the following passage:

"The man who all his lifetime was held in the grasp of an inexorable disease, the most sad that can afflict humanity, should not be judged too harshly for his shortcomings. Moreover, modern physiological science has shown conclusively that inebriety is not always the result of vicious habits and indulgences, but frequently the symptom of disease, as we feel assured was the case with the subject of this paper."

This is so applicable to Kean that I have introduced it here, in mitigation of what is deemed unpardonable in the actor when his exhausted nervous system, strained to the utmost tension, induces him to seek the treacherous aid of stimulants. The brain worker of any other walk or profession is excused when incapacitated by prostration on the ground of overwork; not so the actor—Punch has no feelings! I have no doubt that little Davy often suffered as much from the reaction of emotion, simulated, but nevertheless exhausting, as ever his mammoth friend, the learned Doctor, did.

As I gaze on the pitiable face of him, the waif, the reputed chick of Mother Carey, a stormy petrel indeed, but perhaps the first really great tragedian that trod the English stage, and at the same time recall my experiences with one of a similarly erratic brain, I am convinced that Kean's aberrations were constitutional, and beyond his control. The blots in the 'scutcheon of genius, like spots on the sun, are to us dim-eyed gropers in the vast Mystery incomprehensible, inscrutable! Who shall say that even our very evils, still existing in defiance of man's mightiest efforts to extirpate them, are not a part of the All-wise economy?

Whilst pondering the ills of men like Edmund Kean, we must not forget the sacred precept: "He that is without sin among you, let him first cast a stone."

To those who are interested in theatrical history, the following meager sketch of my father may not be satisfactory; for though the greater part of my boyhood was passed in close attendance upon him, his career, professional and personal, has been so fully discussed by able annalists of the stage that little, if anything, can be told to enlighten the reader regarding the erratic course of that extraordinary actor, whose portrayal of all serious emotions thrilled and charmed, while his eccentricities puzzled, the playgoers of his time. My recollections of him are somewhat somber; and though many of them possess a certain grotesque humor, their recital could serve no better purpose than to gratify the curious or make the unskillful laugh, and therefore would be worthless.

His "oddities" were sources of suffering to him, and it is not for the son to publish what the sire—could he have done so—would have concealed. It may not be deemed unfilial in me, however, to recount a few episodes which may tend to explain away much that was imputed to vices of the blood in him whose memory is still revered by many who knew him well, and will ever be a veneration to me who knew him best.

To comprehend the peculiar temperament with which my father charmed, roused, and subdued the keenest and the coarsest intellects of his generation, one should be able to understand that great enigma to the wisest, *Hamlet*. Bulwer has somewhere said:

> Genius, the Pythian of the Beautiful,
> Leaves her large truths a riddle to the dull;
> From eyes profane a veil the Isis screens,
> And fools on fools still ask—what *Hamlet* means.

To my dull thinking, Hamlet typifies uneven or unbalanced Genius. But who shall tell us what genius, of any sort whatever, means? The possessor, or rather the possessed, of it is, as Hamlet was, more frequently its slave than its master, being irresistibly, and often unconsciously, swayed by its capriciousness. Great minds to madness closely are allied. Hamlet's mind, at the very edge of frenzy, seeks its relief in ribaldry. For a like reason would my father open, so to speak, the safety valve of levity in some of his most impassioned moments. At the instant of intense emotion, when the spectators were enthralled by his magnetic influence, the tragedian's overwrought brain would take refuge from its own threatening storm beneath the jester's hood, and, while turned from the audience, he would whisper some silliness or "make a face." When he left the stage, however, no allusion to such seeming frivolity was permitted. His fellow actors who perceived these trivialities, ignorantly attributed his conduct at such times to lack of feeling; whereas it was the extreme excess of feeling which thus forced his brain back from the very verge of madness. Only those who have known the torture of severe mental tension can appreciate the value of that one little step from the sublime to the ridiculous. My close acquaintance with so fantastic a temperament as was my father's so accustomed me to that in him which appeared strange to others, that much of Hamlet's "mystery" seems to me no more than idiosyncrasy. It likewise taught me charity for those whose evil or imperfect genius sways them to the mood of what it likes or loathes.

Reserved and diffident, almost bashful, when away from home, my father behind his locked doors and bolted shutters was as gleeful as a child. Soon after sunrise he would dig in his garden, whistling while he worked; but when visitors were announced, an unconscious selfishness made him deny himself to all callers. Contented within his family circle, he could not appreciate the necessity for any extraneous element there; hence, his wife and children became isolated and were ill at ease in the presence of others than their own immediate relatives.

The effects of his unfortunate disposition for seclusion was never eradicated; the family in consequence suffered a sense of estrangement, while it caused those who knew my father superficially to deem him moody or morose. He was not, although a man of moods undoubtedly he was. Only when the spirit moved him could he render justice to his work, and sometimes, when not i' the vein, he would refuse to act or, without a word of warning, would quit the crowded theatre to be lost to the world for days; reimbursing his manager afterward, however, by performing without more remuneration than was sufficient to defray his own small expenses. On one such occasion, when his engagement was advertised to begin the first of April, an erring fancy impelled him to walk some distance from the city at the time when he should have been in the theatre. The audience, supposing his nonappearance to be a managerial trick to fill the house with "April fools," was loudly indignant. The manager endeavored to pacify his patrons by promising on his honor that Mr. Booth should not set foot upon that stage while he controlled it. This was received with hisses by his hearers, who left the theatre determined to remain away from it until, in compliance with their demand, the appearance of Mr. Booth (his heroic given names, Junius Brutus, were never used in the playbills with his consent) was again announced. He was greeted with affectionate enthusiasm on his return, and he acted finely throughout the engagement. At the time of this occurrence he had left me at home, in compliance with my mother's wish that "Edwin should remain at school." But soon a message came for me to go to him. Though I was not his favorite, my presence seemed necessary to him at his work, although at other times he almost ignored me, perhaps because his other children were more vivacious and amused him. His reception of me was not very cordial—"Did you bring your schoolbooks?" They were in my trunk, but were seldom looked at; his play books were my more congenial studies. This was his only greeting; yet throughout my long association with him, a motherlike solicitude for me tempered his most irrational moods. He wished none of his children to follow his calling. Not that he considered it unworthy, but its effect upon his nervous system caused him so much distress that he preferred they should engage in some more healthful work, anything that was *true,* rather than that they should be of that unreal world where nothing is but what is not. According to his program my vocation should have been that of a cabinetmaker (a notion suggested by the lease of his farm to one of that trade), but, much to his chagrin, accident ordained for me a different pursuit.

Strange as it may seem, chance, not predilection for the stage, determined my way of life. After my début in the very small part of Tressel, he "coddled" me—gave me gruel (his usual meal at night when acting) and made me don his worsted nightcap, which when his work was ended he always wore as a protection for his heated head, to prevent me from taking cold after my labors, which were doubtless very exhausting on that occasion, being confined to one brief scene at the beginning of the play! At that time there seemed to be a touch of irony in this overcare of me, but *now,* when I recall the many acts of his large sympathy, it appears in its true character of genuine solicitude for the heedless boy who had drifted into that troublous sea, where without talent he would either sink or, buoyed perhaps by vanity alone, merely flounder in its uncertain waves.

During my second season on the stage, he doubtless determined to test my "quality," and one evening, just as he should have started for the theatre to prepare for his performance of Richard III, he feigned illness; nor would he leave the bed where he had been napping (his custom always in the afternoon), but told me to go and act Richard for him. This amazed me; for my experience as yet had been confined to minor parts. But he could not be coaxed to waver from his determination not to act that night, and as it was time for the manager to be notified, there was no course to pursue but to go to the theatre to announce the fact. "Well," exclaimed the manager, "there is no time to change the bill; we must close the house—unless *you* will act the part." The stage director and several actors present urged me to try it, and before my brain had recovered from its confusion they hurried me into my father's dress and on to the stage, in a state of bewilderment. My effort was not altogether futile, for it satisfied my father that his boy's prospects were fair for at least a reputable position in the profession. Thenceforth he made no great objection to my acting occasionally with him, although he never gave me instruction, professional advice, or encouragement in any form: he had doubtless resolved to make me work my way unaided; and though his seeming indifference was painful then, it compelled me to exercise my callow wits; it made me *think!* And for this he has ever had my dearest gratitude.

During my constant attendance on him in the theatre he forbade my quitting his dressing room—where he supposed my school lessons were studied. But the idle boy, ignoring Lindley Murray and such small deer, seldom seeing the actors, listened at the keyhole to the garbled text of the mighty dramatists, as given in the acting versions of the plays. By this means at an early age my memory became stored with the words of *all* the parts of every play in which my father performed. In after years the authors' true text became my more careful study.

To see my father act, when he was in the acting mood, was *not* "like reading Shakspere by flashes of lightning" that could give but fitful glimpses of the author's meaning; but the full sunlight of his genius shone on every character that he portrayed, and so illuminated the obscurities of the text that Shakespeareans wondered with delight at his lucid interpretation of passages which to them had previously been unintelligible. At his best he soared higher into the realm of Art sublime than any of his successors have reached; and to those who saw him then it was not credible that any of his predecessors could have surpassed him. His expressions of terror and remorse were painful in the extreme, his hatred and revenge were devilish, but his tenderness was exquisitely human. As Richard and Lear he reluctantly, though valiantly, contested the crown with Kean at the zenith of the latter's fame, but threw away his more than half-won victory as 'twere a careless trifle. Indeed, he ever seemed to muse with Omar Khayyám thus:

> The worldly hope men set their hearts upon
> Turns ashes—or it prospers; and anon,
>   Like snow upon the desert's dusty face,
>   Lighting a little hour or two—is gone!

and tossed aside his triumphs with indifference.

Whatever the part he had to personate, he was from the time of its rehearsal until he slept at night imbued with its very essence. If Othello was billed for the evening he would perhaps wear a crescent pin on his breast that day; or, disregarding the fact that Shakespeare's Moor was a Christian, he would mumble maxims of the Koran. Once, when he was about to perform *Othello* in Baltimore, a band of Arabs visited that city to exhibit their acrobatic feats and jugglery. To my mother's great disgust, but to the infinite delight of her children, my father entertained the unsavory sons of "Araby the blest" in the parlor. As a linguist he was proficient, and among his many tongues he had acquired some use of Arabic, in which he conversed with his guests, or rather with their spokesman, Budh, whose name suggested consanguinity; "for," said he, "Booth and Budh are from the same root." If Shylock was to be his part at night, he was a Jew all day; and if in Baltimore at the time, he would pass hours with a learned Israelite who lived near by, discussing Hebrew history in the vernacular and insisting that, although he was of Welsh descent, that nation is of Hebraic origin—a belief for which there is some foundation. As the pirate Bertram, he once reproved me for scolding a Negro messenger boy who unwittingly crossed the stage in view of the audience, by saying: "Let him alone, sir! Let him alone! He is one of my gang."

My last experience of his vagaries was at our final parting on the ship that bore him forever from me. He asked a sailor on deck to take his luggage to his cabin. The fellow replied: "I'm no flunky." "What are you, sir?" demanded my father. "I'm a thief," responded the brute. Instantly the actor assumed his favorite part of Bertram at this cue, and said: "Your hand, comrade, I'm a pirate!" The sailor laughed and rejoined, "All right, my covey; where's your traps?" and carried the trunk to the stateroom. My father's influence on the lowest minds was as great as it was strong over the highest intellects with which he came in contact.

He disliked to assume those characters (especially historical ones) to which his size was not adapted. Being requested by his old friend and manager, Wemyss, to study *Richelieu* for the latter's benefit, my father replied: "No, sir! No. The Cardinal was tall and gaunt; I cannot look him. Nonsense! Announce me as Jerry Sneak or John Lump—not Richelieu." (The comic characters named were the only two that my father retained in his repertory; and 'twas pity that he did so.) Wemyss coaxed and finally prevailed. An old red gown was found in the very limited wardrobe of the theatre, my father having no appropriate costume for the part, and thus shabbily attired, His Eminence with Father Joseph appeared before an expectant audience. The dialogue hitched and halted

for a while, until, losing self-control, Richelieu seized his
companion by the arms and waltzed him about the stage, to
the amazement of the spectators and the dismay of Wemyss,
who quickly lowered the curtain and frantically tore the hair
of his wig, as the star coolly inquired: "Well, my boy, how
d'ye like my Richelieu?" He disappeared for several days
after this freak, to return with welcome to the scene of his
mad exploit.

Favorite actors were then permitted many extravagances
which would not be tolerated now, and too often they abused
the privilege granted by an indulgent public; but such was
not my father's error. Although his eccentricities were invariably attributed to the effect of alcohol, the charge was
mainly false.

> As much as wine did play the Infidel,
> And rob him of his robe of honor,

it should be known that the fineness of his organization was
so acute that a bottle of porter, his favorite beverage when
fatigued, or a single glass of brandy and water, would excite
him as much as five times the quantity would affect another.
A single drop of the liquor which the dullard absorbs with
impunity will often disturb and distract the finest intellect.
The vagaries here rehearsed were due solely to his peculiarly
sensitive temperament. How often has the desire to hide
myself almost mastered my own will when, mentally or
physically unfit, I have been duty-bound to entertain an
audience! If a serious actor suffers thus, what must a comic
one endure when, racked with pain or grief, he is forced to
laugh and amuse the public while his heart aches? "Alas!
poor Punchinello!" That name recalls an incident which
shows how humble an estimate my father had of the social
position of an actor. On our way to his rehearsal one day,
he was accosted by almost everyone we met. To my frequent
inquiries, "Father, who is that?" he replied, "Don't know,"
until, wearied by my importunities, he exclaimed impatiently:
"My child, I do not know these people! But everybody
knows 'Tom-fool'!"

He seldom spoke of actors or the theatre; indeed, it is
doubtful if any actor's family knew so little of theatrical
affairs or gossip as did his. But once after reading *Coriolanus*
to me until far into the morning, he spoke of the marvelous
acting of Edmund Kean—the only time he ever indulged me
with even a glimpse of his reminiscences. The reading of
Coriolanus was superb; but to my eager question, "Why don't
you act that part?" he replied, "Nonsense! 'Twould seem

absurd for one of my inches to utter such boastful speeches. I cannot look Coriolanus." This imaginary obstacle, his size, prevented his more frequent performances of Othello and Macbeth, although his treatment of both was eminently Shakespearean and profoundly affecting. Though low in stature, he seemed to tower ten feet high when, as Brutus, he cursed "the monster, Tarquin"; and so it was in many instances when, in other parts, the flight of passion lifted him above the level of ordinary actors. In extolling the virtues of the dead Lucretia, and in sentencing the unfilial Titus to the ax, his pathos not only moved the audience to tears and sobs, but often even the Roman citizens on the stage were known to sniff and rub their noses furtively. Seriously to affect a stage mob denotes unusual, if not extraordinary, magnetism in the speaker.

The following incident relative to this play, Payne's *Brutus*, may serve to illustrate further my father's absorption in his work. In the last scene, when all was hush as death, and while Brutus (my father) was holding his son Titus (myself) in close embrace at their final parting, a senseless fellow in front made some rude remark which disturbed both audience and actors. Raising his head from off my breast, my father, without lapsing from the stern Roman character of judge, and with a lightning glance toward the fellow, said: "Beware. I am the headsman!" It was like a thunder shock. All in front and on the stage seemed paralyzed, until the thunders of applause that followed broke the spell; the scene thenceforward proceeded without interruption, and ended, as it should end, in tearful silence.

The characters of Brutus, Sir Giles Overreach, Richard III, Cassius, Bertram, Shylock, Pescara, and Sir Edward Mortimer are more distinct in my remembrance of my father's impersonations than others of his large repertory. They are vivid, deathless, in my memory; and for many years it required my most watchful care to avoid too close a following of his rendering of them, which would but make me ridiculous in my own esteem, even if it escaped the censure of the few who might remember the great personator of those characters. Take, for example, his mad challenge to Lord Lovel when as Sir Giles he dashed like lightning from the scene and as quickly returned to ask with vivid lips and chilling voice, "Are you pale?" at which not only the pit rose at him as for Kean, but the whole audience frequently started to its feet in amazement and with cheers. The effect was electrical—indescribable! To reproduce such a scene as he gave it is simply impossible, and all attempts to do so by his many imitators were ridiculous.

My father's mind was quick to apprehend the Master's subtlest and sublimest conceptions; his frame was vigorous and able to perform the weightiest tasks. Although his simulated wrath was fearful, his real anger was always "yokèd with a lamb." Even in his most angry moods there seemed to linger upon his lips the Christlike words of Coleridge:

> He prayeth best who loveth best
> All things, both great and small;
> For the dear God that loveth us—
> He made and loveth all.

The Actor:
A Poetical Epistle

by

ROBERT LLOYD

The Actor

ACTING, dear *Bonnell*, it's Perfection draws
From no Observance of mechanic Laws.
No settled Maxims of a fav'rite Stage,
No Rules deliver'd down from Age to Age,
Let Players nicely mark them as they will,   5
Can e'er entail hereditary Skill.
If 'mongst the humble Hearers of the Pit,
At some lov'd Play the old Man chance to sit,
Am I pleas'd more because 'twas acted so
By *Booth* and *Cibber* thirty Years ago?   10
The Mind recalls an Object held more dear,
And hates the Copy that it comes so near.
Why lov'd we *Wilks's Air, Booth's* nervous Tone?
In them 'twas natural, 'twas all their own.
A *Garrick's* Genius must our Wonder raise,   15
But gives his Mimic no reflected Praise.
Thrice happy Genius, whose unrival'd Name
Shall live for ever in the Voice of Fame!
'Tis thine to lead with more than magic Skill,
The Train of captive Passions at thy Will;   20
To bid the bursting Tear spontaneous flow
In the sweet Sense of sympathetic Woe.
Through ev'ry Vein I feel a Chilness creep,
When Horrors such as thine *have murder'd Sleep.*
And at the old Man's Look and frantic Stare   25
'Tis *Lear* alarms me, for I see him there.
Nor yet confin'd to tragic Walks alone
The comic Muse too claims thee for her own.
With each delightful Requisite to please,
Taste, Spirit, Judgment, Elegance, and Ease,   30
Familiar Nature forms thy only Rule,
From *Ranger's* Rake to *Drugger's* vacant Fool.
With Powers so pliant, and so various blest,
That what we see the last, we like the best.
Not idly pleas'd at Judgment's dear Expence   35
But burst outrageous with the laugh of Sense.

PERFECTION's Top with weary Toil and Pain
'Tis Genius only that can hope to gain.
The Play'r's Profession (tho' I hate the Phrase,
'Tis so *mechanic* in these modern Days)   40
Lies not in Trick, or Attitude, or Start,
Nature's true Knowledge is his only Art.
The strong-felt Passion bolts into the Face,
The Mind untouch'd, what is it but Grimace?
To this one Standard make your just Appeal   45
Here lies the golden Secret; learn to FEEL.
Or Fool or Monarch, happy or distrest,
No Actor pleases that is not *possess'd*.

ONCE on the Stage in *Rome's* declining Days,
When Christians were the Subject of their Plays,   50
Ere Persecution dropp'd her iron Rod,
And Mortals wag'd an impious War with God,
An Actor flourish'd of no vulgar Fame,
Nature's Disciple, and *Genest* his Name.
A noble Object for his Skill he chose,   55
A Martyr dying midst insulting Foes.
Resign'd with Patience to Religion's Laws,
Yet braving Monarchs in his *Saviour's* Cause.
Fill'd with th' Idea of the sacred Part,
He felt a Zeal beyond the reach of Art,   60
While Look and Voice, and Gesture all exprest
A kindred Ardour in the Player's Breast,
Till as the Flame thro' all his Bosom ran,
He lost the Actor and commenc'd the Man:
Profest the Faith, his pagan Gods denied,   65
And what he acted then, he after died.

THE Player's Province they but vainly try,
Who want these pow'rs *Deportment, Voice,* and *Eye*.

THE Critic Sight 'tis only *Grace* can please
No Figure charms us if it has not *Ease*.   70
There are who think the Stature all in all,
Nor like the Hero if he is not tall.
The feeling Sense all other Wants supplies,
I rate no Actor's Merit from his Size.
Superior Hight requires superior Grace,   75
And what's a Giant with a vacant Face?

THEATRIC Monarchs in their tragic Gait
Affect to mark the solemn Pace of State.

One Foot put forward in Position strong,
The other like its Vassal dragg'd along.   80
So grave each Motion, so exact and slow,
Like wooden Monarchs at a Puppet-Show.
The Mien delights us that has native Grace
But Affectation ill supplies its Place.

UNSKILFUL Actors, like your mimic Apes,   85
Will writhe their Bodies in a thousand Shapes;
However foreign from the Poet's Art,
No tragic Hero but admires a Start.
What though unfeeling of the nervous Line,
Who but allows his *Attitude* is fine?   90
While a whole Minute equipoiz'd he stands,
Till Praise dismiss him with her echoing Hands.
Resolv'd though Nature hate the tedious Pause,
By Perseverance to extort Applause.
When *Romeo* sorrowing at his *Juliet's* Doom,   95
With eager Madness bursts the canvass Tomb,
The sudden Whirl, stretch'd Leg, and lifted Staff,
Which please the Vulgar, make the Critic laugh.

To point the Passion's Force, and mark it well,
The proper Action Nature's Self will tell.   100
No pleasing Pow'rs Distortions e'er express,
And nicer Judgment always loaths Excess.
In Sock or Buskin who o'erleaps the Bounds,
Disgusts our Reason, and the Taste confounds.

OF all the Evils which the Stage molest   105
I hate your Fool who overacts his Jest.
Who murders what the Poet finely writ,
And like a Bungler haggles all his Wit,
With Shrug, and Grin, and Gesture out of Place,
And writes a foolish Comment with his Face.   110
Old *Johnson* once, tho' *Cibber's* perter Vein,
But meanly groupes him with a num'rous Train,
With steady Face, and sober hum'rous Mien,
Fill'd the strong Outlines of the comic Scene.
What was writ down, with decent Utterance spoke,   115
Betray'd no Symptom of the conscious Joke;
The very Man in Look, in Voice, in Air,
And though upon the Stage, he seem'd no Play'r.
The Word and Action should conjointly suit,
But acting Words is labour too minute.   120
Grimace will ever lead the Judgment wrong,

While sober Humour marks th' Impression strong.
Her proper Traits the fixt Attention hit,
And bring me closer to the Poet's Wit;
With her delighted o'er each Scene I go,   125
Well-pleas'd, and not asham'd of being so.

'TIS not enough the *Voice* be sound and clear,
'Tis Modulation that must charm the Ear.
When desperate Heroines grieve with tedious Moan,
And whine their Sorrows in a see-saw Tone;   130
The same soft Sounds of unimpassioned Woes
Can only make the yawning Hearers doze.

THE Voice all Modes of Passion can express,
That marks the proper Word with proper Stress.
But none emphatic can that Actor call,   135
Who lays an equal Emphasis on *all*.

SOME o'er the Tongue the labour'd Measures roll
Slow and delib'rate as the parting Toll,
Point ev'ry Stop, mark ev'ry Pause so strong,
Their Words, like Stage-Processions stalk along.   140
All Affectation but creates Disgust,
And e'en in speaking *We* may seem *too* just.
Nor proper, *Thornton*, can those Sounds appear,
Which bring not Numbers to thy nicer Ear;
For them in vain the pleasing Measure flows   145
Whose Recitation runs it all to Prose;
Repeating what the Poet sets not down,
The Verb disjointing from its friendly Noun.
While Pause, and Break, and Repetition join
To make a Discord in each tuneful Line.   150

SOME placid Natures fill th' allotted Scene
With lifeless Drone, insipid and serene;
While others thunder ev'ry Couplet o'er,
And almost crack your Ears with Rant and Roar.
In so much Noise but little Sense is found,   155
As empty Barrels make the greatest Sound.

MORE Nature oft and finer Strokes are shown,
In the low Whisper than tempestuous Tone.
And *Hamlet's* hollow Voice and fixt Amaze,
More powerful Terror to the Mind conveys,   160
Than he, who swol'n with big impetuous Rage,
Bullies the bulky Phantom off the Stage.

THE Modes of Grief are not included all
In the white Handkerchief and mournful Drawl;
A single Look more marks th' internal Woe,   165
Than all the Windings of the lengthen'd Oh.

UP to the *Face* the quick Sensation flies,
And darts its meaning from the speaking Eyes;
Love, Transport, Madness, Anger, Scorn, Despair,
And all the Passions, all the Soul is there.   170

IN vain *Ophelia* gives her Flowrets round,
And with her Straws fantastic strews the Ground;
In vain now sings, now heaves the desp'rate Sigh,
If Phrenzy sit not in the troubled Eye.
In *Cibber's* Look commanding Sorrows speak,   175
And call the Tear fast trick'ling down my Cheek.

HE who in Earnest studies o'er his Part
Will find true Nature cling about his Heart.
All from their Eyes impulsive Thought reveal,
And none can want Expression, who can feel.   180

THERE is a Fault which stirs the Critic's Rage,
A Want of due Attention on the Stage.
There have been Actors, and admir'd ones too,
Whose tongues wound up set forward from their cue.
In their own Speech who whine, or roar away,   185
Yet unconcern'd at what the rest may say.
Whose Eyes and Thoughts on diff'rent Objects roam
Until the Prompter's Voice recall them home.

DIVEST yourself of Hearers if you can,
And strive to speak, and be the very Man.   190
Why should the well-bred Actor wish to know
Who sits above To-night, or who below.
So mid th' harmonious Tones of Grief or Rage,
Italian Squallers oft disgrace the Stage.
When with a simp'ring Leer, and Bow profound,   195
The squeaking *Cyrus* greets the Boxes round;
Or proud *Mandane* of imperial Race,
Familiar drops a Curtsie to her Grace.

To suit the Dress demands the Actor's Art,
Yet there are those who over-dress the Part.   200
To some prescriptive Right gives Settled Things,
Black Wigs to Murd'rers, feather'd Hats to Kings.

But *Michel Cassio* might be drunk enough,
Tho' all his Features were not grim'd with Snuff.
Why shou'd *Pol Peachum* shine in sattin Cloaths?   205
Why ev'ry Devil dance in scarlet Hose?

BUT in Stage-Customs what offends me most
Is the Slip-door, and slowly-rising Ghost.
Tell me, nor count the Question too severe,
Why need the dismal powder'd Forms appear?   210

WHEN chilling Horrors shake th' affrighted King,
And Guilt torments him with her Scorpion Sting;
When keenest Feelings at his Bosom pull,
And Fancy tells him that the Seat is full,
Why need the Ghost usurp the Monarch's Place,   215
To frighten Children with his mealy Face?
The King alone should form the Phantom there,
And talk and tremble at the vacant Chair.

IF *Belvidera* her lov'd Loss deplore,
Why for twin Spectres bursts the yawning Floor?   220
When with disorder'd Starts, and horrid Cries,
She paints the murder'd Forms before her Eyes,
And still pursues them with a frantic Stare:
'Tis pregnant Madness brings the Visions there.
More instant Horror would enforce the Scene,   225
If all her Shuddrings were at Shapes unseen.

POET and Actor thus with blended Skill,
Mould all our Passions to their instant Will;
'Tis thus, when feeling *Garrick* treads th' Stage,
(The speaking Comment of his *Shakespear's* Page.)   230
Oft as I drink the Words with greedy Ears,
I shake with Horror, or dissolve with Tears.

O NE'ER may Folly seize the Throne of Taste,
Nor Dulness lay the Realms of Genius waste.
No bouncing Crackers ape the Thunder's Fire,   235
No Tumbler float upon the bending Wire.
More natural Uses to the Stage belong,
Than Tumblers, Monsters, Pantomime, or Song.
For other Purpose was that Spot design'd;
To purge the Passions and reform the Mind,   240
To give to Nature all the Force of Art,
And while it charms the Ear to mend the Heart.

Thornton, to Thee I dare with Truth commend,
The decent Stage as Virtue's natural Friend.
Tho' oft debas'd with Scenes profane and loose,   245
No Reason weighs against its proper Use.
Tho' the lewd Priest his sacred Function shame,
Religion's perfect Law is still the same.

SHALL they who trace the Passions from their rise
Shew Scorn her Features, her own Image Vice;   250
Who teach the Mind its proper Force to scan,
And hold the faithful Mirrour up to Man,
Shall their Profession e'er provoke Disdain,
Who stand the formost in the normal Train.
Who lend Reflexion all the Grace of Art,   255
And strike the Precept home upon the Heart.

YET, hapless Artist, tho' thy Skill can raise
The bursting Peal of universal Praise,
Tho' at thy Beck, Applause delighted stands,
And lifts *Briareus'* like her hundred Hands.   260
Know Fame awards Thee but a partial Breath,
Not all thy Talents brave the Stroke of Death.
Poets to Ages yet unborn appeal,
And latest Times th' eternal Nature feel.
Tho' blended here the Praise of Bard and Play'r,   265
While more than Half becomes the Actor's Share,
Relentless Death untwists the mingled Fame,
And sinks the Player in the Poet's Name.

THE pliant Muscles of the various Face,
The Mien* that gave each Sentence Strength and Grace,   270
The tuneful Voice, the Eye that spoke the Mind,
Are gone, nor leave a single Trace behind.

* Printed as "Mein" in the 1760 edition.

NOTES ON CONSTANT COQUELIN

Constant Coquelin (1841-1909) was the most versatile and accomplished comedian of his time. At the Conservatory in Paris he was the favorite pupil of Régnier; and he was also a close student of the methods of Samson. He won the first prize for comedy at the Conservatory; and he made his first appearance at the Théâtre Français in 1859. He was only twenty-three when he was elected an associate of the Comédie-Française. He early distinguished himself, especially in the series of brilliant parts which Molière had composed for his own acting; and he displayed his extraordinary range of characterization in a host of plays by the leading French dramatists of the day. He went to England with the Comédie-Française in 1879; he played later in all the chief countries of Europe; and in 1888 he paid the first of several visits to the United States. In 1892 he resigned from the Comédie-Française, and not long thereafter he became the manager of the Porte Saint-Martin theatre. Here he produced *Cyrano de Bergerac* in 1907, a poetic play written for him and, so to speak, around him, specially devised to set off the manifold facets of his histrionic genius. He did not survive to appear in *Chantecler,* which Rostand had also composed expressly for him.

He was a prominent figure in Parisian life, being an intimate friend of many of the chief politicians, painters, and poets. He was an appreciative collector of works of art; and he was also an acute critic of literature. He delivered lectures on several of the plays of Molière and on several of the contemporary French poets with whom he was intimate; and these addresses were published one after another as they were delivered. In New York he read before the Nineteenth Century Club a brilliant essay on "Molière and Shakspere."

Three times Coquelin discussed his own calling, twice in lectures, "L'Art et le Comédien," published in 1880, and "L'Art du Comédien," published in 1886; and once in a pamphlet, *Le Comédien,* published in 1882, in which he repelled a bitter attack made on his profession by M. Octave Mirbeau.

The first of his two lectures was translated by Miss Abby Langdon Alger and published in 1881 by Roberts Brothers. Miss Alger's rendering has been carefully revised for the present reprint and slightly condensed by the omission of a few quotations.

Coquelin begins his plea for his profession by a declaration of the importance and the dignity of the art which he adorned. He claims that the actor is not a copyist, but truly a creator. This contention may be supported by citing part of a letter written by Coleridge to the elder Charles Mathews (and quoted by H. B. Irving in his paper on "The Calling of the Actor"):

"A great actor, comic or tragic, is not to be a mere copy, a facsimile, but an imitation of nature; now an imitation differs from a copy in this, that it of necessity implies and demands a difference, whereas a copy aims at identity; and what a marble peach on the mantelpiece, that you take up deluded and put down with a pettish disgust, is compared with a fruit-piece of Van Nuysen's, even such is a mere copy of nature, with a true histrionic imitation. A good actor is Pygmalion's statue, a work of exquisite art, animated and gifted with motion; but still art, still a species of poetry."

Equally illuminating is a passage in the brief but stimulating essay, "On the Stage" prefixed to Fanny Kemble's *Notes on Some of Shakespeare's Plays,* published in 1882. The actress-authoress declared that the art of acting "has neither fixed rules, specific principles, indispensable rudiments, nor fundamental laws; it has no basis in positive science, as music, painting, sculpture, and architecture have; and differs from them all, in that the mere appearance of spontaneity, which is an acknowledged assumption, is its chief merit. And yet—

> This younger of the sister arts,
> Where all their charms combine

requires in its professors the imagination of the poet, the ear of the musician, the eye of the painter and sculptor, and over and above these a faculty peculiar to itself, inasmuch as the actor personally fulfills and embodies his conception; his own voice is his cunningly modulated instrument; his own face the canvas whereon he portrays the various expressions of his passion; his own frame the mould in which he casts the images of beauty and majesty that fill his brain; and whereas the painter and sculptor may select, of all possible attitudes, occupations and expressions, the most favourable to the beautiful effect they desire to produce and fix, and bid it so remain fixed for ever, the actor must live and move through a temporary existence of poetry and passion, and preserve throughout its duration that ideal grace and dignity of which the canvas and the marble give but a silent and motionless image" (pp. 15-16).

In the course of this lecture Coquelin asserts his own conviction that Diderot is absolutely in the right in maintaining that the actor must never allow himself to be carried away by his emotion while he is engaged in portraying it. Diderot's *Paradoxe sur le Comédien* was not published until 1830; it is a one-sided dialogue between a man of straw and the speaker who presents Diderot's own uncompromising opinions. Mr. Walter Herries Pollock made a careful translation issued in 1883, with a preface by Sir Henry Irving in which the English actor ardently combated the French philosopher's theory. More than once, after the publication of this translation, Irving and Coquelin debated the question in various periodicals, British and American, notably in *Harper's Weekly* for November 12, 1889.

Mr. Francis Wilson, in his *Joseph Jefferson; Reminiscences of a Fellow-Player,* records that the American comedian held both contestants to be in the right, each from his own experience: "I have no doubt that the Englishman could not act if he did not feel, and that the Frenchman would be very inferior if he did feel. You remember Shakespeare's advice to the players in *Hamlet.* I understand he means by that that no matter how you are overcome by your emotions you must take care and maintain coolness and clearness. For my part, I like to have the heart warm and the head cool" (p. 141).

Yet there is significance in the account—cited by Mr. Wilson (pp. 330-31) from Mr. Henry Watterson's tribute to Jefferson— of a performance which was marred by the actor's failure to abide by his own rule: "He was playing Caleb Plummer, and in the scene between the old toy-maker and his blind daughter, when the father discovers the dreadful result of his dissimulation—at the very crucial moment there was an awkward twitch and, the climax quite thwarted, the curtain came down. 'Did you see that?' he said, as he brushed by me, going to his dressing-room. 'No,' said I, following him. 'What was it?' He turned, his eyes still wet, and his voice choked. 'I broke down,' said he, 'completely broke down. I turned away from the audience to recover myself. But I could not, and had the curtain rung.' The scene had been spoilt because the actor had been overcome by a sudden flood of real feeling, whereas he was to render by his art the feeling of a fictitious character and so communicate this to his audience."

It may be noted also that in a review of the American translation of Coquelin's first lecture contributed to the *New York Times* for January 16, 1881, Lawrence Barrett adduced an example of the perfect self-control of Junius Brutus Booth in one of the most moving episodes of *King Lear.* Barrett derived the anecdote from William Warren, who was playing Kent to Booth's Lear. "At the close of one of Booth's tenderest speeches, when the whole house was in tears, he leaned upon his companion's shoulder and whispered in his own natural voice, 'William, you ought to have been out fishing with us today'; and then resumed his part with all his old power.

The widespread interest aroused by the publication of Mr. Pollock's translation of Diderot's *Paradox* led Mr. William Archer to collect all the evidence scattered through theatrical biography and dramatic criticism and also to send a questionnaire to a host of living British and American actors and actresses. As a result of this indefatigable investigation Mr. Archer was enabled to prepare *Masks or Faces? A Study in the Psychology of Acting* (London and New York: Longmans, Green & Co., 1888), to which every student of the stage may be referred for a judicious weighing of the testimony on one side and the other and for an acute analysis of the underlying principles.

Toward the end of his lecture Coquelin asked that the art of the actor should be as adequately rewarded as the other arts and that the tragedian and the comedian should be admitted to the Legion of Honor as freely as the author, the painter, or the sculptor. When this plea was made no actor had been decorated with the coveted cross, although this honor had been conferred upon Régnier after he had left the stage to devote himself to his work as a teacher in the Conservatory. It is pleasant to be able to record that the prejudice against which Coquelin protested gave way at last and that in 1882 the dean of the Comédie-Française, Got, also a professor in the Conservatory, but still in the active exercise of his profession as an actor, was admitted to the Legion of Honor. Since then this coveted distinction has been conferred on a score of other actors—although Coquelin always refused to accept it, lest it be supposed that he had made his appeal on his own behalf.

NOTES ON TALMA

Lekain (1729-1778) was the foremost tragic actor of France in his generation, as Talma was the foremost tragic actor of the succeeding generation. He owed to the friendly admiration of Voltaire his admission into the Comédie-Française when he was only twenty-one. He had against him certain physical disadvantages; and he had in his favor a rich, warm voice, which he cultivated assiduously until it became a supple instrument for rendering passion. At Voltaire's suggestion he was invited to Potsdam by Frederick the Great. To him and to Mlle. Clairon were due two important reforms in the French theatre: the striking advance in the propriety of costuming and the clearing of the stage of the Théâtre Français of the mob of courtiers who had until then been privileged to occupy seats in close proximity to the actors.

Talma (1763-1826) spent a part of his youth in England; and he made his first appearance at the Théâtre Français in 1787, when he was twenty-four. He excelled in the chief characters of French classicist tragedy; and he gave them an external verisimilitude by donning flowing white robes designed for him by his friend David, the painter. During the French Revolution he became intimate with Napoleon I, retaining this friendship even after the establishment of the Empire. When Napoleon went to meet the Czar at Erfurt in 1808 he took with him Talma and others of the Comédie-Française, telling him that they were to perform "before a parterre of Kings." He survived to behold the beginnings of the Romanticist revolt which was to overthrow the rigorous code of the Classicists, and both Victor Hugo and the elder Dumas have recorded the admiration they felt for his skill as an actor.

The autobiography of Lekain, edited by his son, first appeared in Paris in the year X. When the volume was included in 1825 in a series of dramatic memoirs, there was prefixed to it a paper entitled "Reflections on Lekain and on the Actor's Art," by Talma. This essay revealed the fact that Talma had thought profoundly about the art which he brilliantly adorned and that he was able to present his thoughts skillfully. The significance and the importance of what Talma had written was immediately recognized; and in all later French discussion of the principles and the practice of the histrionic art the words of the great French tragedian were frequently cited.

At the suggestion of Sir Henry Irving, whose position at the head of the British stage was as undisputed as had been Talma's leadership in the French theatre, the essay was translated by some person unknown and published in 1877 in a British monthly, *The Theatre*. From this magazine the anonymous translation was reprinted as a pamphlet entitled *Talma on the Actor's Art*, issued in 1883 with a preface by Sir Henry Irving. This publication brought the paper to the attention of the English-speaking public for the first time; and its own merits and the eulogy bestowed upon it by Irving evoked a host of reviews in the British and American periodicals of the time.

As might be expected, most of these ephemeral criticisms were valueless. One of them, however, that which appeared in the *Saturday Review,* was a solid contribution to the subject. It was written by a lifelong student of the theory and practice of the art of acting, Fleeming Jenkin, professor of engineering in the University of Edinburgh. He was a man of varied intellectual interests, as must be well known to all those who may have read the memoir affectionately written by his former pupil, Robert Louis Stevenson. This brief biography was prepared as an introduction to the two volumes in which the literary and scientific papers of Fleeming Jenkin were collected. These volumes were published in London in 1887 by Longmans, Green and Co.; and they replevined from the swift oblivion of the back number two articles on the acting of Mrs. Siddons and this review of Talma's essay. It is by the kind permission of Mrs. Fleeming Jenkin and of Longmans, Green and Co. that this paper is here printed as a most useful commentary on both Talma and Irving.

The discussion of the principles and the practice of his art by an artist who can analyze his instinctive and intuitive processes is always useful to all who seek to inquire into the secrets of the craft; but these analyses tend to the undue consideration of technique, and they are vital only where the artist happens also to possess range as well as depth of vision. This double qualification is Talma's as obviously as it was also Samson's and Coquelin's. On the other hand Mrs. Siddons and Salvini, mighty as they were in the impersonation of great characters, were incompetent to analyze these very parts; and Mrs. Siddons' essay on Lady Macbeth is as empty as Salvini's paper on Othello.

Talma has luminously indicated what an actor must do to make himself master of a part; and it is interesting to supplement this with Coquelin's account of his own method of getting inside the skin of a character, as he once gave it to an interviewer: "When I have to create a part, I begin by reading the play with the greatest attention five or six times. First, I consider what position my character should occupy, on what plane in the picture I must put him. Then I study his psychology, knowing what he thinks, what he is morally. I deduce what he ought to be physically, what will be his carriage, his manner of speaking, his gesture. These characteristics once decided, I learn the part without thinking about it further; then, when I know it, I take up my man again and, closing my eyes, I say to him, 'Recite this for me.' Then I see him delivering the speech, the sentence I asked him for; he lives, he speaks, he gesticulates before me; and then I have only to imitate him."

NOTES ON H. C. FLEEMING JENKIN

The paper on "Mrs. Siddons as Lady Macbeth" first appeared in the *Nineteenth Century* for 1878; and that on "Mrs. Siddons as Queen Katharine, Mrs. Beverley, and Lady Randolph" was contributed to *Macmillan's Magazine* for April 1882. Both of them were reprinted in the first volume of *Papers Literary, Scientific, &c.* by Fleeming Jenkin, F.R.S., LL.D., Professor of Engineering in the University of Edinburgh. Edited by Sidney Colvin and J. A. Ewing, F.R.S. London, and New York: Longmans, Green and Co., 1887.

The outline of Mrs. Siddons' life which constitutes the first section of the Introduction is amended and amplified from a paper contributed to the second volume of *Actors and Actresses of Great Britain and the United States from the days of David Garrick to the Present Time*, edited by Brander Matthews and Laurence Hutton and published in five volumes in New York in 1886-7. The outline of Fleeming Jenkin's life which constitutes the second section of the Introduction has been specially prepared for this occasion.

There are half a dozen biographies of Mrs. Siddons, of which the most valuable are those by Campbell and Boaden; and she figures amply in the theatrical criticism of her time. And there are interesting glimpses of her to be gleaned from Mme. D'Arblay's *Diary*, Macready's *Reminiscences*, Leigh Hunt's *Autobiography*,

Moore's *Diary,* Boswell's *Johnson,* and *The Memoirs of Charles Mayne Young.* In view of the fact that contemporary critics were sometimes inclined to comment on the tendency of all the Kemble family to make pauses of a length then unusual, it may be worth while to quote the opinion of a comedian of the generation which has just passed off the stage. In one of his conversations with Francis Wilson, Joseph Jefferson declared that the eloquent pauses of Mrs. Siddons were as effective as her eloquent speeches, since a play "passes so swiftly that unless you give the minds of the auditors a chance to rest upon the important themes and speeches —time to receive the proper impression, as acid upon copper— there can be no effect or result. I learn something about my art every night and have but recently verified the justice of the old-time claim for eloquent pauses. Mrs. Siddons was right, when she said that the secret of acting was proper pauses. George Henry Lewes, who knew more about acting than most critics, added cleverly that one must pause without seeming to do so and without making a wait." (*Joseph Jefferson: Reminiscences of a Fellow Player.* By Francis Wilson, New York, 1906, p. 28.)

The fame of Mrs. Siddons as the greatest tragic actress of the English-speaking stage is so firmly established that there is no need to buttress it by any added record of the impression made by her upon her contemporaries. Yet it may not be a work of supererogation to append here the lines in which Charles Lamb recorded the impression she had made upon him:

> As when a child on some long winter's night,
>   Affrighted, clinging to its grandma's knees,
> With eager wondering and perturbed delight
>   Listens strange tales of fearful dark decrees
> Mutter'd to wretch by necromantis spell;
>   Or of those hags, who, at the watching time
>   Of murky midnight, ride the air sublime,
> And mingle foul disguise with fiends of hell,
>   Cold horror drinks its blood! anon the tear
> More gentle starts, to hear the beldame tell
> Of pretty babes that lov'd each other dear,
> Murder'd by cruel uncle's mandate fell;
>   Ev'n such the shiv'ring joys thy tones impart,
>   Ev'n so thou, Siddons, meltest my sad heart.

NOTES ON WILLIAM GILLETTE

This address was delivered at the fifth joint session of the American Academy of Arts and Letters and of the National Institute of Arts and Letters, held in Chicago on November 14, 1913; and it was afterward written out for publication in the seventh number of the proceedings of the Academy and Institute (pp. 16-24).

In this paper there are four points made with special emphasis, as though to challenge contradiction. These may be summarily described as the assertions

(A) that a play has to be seen to yield up its dramatic value;

(B) that the manager of a theatre must be commercial or crazy;

(C) that the actor must convey the illusion that what he is doing is then done for the first time; and

(D) that an actor is most successful when he can infuse his part with his own personality.

Any reader inclined to pick up the glove of the challenger and to impale himself upon one or another of these points will do well to remember that they are each of them supported by authorities not lightly to be impeached.

(A) Goethe in his *Conversations with Eckermann* dwelt more than once on the difficulty, not to say the impossibility, of judging a play from a mere perusal of the manuscript and of estimating the effect which might be produced by an actual performance. Molière, in the preface to the *Précieuses Ridicules,* explained his original intention not to publish that play as due to his knowledge that a large portion of the beauties which had been found in it depended on the gestures and on the voices of the performers, and that therefore he felt disinclined to print his play in a book wherein it would be deprived of these necessary ornaments. The younger Dumas, in the preface to the *Père Prodigue,* declared dramatic effect to be sometimes so intangible that the spectator cannot find in the printed text the point which delighted him in the performance of a play and which was due perhaps to "a word, a look, a gesture, a silence, a purely atmospheric condition."

Although anyone holding in his hand the words and music of a song does not actually possess that song until it is really sung by a human voice in accord with those directions, yet there are experts whom insight and experience enable to make a better guess at the probable effect of the unsung song than would be possible to the average lover of music devoid of this equipment; and in like manner there are a few readers of plays possessing a similar insight and experience which enable them to make a better guess at the effect of the unperformed drama than is possible to the average reader less substantially trained and less gifted with interpretative imagination. Fleeming Jenkin, so Robert Louis Stevenson recorded in his memoir of his friend, was "one of the not very numerous people who can read a play: a knack, the fruit of much knowledge and some imagination, comparable to that of reading score."

(B) In support of this second point, that the manager of a theatre is unwise unless he pays respect to the economic stability of his enterprise, it is possible to cite another of Goethe's remarks to Eckermann. He asserted (May 1, 1825) that Shakespeare and Molière had always a keen eye to the main chance and that "both of them wished, above all things, to make money by their theatres. . . . Nothing is more dangerous for the well-being of a theatre than when the director is so placed, that a greater or less receipt at the treasury does not affect him personally. . . . It is a property of human nature soon to relax when not impelled by personal advantage or disadvantage." It is perhaps not unfair to suggest that Goethe may have been moved to this declaration by his own experience as manager of the ducal theatre at Weimar, and by his memory of the unsatisfactory results of his occasional refusals to give due weight to the wishes of the playgoers who paid their way in. With these quotations from his table talk may be compared the more deliberate presentation of the case in the prologue to *Faust,* in which the manager is allowed to state his views at length.

(C) In Francis Wilson's *Joseph Jefferson: Reminiscences of a Fellow-Player* there are several passages which bear upon the necessity for creating the Illusion of the First Time. "The actor," said the great comedian, "must not only produce, but in order to make the greatest artistic effect, he must reproduce each time as if he had never produced before" (p. 100). And again, in addressing the students of the American Academy of Dramatic Arts in April 1897, Jefferson told these apprentice players that their profession was "not only one of production but also of reproduction. A writer does not write the same book, a painter does not paint the same picture; but you have to play the same part very often—night after night—and yet play as if you never had played it before" (p. 109).

On one occasion a ten-year-old boy who had seen *Rip Van Winkle* was introduced to Jefferson and informed that he was talking to the performer of the part. The boy looked up at the actor and said in the most childish and frank manner, "Don't you remember that time when your gun fell apart?" And Jefferson joyfully commented: "*That* time, and it had fallen apart for *thousands* of times!" And he told the boy's father that the little lad had paid him the best compliment he had ever had in his life, for "if I made him believe that was the first time that gun had fallen apart, I did much better than I thought I did" (p. 138).

An even more striking illustration of the necessity of creating the Illusion of the First Time is to be found in Jefferson's own *Autobiography* (pp. 443-44) where he reports a conversation between Macready and Mrs. Warner: "My dear Madam," said Macready, "you have acted with me in the tragedy of *Werner* for many years. . . . I have noticed lately that some passages do not produce the effect they formerly did. There is a certain speech especially that seems to have lost its power . . . the one wherein Werner excuses himself to his son for the 'petty plunder' of Stralenheim's gold. In our earlier performances . . . this apology was received with marked favour; and last evening it produced no apparent effect. Can you form any idea why this should be?

Is it that the audience has grown too familiar with the story? I must beg you to be candid with me."

And Mrs. Warner answered: "Since you desire that I should speak plainly, I do not think it is because your audience is too familiar with the story, but because you are too familiar with it yourself. . . . When you spoke that speech ten years ago there was a surprise in your face as though you only then realised what you had done. You looked shocked and bewildered, and in a forlorn way seemed to cast about for words that would excuse the crime; and all this with a depth of feeling and sincerity that would naturally come from an honest man who had been for the first time in his life accused of theft. [But now] you speak it like one who has committed a great many thefts in his life and whose glib excuses are so pat and frequent that he is neither shocked, surprised or abashed at the accusation."

Jefferson heard this anecdote from C. W. Couldock, and he recognized its force at once: "I knew then that I had been unconsciously falling into the same error, and I felt that the fault would increase rather than diminish with time, if I could not hit upon some method to check it. I began by listening to each important question as though it had been given for the first time, turning the query over in my mind and then discussing it, even at times hesitating as if for want of words to frame the reply."

Henry Irving, in an address on "The Art of Acting" delivered at Harvard University in 1885, is in accord with Jefferson: "It is necessary that the actor should learn to think before he speaks; a practice which, I believe, is very useful off the stage. Let him remember . . . that the thought precedes the word. . . . Often it will be found that the most natural, the most seemingly accidental effects are obtained when the working of the mind is seen before the tongue gives it words."

(D) Here again a quotation may be adduced from Wilson's *Jefferson:* "It is a great mistake for the artist to attempt entirely to sink his individuality in the parts he assumes. By so doing he is robbing the audience of that for which they are looking, that for which they admire him" (pp. 221-22). And Ellen Terry, in her appreciation of the Russian Ballet, takes occasion to remark that it used to be said of Henry Irving, "who expressed himself in a multiplicity of parts, that he was always the same Irving. Certainly he was always faithful to himself, whatever he assumed. This is a sign of the presence of genius, not of its absence" (p. 17).

It may be well also to call attention to the fact that nearly all of the great actors have been men of marked individuality and that they have rarely sought to disguise their personalities in their several performances. When they were impersonating any one of the chief characters of the drama they brought into vigorous relief those characteristics which were in accord with their own temperament and therefore within their means of expression. A great actor plays a great part, not necessarily as he thinks that it ought to be played, but rather as he feels that he himself can best play it. Fanny Kemble, it is significant to record, held that her aunt, Mrs. Siddons, "could lay no claim to versatility—it was not in her nature; she was without mobility of mind, countenance, or manner; and her dramatic organisation was in that respect inferior to Garrick's; but out of a family of twenty-eight persons, all of whom made the stage their vocation, she alone preëminently combined the qualities requisite to make a great theatrical performer in the highest degree."

NOTES ON DION BOUCICAULT

Dionysius Lardner Boucicault was born in Dublin, December 26, 1822. He died in New York, September 18, 1890. His father was a French refugee, his mother was Irish, and he inherited racial characteristics from both parents. His first play, *London Assurance,* a five-act comedy, was brought out at Covent Garden on March 4, 1841, when he was not yet twenty. It was immediately profitable, and it held the stage for nearly fifty years. During that half century he was the most popular and most prolific playwright on the English-speaking stage. In 1857 he made his first appearance as an actor, and thereafter he was as successful as a performer as he was as a playwright. He came in time to possess great dexterity as a stage manager; and his own pieces owed not a little of their appeal to the adroitness of their presentation. He spent many of his later years in the United States, where he brought out some of his most attractive plays, skillfully compounded melodramas, with startlingly novel effects, a rising wall in *Arrah-na-Pogue* (1865) and a turning tower in *The Shaughraun* (1874).

The plays to which his name was appended may be divided into groups. In the first of these are his comedies *London Assurance, The Irish Heiress, Old Heads and Young Hearts,* and *Marriage,* which must be called original, although they often contained scenes and characters long familiar on the stage. In the second group are his dramatizations of novels, *Smike* from Dickens and *Jeanie Deans* from Scott. Sometimes he found only the elements of a plot in the tales he took over, modifying its structure to suit himself; thus a novel of Mrs. Gaskell's was the basis of *The Long Strike* and a story of Gerald Griffin's was the basis of *The Colleen Bawn.* In a third division are his adaptations from the French, such as *Kerry* and *Daddy O'Dowd,* in both of which he transferred to Ireland situations invented in France. And in a fourth and final grouping are to be found a dozen plays taken from the French with only the slightest modification: *Louis XI* and *The Corsican Brothers,* which, although he saw fit to put his own name to them, are in fact only clever translations.

It was during one of his visits to England that he delivered at the Lyceum Theatre (lent for the occasion by Henry Irving), to a house-filling audience of actors and actresses, the lecture here reproduced from the stenographic report printed in the *Era* of July 29, 1882. It is to be noted that for several months before his death (eight years later) he had been connected with a school of acting established by A. M. Palmer at the Madison Square Theatre in New York.

Lessing, in the introduction to his *Hamburg Dramaturgy,* had already asserted that "valuable gifts of nature are very necessary to the calling of the actor, but they are by no means sufficient for it; he must every where think with the poet, he must even think for him in places where the poet has shown himself human by his errors."

In commenting on an article by Boucicault, written before this lecture and containing suggestions utilized in its preparation, Coquelin wrote (in *Harper's Weekly* for November 12, 1887):

A man is born with greater or less natural gifts; and the reason why remains a mystery. But he must cultivate his gifts and work out his genius. Mr. Boucicault speaks of that indescribable something which makes an original picture superior to the most perfect copy imaginable. Well, I know in what this indescribable something consists. It consists on the one hand of the author's manner of feeling, which in its turn depends on his personality—that is to say, on something of unknown and, if you like, of divine origin—and on the other hand it consists in his manner of rendering what he feels; that is to say, his artistic process. Now, while he has little or no power over his personality, the artist has every power over his process; and so it came about that Raphael thrice changed his manner.

There is a shrewd and significant passage about the histrionic art in a paper by Bronson Howard entitled "Our Schools for the Stage," published in the *Century* for November 1900:

The phrase "art of acting" has become so familiar, and it trips so lightly off the tongue, that no one needs to think when he uses it. There are many other comfortable phrases like that in the language. Not one "lay" reader in a thousand, probably, ever had a definite idea passing through his head when he was using the words "art of acting." Let me submit an incomplete and superficial, but fairly clear, definition of the phrase—one on which, so far as it goes, we may all agree. Suppose we put it in this shape:

"The art of acting is the art of moving, speaking, and appearing on the stage as the character assumed would move, speak, and appear in real life, under the circumstances indicated in the play."

This seems a reasonable definition; it would meet the views

of nearly every reader, and even the more philosophical playgoer would merely add something about "feeling," "soul," "sympathy," or "magnetism." This last word fills all the chinks, like putty in the work of a bad house-carpenter. Mechanics have the proverb: "Putty makes many a good carpenter." We may paraphrase it: "Magnetism makes many a profound dramatic critic." But the above definition of the art of acting, with or without the philosophical playgoer's embroidery, is absolutely and radically false—for this reason: it lacks the one small word "seeming." It ought to read as follows:

"The art of acting is the art of seeming to move, speak, and appear on the stage as the character assumed moves, speaks, and appears in real life, under the circumstances indicated in the play."

In that word "seeming" lie nearly all the difficulties, the intricacies, the technicalities of acting. The writer is assuming no special or superior wisdom as an "expert"; for every actor, from the greatest of them down to the second-month student, knows that the definition we had first agreed on is inaccurate. Move, speak, and appear as the character does? Real life? One might as well say that a painter's art is to use gray stone to represent an old church in Rome, instead of mere pigments mixed with oil. The painter appeals to the eye by artificial, not by natural, means. So, the actor's art is to make the people in an audience, some of them a hundred feet or more away, think that he is moving, speaking, and appearing like the character assumed: and, in nine cases out of ten, the only way to make them think this is to be not doing it; to be doing something else—something that you would never dream of unless you were taught it, or learned it from long and weary experience without a teacher.

At the Conservatory in Paris the pupil is assigned to the care of an experienced actor-instructor; and during his two or three years of schooling he is under the guidance of this teacher, not being encouraged to profit by the lesson of the other instructors. As a result of this practice the pupil may become simply an echo of his master. This disadvantage was clearly perceived by W. C. Macready during one of his visits to Paris. In his diary, under date of January 21, 1845, he records that he

called on De Fresne, and although with great reluctance, in compliance with his particular wish, accompanied him to the Conservatoire. Heard the pupils of Samson go through their course of theatrical instruction. It is an institution of the government to train pupils (who are elected to the school) for the stage. I was interested, and saw the inefficacy of the system clearly; it was teaching *conventionalism*—it was perpetuating the mannerism of the French stage, which is all mannerism. Genius would be cramped, if not maimed and distorted, by such a course.

It is to be feared that in expressing this condemnatory opinion Macready was characteristically insular. Samson was a remarkable actor and an even more remarkable teacher. He was consulted by Rachel even after she had attained the zenith of her fame; and she is recorded as having said that she felt "lame on one side" when she had not gone over a part with Samson.

Coquelin, who was a pupil of Régnier at the Conservatory, once told an American friend that Régnier did not admire Samson's methods. "But I did—and I took every occasion to study him. In fact, I think I learnt as much from Samson as I did from Régnier."

NOTES ON FRANCES ANNE KEMBLE

Frances Anne Kemble was born in London on November 27, 1809, and she died in London on January 15, 1893. She was the daughter of Charles Kemble; her mother was of French parentage; and at the age of seven she was sent to France, remaining there until she was fifteen, when she returned to her father's house in London. Before she was eighteen she wrote a poetic play, *Francis I,* which was immediately published and ultimately produced. Her father was manager and part-proprietor of Covent Garden Theatre, which had had a series of unsuccessful seasons; and with the hope of retrieving its fortunes Charles Kemble resolved to bring out his daughter as an actress. She was not yet twenty when she made her first appearance on the stage, having previously acted only in private theatricals and only infrequently. She appeared as Juliet, on October 5, 1829, her father playing Mercutio, one of his best parts, and her mother impersonating the Nurse. Her success was immediate and prolonged; and in the course of the theatrical season she acted Juliet more than a hundred and twenty times. In that season also and in the next two she appeared as Portia and Beatrice, Constance and Lady Macbeth, as well as in a dozen other dramas by authors other than Shakespeare. Notable among these modern plays was *The Hunchback* of Sheridan Knowles, in which she acted Julia, a character written for her.

With her father she played engagements in Ireland, Scotland, and in the more important towns of England; and with her father she came to the United States in 1832, making her last appearance in New York in 1834. In this year she married Pierce Butler of Philadelphia; and she was not seen again on the stage for a decade. She spent one winter at her husband's plantation in Georgia. Two daughters were born to her; but unfortunate dissensions took place between her and her husband, and five

years after her marriage she left him and went back to England.
In 1846 she returned to the stage, only to abandon it finally two
years later, for reasons which she has made plain in the preceding
pages. She disliked the theatre, but she loved Shakespeare; and
it was Shakespeare who enabled her to achieve financial independence. In her *Records of Later Life* she has told us that
"in the summer of 1845, I returned to America, where my good
fortune in the success of my public readings soon enabled me to
realise my long-cherished hope of purchasing a small cottage and
a few acres of land in the beautiful and beloved neighbourhood
of Lenox."

Her divorce from her husband was pronounced in 1849; and
thereafter she was known as Mrs. Kemble. It was in 1877 that
she established herself in London, to remain there until her death
in 1893 at the age of eighty-three. She was a ready writer,
master of easy and idiomatic English; and she published many
volumes of prose and verse, most of them more or less autobiographic—her *Journal* in 1835; *A Year of Consolation* in 1847;
her diary of her *Residence on a Georgia Plantation* in 1863; and
her *Records of a Girlhood* in 1878, *Records of Later Life* in 1882,
and *Further Records* in 1891. She issued several volumes of poems.
She wrote half a dozen plays, the first published before she was
twenty; and she wrote one novel, *Far Away and Long Ago,*
published after she was eighty.

In one of his most beautiful sonnets Longfellow expressed the
delight of all who were privileged to hear Mrs. Kemble read the
plays of Shakespeare:—

> O precious evenings! all too swiftly sped!
>   Leaving us heirs to amplest heritages
>   Of all the best thoughts of the greatest sages,
>   And giving tongues unto the silent dead!
> How our hearts glowed and trembled as she read,
>   Interpreting by tones the wondrous pages
>   Of the great poet who foreruns the ages,
>   Anticipating all that shall be said!
> O happy Reader! having for thy text
>   The magic book, whose Sibylline leaves have caught
>   The rarest essence of all human thought!
> O happy Poet! by no critic vext!
>   How must thy listening spirit now rejoice
>   To be interpreted by such a voice!

In one of the papers collected in the volume entitled *Essays in
London and Elsewhere* Henry James, in a prose only less eloquent
than Longfellow's verse, recorded his recollections of Mrs. Kemble
as she appeared to him in the later years of her life in London.
He noted that she was always glad to go to the theatre, although
she often found there only a sorry spectacle; and he added:

Nobody connected with the stage could have savoured less of the "shop." She was a reactionary Kemble enough, but if she got rid of her profession she could never get rid of her instincts, which kept her dramatic long after she ceased to be theatrical. They existed in her, as her unsurpassable voice and facial play existed, independent of ambition or cultivation, of disenchantment or indifference.

"On the Stage" was published in 1863 in the *Cornhill Magazine,* and it was republished as an introduction to her volume of *Notes on Some of Shakespeare's Plays,* issued in 1882. It is as characteristic as anything she ever wrote; and it is as frank and plain-spoken. She knew what she liked and what she disliked; and she knew also her own value, her native gifts and her artistic shortcomings. Her continued success on the stage had not turned her head or tempted her to overestimate her achievement. She dealt with a theme to which she had given deep thought for many years; and her opinions were the result of her own experiences in the theatre itself. In her *Records of a Girlhood* (Chapter XI) she has described how she came to go on the stage and how she felt while she was on it:

My frame of mind under the preparations that were going forward for my début appears to me now curious enough. Though I had found out that I could act, and had acted with a sort of frenzy of passion and entire self-forgetfulness the first time I ever uttered the wonderful conception I had undertaken to represent, my going on the stage was absolutely an act of duty and conformity to the will of my parents, strengthened by my own conviction that I was bound to help them by every means in my power. The theatrical profession was, however, utterly distasteful to me, though acting itself, that is to say, dramatic personation, was not; and every detail of my future vocation, from the preparations behind the scenes to the representations before the curtain, was more or less repugnant to me. Nor did custom ever render this aversion less; and liking my work so little, and being so devoid of enthusiasm, respect, or love for it, it is wonderful to me that I ever achieved any success in it at all. The dramatic element inherent in my organization must have been very powerful, to have enabled me without either study of, or love for, my profession to do anything worth anything in it.

But this is the reason why, with an unusual gift and many unusual advantages for it, I did really so little; why my performances were always uneven in themselves and perfectly unequal with each other, never complete as a whole, however striking in occasional parts, and never at the same level two nights together; depending for their effect upon the state of my nerves and spirits, instead of being the result of deliberate thought and consideration—a study, in short, carefully and conscientiously applied to my work; the permanent element which preserves the artist, however inevitable he must feel the influence of moods of mind and body, from ever being at their mercy.

Mention of *The Duke's Motto,* an adaptation by John Brougham of *Le Bossu,* by Paul Féval, produced by Fechter at the Lyceum in London in 1863, is evidence that this essay was written in the year of its appearance in the *Cornhill*—that is to say at a time when the English stage was given over to adaptations of French plays; adaptations which in Matthew Arnold's words were "tainted with an incurable falsity." She survived to see a new birth of the drama in our language, although even now, after more than half a century, we have no plays in the grand style, no soul-searching, heart-rending tragedies, bold, massive, and enduring.

For a full account of the bad taste displayed by David Garrick in his wanton distortions of the masterpieces of our dramatic literature, see *Shakespeare from Betterton to Irving,* by Professor G. C. D. Odell. In calling Garrick "the most perfect actor that our stage has produced" Mrs. Kemble is in accord with the historians of the English theatre. Garrick had the power and the pathos to represent the principal characters of Shakespeare's noblest plays—of all of them except *Othello,* which he acted only once and never repeated, so dismal was his failure in this exacting part.

"The master of the stage" who pronounced that Mrs. Kemble was "ignorant of the first rudiments of her profession" was William Charles Macready, whose diaries, written solely for his own eye, were unjustifiably published in full by Mr. William Toynbee in two volumes in 1912. From these hasty jottings, set down almost daily for eighteen years (1833-51), we get an intimate revelation of the diarist, with his incessant irritability, his inordinate jealousy, and his uncompromising disparagement of all his contemporaries in the theatre. We discover also his uncertainty of judgment and his swift changes of opinion. In 1836 Macready thought that Miss Kemble was "an impostor in her art." Yet in 1838, after she had married Pierce Butler and left the stage, she sent him one of her plays which he felt to be powerful but repellent; and he confided to his diary that she "was one of the most remarkable women of the present day." Still later, in 1843, after he had met her, he declared that she was "a woman of a most extraordinary mind." Apparently he never saw her act until her return to the stage, and then he delivered the damning verdict, rendered more emphatic by underscoring:

In Mrs. Butler I saw the *proof* that I had been *most honest* and *discriminating* in my original judgment of her. *She is ignorant of the very first rudiments of her art.* She is affected, monotonous, withough one real impulse—never in the feeling of her character, never true in look, attitude, or tone. She can never be an actress; and this I never ventured to think before.

And when she acted Lady Macbeth to his Macbeth in 1848 he felt moved to declare that he had "never seen any one so bad, so unnatural, so affected, so conceited."

It may be noted that Macready had no higher opinion of acting as a profession than had Mrs. Kemble. In 1840 when he was almost at the pinnacle of his professional fame he recorded his own remark, "I had rather see one of my children dead than on the stage." From beginning to end his diaries are besprinkled with expressions not only of his bitter dislike for nearly every one of his fellow professionals but also of his absolute detestation of his profession itself. Yet it is only fair to point out that these ebullitions ought not to be taken too seriously: they could easily be paralleled in the conversation and in the writings of many members of other professions. Lawyers, for example, are sometimes so keenly alive to the disadvantages of their calling that they refuse to allow their sons to follow it.

Mrs. Kemble's tribute to Rachel, probably the only tragic actress of the nineteenth century who deserved to be placed by the side of Mrs. Siddons, is qualified by the assertion that "her intellectual processes were limited to the consideration of the most purely mechanical part of her vocation." This is not supported by the testimony of those who knew Rachel best; Legouvé, for example, in his lecture on his own *Medée,* gave a most suggestive instance of her fine dramatic intelligence. Apparently Rachel, in spite of the deficiencies of her education and of the vulgarity of her character, had a mind of unusual acuteness.

Mrs. Kemble here seems to imply that the actor is alone among artists in achieving results by instinct or intuition. But surely in all the arts, the most accomplished of craftsmen and the most inspired are continually building better than they know. They may be unaware not only of the reasons for what they have done but even of the full meaning of what they have actually succeeded in doing. We moderns find many things in the masterpieces of the past which we may be assured their authors did not deliberately purpose to put there—but which nevertheless they must have put there, since no one else could have done it.

NOTES ON FRANCISQUE SARCEY

As Sarcey has here pointed out, the organization of the Comédie-Française is a development from that of the French strolling players of three centuries ago; and it is substantially identical with the primitive organization of the earliest companies of actors in Italy and in England. In those distant days there was no responsible manager engaging all the performers and conducting the enterprise for his own profit and at his own risk. Half a dozen or half a score of the more important actors, after paying salaries to the few who were relatively unimportant, divided the receipts among themselves, share and share alike. They were a self-governing community of equals, although one of them was necessarily acknowledged as their chief.

As this was the case in France in the time of Molière, so it was in England in the time of Shakespeare, who was one of the sharers in the company of which Burbage was the head. The somewhat intricate arrangements between these associated players and the owners of the playhouse are explained clearly in Professor Ashley H. Thorndike's *Shakespeare's Theater* (New York: 1916). And the similar organization of the wandering Italian companies is described in Mr. H. C. Chatfield-Taylor's *Goldoni* (New York: 1913).

Detailed information about the habits and customs of the French companies, whether they were strolling in the provinces or settled in Paris, can be found in *Le Théâtre Français,* written by Samuel Chappuzeau, published in 1674, and reissued in 1876 with a solidly documented introduction by Georges Monval. As interesting and even more instructive is Eugène Despois' elaborate explanation of the conditions of the theatre in France in the reign of Louis XIV (Paris: 1875).

No one of these books is as valuable and as revelatory as is the *Register* of La Grange, in which that loyal follower of Molière set down day by day the titles of the plays performed, the takings at the door of the theatre, and his own share thereof. Sometimes we can read in this otherwise dry daybook an entry which brings out suddenly the high regard in which Molière was held by his associates. For example, when the company was unexpectedly dispossessed from the theatre in the Petit Bourbon and was forced to wait for three months in comparative idleness while the theatre in the Palais Royal was being repaired and made ready for them, the rival companies of the Hôtel de Bourgogne and of the theatre in the Marais sought in vain to lure away certain of the more attractive actors and actresses; and there is a note of sincere affection in the simple words with which La Grange recorded the fruitless result of these temptations.

> The whole company kept together; all the actors loved the Sieur de Molière, their chief, who united to extraordinary merit and capacity an honesty and an engaging manner which compelled them all to protest to him that they wished to share his fortunes and that they would never quit him, whatever proposals might be made to them and whatever advantages they could find elsewhere.

Molière, it must be noted again, was not in any modern sense the manager of the company; he was only its foremost comedian and its guiding spirit, and he was content to receive only his equal share of the receipts, a share augmented only now and then by small sums specially appropriated by the votes of his appreciative comrades.

In the *Apology for the Life of Colley Cibber* we can see how the partnership of a few leading performers in the control of the theatre was slowly succeeded by the passing of the management into the hands of one man. And to-day in this twentieth century of ours, the Comédie-Française is almost the only long-enduring institution in which the performers are themselves in power. Yet it is to be recorded that even now there are occasions when a company of actors and actresses, left in the lurch by the failure of their employer, have chosen to fill their engagements as a commonwealth, the minor players taking their humble salaries and the leading players distributing among themselves such moneys as may remain after all the expenses are met.

NOTES ON EDWIN BOOTH

In 1885-86 there appeared a series of five volumes edited by Brander Matthews and Laurence Hutton and entitled *Actors and Actresses of Great Britain and the United States from the days of David Garrick to the present time.* The successive volumes contained brief critical biographies of about eighty performers of acknowledged prominence; Edwin Booth kindly consented to write out his recollections of his father, Junius Brutus Booth. Henry Irving undertook to prepare a paper on Edmund Kean, who had been the triumphant rival of Junius Brutus Booth, but he found himself unable to do this; and the editors were fortunate enough to persuade Edwin Booth to prepare both papers. In his "Memories of Edwin Booth," now included in a collection of essays called *The Principles of Playmaking and other essays,* the senior editor of the series to which Booth contributed these two articles recorded:

> Even when he had set down what was in his heart he hesitated to let the manuscript pass out of his own hands. When Hutton was at last empowered to carry it off, he brought it to me; and it made glad our editorial souls. It was not at all in accord with the pattern accepted by the professional writers who had prepared the articles for the earlier volumes. . . .
>
> It was thrown on paper in haste; it had not been modified by second thoughts; it had the flowing ease of a familiar letter; its sentences were sometimes entangled; and its punctuation was eccentric. But these external inadvertences were negligible. We had Booth's own manuscript copied faithfully, whereupon we made the few adjustments necessary to bring it into conformity with the conventions of literature. The result

stood forth as an admirable piece of writing, individual in expression, full of flavor, and rich in sympathetic understanding. . . .

Encouraged by our editorial appreciation, Edwin Booth wrote out for us his impressions of Kean, inspired in some measure by the study of Kean's death mask. He told us that although Edmund Kean and Junius Brutus Booth had been rivals in London, there was no personal enmity in their contest for the crown, and when they came together again in America their meeting was not only friendly but cordial. That the two great actors were not hostile to each other was made certain by this glowing tribute to Edmund Kean written by the son of Junius Brutus Booth, as it had been made probable years before by the appearance of Junius Brutus Booth as the Second Actor in support of the Hamlet of Edmund Kean's son.

Doubtful as Edwin Booth had been as to his ability to put on paper adequately his impressions of Kean and Booth, he was keenly interested in their reception by his friends after they were printed in the third volume of our *Actors and Actresses*. In the correspondence lovingly collected by his daughter he is constantly mentioning his "little sketches," anxious to learn what his friends thought of them. As an actor he was surfeited with newspaper criticism, and he had come to pay little attention to it; but as a writer he wanted to see every journalistic review of our volume which might comment on his two contributions. It is amusing, in fact it is almost pathetic, to note the new interest which the writing of these two articles had brought into his life when he was beginning to be wearied, and to observe the eagerness with which he awaited any casual comment on what he had written.

In an autograph letter of Edwin Booth dated 1881, and offered for sale by a dealer, there is a paragraph in which he criticizes an engraving of Junius Brutus Booth as Richard III:

Rowse's Portrait of which you have made a perfect Copy I think, is not strictly speaking an exact likeness of Father, the lower part of the face is incorrect, but nevertheless it brings Father vividly to the mind's eye—the effect is striking indeed, with the exception named, it is marvellously like my Father even to his feet. Father's nose was broken at the Bridge, Rowse places the deformity below it, towards the tip, and Father's lips when compressed formed a clear-cut line not the curve as shown in the portrait. . . . Take it as a whole it is an admirable illustration of him in the character of Richard. I always regretted the introduction of the Cap and Feathers for he never used them in that scene, nor did he ever use a Cap in that Rôle."

Edmund Kean was born in London, March 17, 1787 and he

died in Richmond in the outskirts of London on May 15, 1833. His parentage is uncertain and his education was desultory. He was only two years old when he first appeared on the stage. He spent his youth acquiring experience in strolling companies in the provinces, giving imitations and performing in pantomimes. In Belfast in the season of 1804-5, when he was only eighteen, he appeared in support of Mrs. Siddons, disgusting her the first time by his inaccuracy and inattention and astonishing her the second time by his vigor and fire. He seems to have made little impression until he was thirty; but when he acted Shylock at Drury Lane on January 26, 1814 his genius burst forth and he took his place at once as the foremost tragic actor of his time. Coleridge declared that "seeing Kean act was like reading Shakespeare by flashes of lightning"; and Byron hailed him as

> The sun's bright child;
> The genius that irradiates thy mind,
> Caught all its purity and light from heaven!
> Thine is the task, with mastery most perfect,
> To bind the passions in thy train.

At Drury Lane he followed Shylock with Richard III, Hamlet, Othello, and Iago. To these, in the next two years, he added Macbeth, Romeo, and Sir Giles Overreach (in Massinger's *New Way to Pay Old Debts*. It was for Kean that John Howard Payne wrote *Brutus, or the Fall of Tarquin;* and this was one of the tragedies he acted during a visit to Paris. He came to America in the fall of 1820, and again in 1825. His life was irregular, and he failed to husband his strength. He was greatly enfeebled when he made his last appearance at Covent Garden in March 1833; and he died two months later.

Junius Brutus Booth was born in London on May 1, 1796 and he died on a Mississippi steamboat on its way to Cincinnati on November 30, 1852. He began to act when he was seventeen; he made his first appearance in London at Covent Garden on February 12, 1817, playing Richard III, and was instantly hailed as a rival to Edmund Kean. He paid his first visit to America in the fall of 1821, returning to England in 1825. After acting also in Rotterdam, Amsterdam, and Brussels he came to the United States a second time; this was in 1827, and in 1828 at New Orleans he acted Oreste in French in Racine's *Andromaque*. In 1831 he was the manager of a theatre in Baltimore; and when Charles Kean, the son of his old rival, appeared there as Hamlet he voluntarily assumed the part of the Second Actor.

In 1836 he went back to England for a brief visit, playing at Drury Lane; but in 1837 he returned finally to America, taking up his residence on a farm near Baltimore. He made occasional professional tours during the next fifteen years, even venturing to

California in 1852. He made his last appearance in New Orleans on November 19 of that year; and he died only eleven days later.

NOTES ON ROBERT LLOYD

Robert Lloyd (1733-64) was educated at Westminster, where he was a schoolmate of Cowper, George Colman (the elder), and Charles Churchill. In his short life he composed abundantly in prose and verse, translated, and earned a scanty living as a hack writer for the booksellers. He was more than once imprisoned for debt, in spite of the aid of Garrick and of Churchill. Both Cowper and Churchill wrote poetic epistles to him; and in association with him they founded the Nonsense Club, which dined together once a week and which seems to have been a juvenile mutual admiration society. Certainly its members were constantly finding occasion to praise one another in print. In 1774, ten years after his death, a more or less complete edition of his Poetical Works was published.

The Actor appeared in 1760, and it apparently achieved a certain popularity, for a fourth edition was issued four years after the first. The year after the publication of *The Actor* Churchill sent forth *The Rosciad,* a work of far more substance and solidity.

Bonnell Thornton (1724-68) was "an agreeable rattle," in the eighteenth-century phrase. He was called

> sole heir and single
> Of dear Mat Prior's easy jingle.

He collaborated with Cowper and Colman in *The Connoisseur;* and after Colman had translated the comedies of Terence, Thornton undertook to turn into English the comedies of Plautus (published in 1767). He survived Lloyd by four years; and he was buried in Westminster Abbey.

The Actor is pleasantly written, although it lacks the masculine vigor of *The Rosciad* and although Lloyd had not that intimate understanding of the art of acting that gives value to Churchill's satire, even now after a century and a half. Superficial as Lloyd's lines may seem now and then, they are more often sensible; and they carry a useful message to all who seek to master the secrets of the histrionic art.

There is an apparent inconsistency between lines 37-38

> Perfection's Top with weary Toil and Pain
> 'Tis Genius only that can hope to gain,

and line 46:

> Here lies the golden Secret; learn to *feel.*

But the inconsistency is apparent only. The tragic actor must feel—but that is only the beginning of his accomplishment. He can achieve perfection only by toil and pain; that is, by controlling and disciplining his native power. As Lessing put it tersely in the preface to his *Hamburg Dramaturgy:* "valuable gifts of nature are very necessary to the calling of the actor, but they by no means suffice for it. He must everywhere think with the poet; he must even think for him in places where the poet has shown himself human by his errors."

Anna Cora Mowatt, in her *Autobiography of an Actress* (p. 244), has a remark that is pertinent here:

> "I agree with those who maintain that the highest school of art is that in which the actor, Prospero-like, raises or stills tempestuous waves by the magical force of his will—produces and controls, *without sharing,* the emotions of his audience."

In lines 105-126 Lloyd touches lightly upon the clowning in which uninspired and unintelligent comic actors are wont to indulge. And here it may be useful to quote from Fanny Kemble's *Records of a Girlhood:*

> Comedy appears to me decidedly a more mature and complete result of dramatic training than tragedy. The effect of the latter may, as I myself exemplified, be tolerably achieved by force of natural gifts, aided but little by study; but a fine comedian *must* be a fine artist; his work is intellectual, and not emotional, and his effects address themselves to the critical judgment and not the passionate sympathy of the audience. Tact, discretion, fine taste, are quite indispensable elements of his performance; he must be really a more complete actor than a great tragedian need be. The expression of passion and of emotion appears to be an interpretation of nature, and may be forcibly rendered sometimes with but little beyond the excitement of the moment of its imaginary experience on the actor's own sensibility; while a highly educated perfection is requisite for the actor who, in a brilliant and polished representation of the follies of society, produces by fine and delicate and powerful delineations the picture of the vices and ridicules of a highly artificial civilization.

Fanny Kemble was probably moved to this utterance by her own experience as an actress of indisputable endowment and of inadequate education. In tragedy she did not fail, whereas she felt herself unsuccessful in comedy. It is significant that Garrick, equally triumphant in comedy and in tragedy, held the former to be far more difficult and more dangerous. He declares that he could act a serious part whether he felt well or ill, feeling himself supported by the emotion, whereas "Comedy is a very serious thing!"

PUBLICATIONS OF THE DRAMATIC MUSEUM OF COLUMBIA UNIVERSITY IN THE CITY OF NEW YORK

With a view to extending its usefulness beyond the circle of those who could actually visit its library and its model room, the committee in charge of the Dramatic Museum decided in 1914 to enter the field of publication and to issue in limited editions several series of documents dealing with the theory and the practice of the art of the theatre—reprints of inaccessible essays and addresses, translations from foreign tongues, selections from works not altogether dramatic in scope, and original papers. The committee believed that the interest and the value of these writings could be increased by introductions contributed by experts and by an annotation which should be at once succinct and suggestive. They decided that the several series should be uniform and that they should be strictly limited to 333 copies each, 33 being reserved for authors, translators, and editors and 300 being available for subscribers. It seemed best not to sell the volumes separately, and it was found possible to offer a series of four volumes for the subscription price of five dollars.

First Series, 1914. PAPERS ON PLAYMAKING

I. *The New Art of Writing Plays.* By Lope de Vega. Translated by William T. Brewster. With an Introduction and Notes by Brander Matthews.

II. *The Autobiography of a Play.* By Bronson Howard. With an Introduction by Augustus Thomas.

III. *The Law of the Drama.* By Ferdinand Brunetière. Translated by Philip M. Hayden. With an Introduction by Henry Arthur Jones.

IV. *Robert Louis Stevenson as a Dramatist.* By Arthur Wing Pinero. With an Introduction and Bibliographic Addenda by Clayton Hamilton.

Second Series, *1915*. PAPERS ON ACTING

I. *The Illusion of the First Time in Acting.* By William Gillette. With an Introduction by George Arliss.

II. *Art and the Actor.* By Constant Coquelin. Translated by Abby Langdon Alger. With an Introduction by Henry James.

III. *Mrs. Siddons as Lady Macbeth and Queen Katharine.* By H. C. Fleeming Jenkin. With an Introduction by Brander Matthews.

IV. *Reflections on Acting.* By Talma. With an Introduction by Sir Henry Irving; and a review by H. C. Fleeming Jenkin.

Third Series, *1916*. PAPERS ON PLAYMAKING

I. *How Shakespeare Came to Write "The Tempest."* By Rudyard Kipling. With an Introduction by Ashley H. Thorndike.

II. *How Plays Are Written.* Letters from Augier, Dumas, Sardou, Zola, and others. Translated by Dudley Miles. With an Introduction by William Gillette.

III. *A Stage Play.* By Sir William Schenck Gilbert. With an Introduction by William Archer.

IV. *A Theory of the Theatre.* By Francisque Sarcey. Translated by H. H. Hughes. With an Introduction and Notes by Brander Matthews.

V. (Extra volume) A catalogue of Models and of Stage-Sets in the Dramatic Museum of Columbia University.

Fourth Series, *1919*. DISCUSSION OF THE DRAMA

I. *Goethe on the Theatre.* Selections from the conversations with Eckermann; translated by John Oxenford. With an Introduction by William Witherle Lawrence.

II. *Goldoni on Playwriting.* Translated and compiled by F. C. L. van Steenderen. With an Introduction by H. C. Chatfield-Taylor.

III. *Prospero's Island.* By Edward Everett Hale. With an Introduction by Henry Cabot Lodge.

IV. *Letters of an Old Playgoer.* By Matthew Arnold. With an Introduction by Brander Matthews.

Fifth Series, *1926*. PAPERS ON ACTING

I. *The Art of Acting.* By Dion Boucicault. With an Introduction by Otis Skinner.

II. *Actors and Acting.* A discussion by Constant Coquelin, Henry Irving, and Dion Boucicault.

III. *On the Stage.* By Frances Anne Kemble. With an Introduction by George Arliss.

IV. *A Company of Actors.* By Francisque Sarcey. With an Introduction by Brander Matthews.

Manuscripts for the Sixth and Seventh Series as deposited in the Museum by Brander Matthews, July 29, 1926:

Sixth Series. DISCUSSION OF THE DRAMA

I. *The Pleasures of Playgoing.* By Emile Faguet. Translated by Philip M. Hayden. Introduction by Ferris Greenslet.

II. *Lope De Vega.* By George Henry Lewes. Introduction by James Fitzmaurice Kelly.

III. *Eugène Scribe.** By Ernest Legouvé. Translated by Albert D. Vandam.

IV. *Molière and Shakespeare.* By Constant Coquelin. Translated by Florence Hallett Matthews. Introduction by Brander Matthews.

Seventh Series. PAPERS ON ACTING

I. *The Paradox of Acting.* By Denis Diderot. Translated by Walter Herries Pollock. With an Introduction by Henry Irving.

II. *The Actor.†* By Robert Lloyd.

III. *Edmund Kean and Junius Brutus Booth.* By Edwin Booth. Introduction by Lawrence Barrett.

IV. *Poems About Players of the Nineteenth Century.* Chosen by Brander Matthews.

* Hatcher H. Hughes was to have written an introduction to the paper on Scribe.

† G. C. D. Odell was to have written an introduction to *The Actor.*

Index

Index

DRAMABOOKS

Hill and Wang has established DRAMABOOKS as a permanent library of the great classics of the theatre of all countries, in an attractive, low-priced format.

CRITICISM

Date Due

MAY 8 1968			
JAN 13			
DE 20 72			

Library Bureau Cat. No. 1137